ISRAELI HISTORICAL REVISIONISM

Of Related Interest

In Search of Identity: Jewish Aspects in Israeli Culture
Dan Urian and Efraim Karsh

Fabricating Israeli History: The 'New Historians', second revised edition
Efraim Karsh

*Green Crescent over Nazareth:
The Displacement of Christians by Muslims
in the Holy Land*
Raphael Israeli

A Dissenting Democracy: The Israeli Movement 'Peace Now'
Magnus Norell

Israeli Politics and Society Since 1948: Problems of Collective Identity
Efraim Karsh

The Israeli Palestinians: An Arab Minority in the Jewish State
Alexander Bligh

ISRAELI HISTORICAL REVISIONISM

From Left to Right

Editors

ANITA SHAPIRA
Tel Aviv University

and

DEREK J. PENSLAR
University of Toronto

FRANK CASS
LONDON • PORTLAND, OR

First Published in 2003 in Great Britain by
FRANK CASS PUBLISHERS
2 Park Square, Milton Park,
Abingdon, Oxon, OX14 4RN

and in the United States of America by
FRANK CASS PUBLISHERS
270 Madison Ave,
New York NY 10016

Transferred to Digital Printing 2006

Website: www.frankcass.com

Copyright © 2003 Frank Cass Publishers

British Library Cataloguing in Publication Data

Israeli historical revisionism : from left to right
  1. Revisionist Zionism 2. Israel – Historiography 3. Israel –
  History – Errors, inventions, etc.
  I. Shapira, Anita II. Penslar, Derek Jonathan
  956. 9'405'072
        ISBN 0714653799 (cloth)
        ISBN 0714683132 (paper)

Library of Congress Cataloging-in-Publication Data

Israeli historical revisionism : from left to right/editors, Anita
Shapira and Derek J. Penslar.
  p. cm.
Includes index.
  ISBN 0-7146-5379-9 (cloth – ISBN 0-7146-8313-2 (pbk.)
  1. Zionism – Historiography. 2. Jews – Palestine – Historiography.
3. Israel – Historiography. 4. Post-Zionism. I. Shapira, Anita. II.
Penslar, Derek Jonathan.
  DS149 .1775 2002
  320.54'095694'0722–dc21
                                                2002012354

This group of studies first appeared as a special issue of
The Journal of Israeli History (ISSN 1353-1042), Vol. 20, Nos. 2/3,
Summer/Autumn 2001, published by Frank Cass

All rights reserved. No part of this publication may be reproduced, stored in or introduced into a retrieval system, or transmitted, in any form, or by any means, electronic, mechanical, photocopying, recording, or otherwise, without the prior written permission of the publisher of this book.

Contents

Editors' Note		vi
Foreword	Itamar Rabinovich	vii
History and National Liberation	Michael Walzer	1
Left and Right Post-Zionism and the Privatization of Israeli Collective Memory	Daniel Gutwein	9
Historiosophical Foundations of the Historical Strife in Israel	Uri Ram	43
The Strategies of Historical Revisionism	Anita Shapira	62
Zionism and the Counter-Intellectuals	Mark Lilla	77
Zionism, Colonialism and Postcolonialism	Derek J. Penslar	84
Forgetting Europe: Perspectives on the Debate about Zionism and Colonialism	Avi Bareli	99
The Status of Zionist and Israeli History in Israeli Universities	Yoav Gelber	121
History Textbooks and the Limits of Israeli Consciousness	Amnon Raz-Krakotzkin	155
Contributors		173
Index		175

Editors' Note

It has been some 15 years since the beginning of the Israeli historians' controversy over the creation of the State of Israel, the 1948 War and its aftermath, Israel's attitude towards Holocaust survivors, the "melting pot" absorption policy, and similar subjects. The attack on Zionist historiography came initially from what was dubbed the "post-Zionist" radical left. More recently, the controversy has broadened to include a critique from the right. This volume is based on papers presented at two conferences on "Israeli Historical Revisionism: From Left to Right," the first held in Tel Aviv on 24 January 2001, and the second in New York on 25–26 February 2001, organized by Brandeis University, the American Jewish Committee, the Zalman Shazar Center for Jewish History and Tel Aviv University. These conferences were distinguished by the multifaceted nature of the discussion, with the Zionist "center" in defense against both extremes. This diversity of approaches is reflected in this volume, which includes contributions from most of the participants in the conferences, joined by some additional writers, giving some new perspectives on the old controversy.

Anita Shapira
Tel Aviv University

Derek J. Penslar
University of Toronto

Foreword

Among the many strands of the current intellectual, academic and political debates in and about Israel, the controversies generated by the rise of revisionist schools of Israel's historiography stand out as particularly rich and animated.

Revisionist historiography is grounded in a political or ideological position regarding the present and the future. All historical writing entails an element of revision: there is no point in publishing works that do not revise or alter our view of the issue under consideration. But revisionism is different from revision. If revision is the end point of a voyage that begins with a question mark, revisionism is a process that seems to depart from a firm conviction. Broadly speaking, Israel's traditional historiography has been challenged in the last two decades from both left and right. Both challenges have been passionate and often overstated, but both have contributed to an important reassessment of established views and concepts.

The sponsors and organizers of the conference in New York which gave birth to this volume had three purposes in mind: to enable some of the parties to these debates to converse with each other; to evaluate the state of the debate; and to expose it to an interested audience in New York. The printed volume enables us to reach a much larger audience.

It is my pleasant duty to thank Tel Aviv University's three partners in this endeavor, Brandeis University, the American Jewish Committee and the Shazar Center for Jewish History in Jerusalem, for their cordial and effective cooperation.

Itamar Rabinovich
President, Tel Aviv University
October, 2002

History and National Liberation

Michael Walzer

Every national-liberation movement has to rewrite the history of the nation it aims to liberate. A new history is always necessary — so as to make liberation a more plausible project than it is likely to appear given the traditional history. For nations that are forced to endure conquest, oppression, servitude or exile over long periods of time gradually accommodate themselves to their condition, and historical literature is one of the key means of their accommodation. They tell themselves a story that explains their weakness and defeat, like the Jewish story according to which exile is a "punishment for our sins," or they tell a different kind of story suggesting that they have, after all, higher goals than statehood and political sovereignty. The liberationist historians have to "untell" these stories and provide different ones, commonly ones that celebrate heroism-even-in-defeat and stubborn resistance thereafter and that are pointed towards a future national revival. We can see this in many cases, and Zionism, despite all the peculiarities of Jewish life, is one among them.

Zionist historians tended, like Zionists generally, to "negate the exile" rather than to find stubbornness and heroism within it (a mistake, I think, and one that I will come back to at the end of this article); they leapfrogged backwards to the biblical years and, even more, to the Hasmonean state and the revolts that followed its demise. I will not try here to discuss the scholarly exemplars of this new history, like Yehezkel Kaufmann's account of the biblical period or Joseph Klausner's studies of the Second Temple years. More important, for our purposes today, are the popular and schoolbook histories. Growing up in an American Zionist household, for example, I was raised on stories of the Maccabees and Bar-Kokhba, stories that gave the lives of these ancient figures immediate political relevance. Judah Maccabee was a fighter for national liberation and (since we were also Reform Jews) for toleration and religious freedom. The actual religious foundations of the revolt, the zealotry of the *hasidim*, figured hardly at all in the stories I read; the destruction of heathen temples and the forced conversion of the Idumeans were never mentioned. Though this was popular history (and historical fiction, as in Howard Fast's novel *My Glorious Brothers*), I assume that it had some basis in more serious writing. And it was not wholly wrong, only one-sided; in the older history it was the political meaning of the Maccabean revolt that had been actively repressed.

The Maccabees were important not only because of their courageous struggle but also because of the state they founded — which turned out to be (unexpectedly, perhaps, given their original motivation) a "normal" state, a Hellenistic principality, which had military and diplomatic relations with other states in the international society of its time. The early contacts with Rome and the (possibly fictitious) exchange of letters with the Spartans were especially interesting in the Zionist retelling because they suggested a politics so wonderfully different from the fears and resentments, the "all the world against us" sensibility, of *galut* Jews. In those years it was an exhilarating thought: a Spartan–Maccabee alliance! (Even then, of course, I would have preferred Athens as an ally.)

Bar-Kokhba is another interesting case: the revolt named after him figured centrally and often in Zionist writing and then was the subject of an early revisionist effort (Yehoshafat Harkabi's 1980 critique). In the rabbinic world, the politics of the Bar-Kokhba revolt was mostly ignored; Bar-Kokhba himself was treated critically (or, sometimes, fantastically, as a mythic figure whose superhuman feats make it impossible to understand his final failure). But among the writers of the *Haskalah* and then among Zionist writers and publicists, he came into his own — or what we were told was his own. The revolt he led, writes Harkabi, "became a model for breaking the yoke of foreign rule. ... The national movement sought an example of a positive, militant heroism to counterbalance the negative heroism of Jews who gave their lives as martyrs."[1] Because it made such a striking contrast with exilic passivity, the very recklessness of the revolt was celebrated; its disastrous but predictable outcome was played down. As that last sentence suggests, I have mostly accepted Harkabi's critique of the Bar-Kokhba "syndrome"; his book seems to me a fairly striking example of revisionist success.

For Zionist writers the history of the martyrs was not, could not be, real national history. Since the suppression of the Bar-Kokhba revolt, David Ben-Gurion argued, "we have had 'histories' of persecution, of legal discrimination, of the Inquisition and pogroms, of ... martyrdom, but we have not had Jewish history anymore, because [the] history of a people is only what the people create as a whole. ..."[2] This is a literal and extraordinary "untelling" of history; it is certainly wrong, since the real exilic story is not one of persecution and death (though there was enough of that) but of survival over many centuries, across many countries; and it is a remarkable story of political adaptability, innovation and collective stubbornness. A non-Zionist historian like Simon Dubnow could recognize this and make medieval Jewish autonomy into a modern political program. But autonomy is not independence; Zionists needed to tell a different story.

The story resumes in the modern period: from Bar-Kokhba to Joseph Trumpeldor, with not much in between. These two figures (and others too, of course) are "written up" so as to make them the very opposites of the *galut* Jew. Trumpeldor, who died reciting a Hebrew version of "dulce et decorum est pro patria mori," is specifically the opposite of the religious martyr: he gives his life for his country, not his God.[3] I have always imagined him alongside Nathan Hale, a hero of the American Revolution, who, standing on the gallows, regretted that he had only one life to give for his country. In Nietzsche's precise meaning, the telling of these stories is monumental history, focused on the great deeds of great men and, in the modern age, great women too. In my youth, Hannah Senesh was the great woman, and Marie Syrkin's popular history *Blessed Is the Match* was the crucial text; the book worked its magic: the first time I brought my daughters to Israel, I took them to visit Hannah Senesh's grave on Mt. Herzl. I dread the revisionist assault on Syrkin and Senesh.

No national-liberation movement could succeed without a historical "untelling" and retelling of the sort I have just described. But once the movement has succeeded, a revisionist critique of this history is inevitable; it is indeed a sign of success. I am not sure what determines the timing of the revisionist enterprise. Harkabi's critique of the Bar-Kokhba syndrome was driven by political events — by the peace treaty with Egypt and the refusal of the Begin government to deal in a similar way with the Palestinians. Revisionism is commonly politically driven, just as liberationist history is, but the driving forces are not usually so particular; they have more to do with psychology and ideology than with day-to-day politics.

Once liberation has been won, once the state has been established, the heroism of the founders, and of their legendary predecessors, begins to seem exaggerated. It is a burden on later generations to measure up to such an extraordinary standard — or to feel obliged to respond with the appropriate sentiments to the sentimentality of a very different time. Nationalism itself is a burden for people whose nation-state is, so to speak, already achieved. A new generation of historians and publicists casts off the burden; some of its members launch a scholarly critique of liberationist history (there is now a large cadre of professors, which the liberation movement never had); some of the critics are more interested in political polemic. But no revisionist lives, any more than the liberationists did, in an ivory tower. Even the most academic histories have a public purpose and a popular impact; they undercut the schoolbook accounts; they require the rewriting of the texts.[4]

This rewriting is always controversial, sure to be contested. The revisionists deny the stories that "everyone's" parents and grandparents believed. They mock the old commitments. They expose the dark side of national liberation, the crimes committed in its name, the repressed divisions, the factional self-interest that was always disguised as the common good. All this, as I have said, is natural and normal. And it goes on (will go on) for a very long time. As I was working on this essay, I came across a *New York Times* review of a new book on the American Revolution; the review is entitled "The Founding Villains," and the book sounds very much like books currently coming out in Israel — which suggests that revisionism's work is never done. In the United States, at least, liberationist history endures and still requires (or, at least, still gets) critical analysis more than 200 years after the liberation.[5]

It is another sign of normality that the intellectual and political establishments, produced by the success of national liberation, respond to revisionism in a double way: they are both defensive and concessionary — more defensive than concessionary, perhaps, but they are not, at any rate, militant or absolutist. After all, the representatives of the establishment are also professors, and they have won the battle (that's what it means to be established), and so they do not have to insist on the heroism and moral rectitude of every warrior in the grand struggle or on the rightfulness of every decision made in its course. So the revisionists win a number of partial victories, and the textbooks are, or will be, partially rewritten. The precise extent of their victory is determined, I think (perhaps naively), by the strength of their arguments and their evidence — even though many of the revisionists (Benny Morris being the notable exception) are committed to a postmodern ideology that denies the determining force of arguments and evidence. Still, they pile up footnotes as if they were good positivists, as if they were not producing just another "narrative" but were really trying to get things right, and I suspect that it will be their footnotes that ultimately win or lose the game. No doubt, the skillfulness of their rhetoric and their ability to mobilize political support will also play a part, as they tell us, but their footnotes will be critical. The limits of whatever victories they win will be fixed by their own exaggerations and evasions, by the extent to which their new history is seen to be determined not by their evidence but by their political agenda. Revisionism's agenda varies over time, but it is generally leftist in character — even though the liberationist movement itself was leftist, or claimed to be: the revisionists dispute the claim (as in Zeev Sternhell's *Founding Myths*).[6] They also defend a "new left," committed to a demystified, postnational society.

I should add one further note on the revisionist enterprise: its future course, even its future content, will be determined by what happens over the next 100 years (or more) in and to the State of Israel. Recent American revisionists describe the revolutionary war as the first episode in the history of

American imperialism. That is not a charge that revisionists' writing, say, 50 years after the revolution, in 1826, would have been inclined to make; they would hardly have been able to imagine it. All history is backward looking, and it matters a great deal from where one is looking back. If there ever is an Israeli–Palestinian peace, the revisionist enterprise would look very different than it does today.

Meanwhile, however, revisionism has inspired strong hostility. And now my story takes a curious turn (though this turn too is common to other stories): the fiercest response has not come from the national-liberation establishment but from the establishment's own right-wing opposition. The American parallel to this, which may cast some light on what has just begun in Israel, is the bitter attack on our newer or newest historians, which was originally launched, and has since been sustained, by the "neoconservatives" and the right generally. The new historians offer, let us say, a new account of the Indian wars, and they propose to rewrite the school texts accordingly. They are then bitterly attacked in the name of patriotism and "traditional" values. But what are America's traditional values? The ones that we celebrate today are the values that led to the revolution, the founding of the republic, its progressive democratization, the abolition of slavery, the acceptance of mass immigration, the civil rights movement, and so on. And the historical counterparts of the right-wing historians who today defend American values opposed in their own time everything that those values produced. Now the anti-revisionists insist that America's history, at least its textbook history, must be told as the progressive enactment of freedom, without any perverse exploration of American racism or nativism, indeed, without qualification or critique. But that does not mean that they are defenders of freedom. They may just be opponents of qualification and critique.[7]

The Israeli story is made more complicated by the mixed political/religious character of the anti-revisionist campaign. At the very moment when (some) secular leftists are revising and criticizing a history in which they and their historical counterparts played a large role, religious rightists are claiming a place they mostly did not have in the success of national liberation. But the story is curiouser and curiouser: for the right-wing anti-revisionist campaign also represents a denial — I will not say unconscious but certainly unacknowledged — that national liberation has actually been a success. The fierceness of anti-revisionism is motivated by the old exilic "all the world against us" sensibility. Its protagonists insist that Zionism has not, in fact, made Israel normal. The country is besieged. The *goyim* still hate us. We still hate ourselves: the country has been betrayed by its own intellectual elites, seduced by Western liberalism.[8] The intellectual and emotional mobilization that Zionism's monumental history was meant to inspire, and did inspire, is still necessary; we cannot accept the risks of a critical history.

This is the political version of anti-revisionism. There is also a more explicitly religious version, which bears some resemblance to the defense of "Asian values" in the contemporary Far East; it is also directed against the modern and postmodern West (secular, democratic, feminist, environmentalist, and so on). In the Israeli case, the self-critical style and the postnational commitments of the revisionist historians are taken to be a threat to the Jewishness of the Jewish state (though I would have thought they could also be taken as proof that there are still Jews in the Jewish state). And here again, the ostensible defense of liberationist history and old-fashioned Zionism conceals, or does not quite conceal, an exilic political sensibility — the wish that Israel could be, so to speak, a big *kahal* (the medieval Jewish community), a *kahal* with an army, and not the modern democratic state that was the goal of national liberation.

But was it actually the goal? That has been questioned by both revisionist and anti-revisionist writers, who often agree in their emphasis on the *nationalism* of national liberation. They simply attach different value signs to it: minus signs for the revisionists, plus signs for the anti-revisionists. They could both be wrong; I suspect they often are and that *liberation* was more central to national liberation than they allow. Let us consider for a moment Ben-Gurion's vision of Israeli statehood, cited from a speech given in December 1947 to members of Mapai, just after the UN vote in favor of partition:

> We must think in terms of a state, in terms of independence, in terms of full responsibility for ourselves — and for others. In our state there will be non-Jews as well — and all of them will be equal citizens; equal in everything without any exception; that is, the state will be their state as well. ... The attitude of the Jewish state to its Arab citizens will be an important factor ... in building good neighbourly relations with the Arab States. If the Arab citizen will feel at home in our state, and if his status will not be in the least different from that of the Jew ... and if the state will help him in a truthful and dedicated way to reach the economic, social, and cultural level of the Jewish community, then Arab distrust will accordingly subside and a bridge to a Semitic, Jewish–Arab alliance will be built.[9]

That is a good description of the liberationist goal (which also suggests the real limits of Zionist success). There may be condescension in Ben-Gurion's line about "cultural level," though a later sentence in the speech indicates that he was talking chiefly about equalizing state expenditure for cultural affairs in the

Arab and Jewish sectors. In any case, Ben-Gurion was far more condescending towards Jewish immigrants than he was towards Arab citizens. And in both cases, the Zionist project was equal citizenship. Revisionist historians justly criticize the reiterated failure to fulfill this project, though I think they underestimate the difficulties involved. But the anti-revisionists are not focused on such complaints; they simply have a different project.

I would describe it this way: they imagine a Jewish state as it was imagined during the centuries of exile. Gentiles would be allowed to live in this state (hence it would not be just a big *kahal*), but only in something like the subordinate status of the *ger toshav* (resident alien) — which was the status that Jews aspired to in Europe in the days before emancipation. Perhaps this is unfair; anti-revisionism is a critical enterprise whose protagonists are a bit shy about revealing their positive program (Yoram Hazony's *The Jewish State* is a model of radical reticence). But certainly the program falls short of equal citizenship. And in that sense it is a quintessentially exilic program, for equal citizenship, in the centuries before emancipation and sovereignty, was not part of the experience of the Jews, nor was it ever a feature of their aspiration. I began by saying that I thought the "negation of the exile" was a mistake. It was also a failure, and we should think of right-wing anti-revisionist history as the return of the negated. This return is natural enough: one of the great achievements of national liberation was the "ingathering of the exiles" — the achievement is disputed by revisionist historians, but it is an achievement nonetheless — and the political attitudes and practices of the exile were also gathered in. These must now be confronted. The liberationists rejected the exile, without confronting it; the revisionists have ignored it. If there is to be an anti-anti-revisionism, one last history in the series I have described, historians will have to engage the exilic years; they will have to find some way to recognize and admire the strengths of stateless Jewry — its intense mutuality and political flexibility; and also, finally, to acknowledge and deal with its pathologies — parochialism, chauvinism, fear and hatred of the *goyim*. This, I suggest, is the necessary next stage in the everlasting historical wars.

NOTES

1 Yehoshafat Harkabi, *The Bar Kochba Syndrome*, trans. Max Ticktin (Chappaqua, NY, 1983), p. 103.
2 Quoted in Amnon Rubinstein, *The Zionist Dream Revisited* (New York, 1984), p. 7.
3 For a revisionist account of the centrality of this theme in nationalist thought, see Yael Tamir, "*Pro patria mori!*: Death and the State," in Robert McKim and Jeff McMahan (eds.), *The Morality of Nationalism* (New York, 1997), pp. 227–41.
4 Uri Ram offers a different, more ideologically revisionist, account of revisionism in "Postnational Pasts: The Case of Israel," *Social Science History*, Vol. 22, No. 4 (Winter 1998), pp. 513–45.

5. William R. Everdell, "The Founding Villians," *New York Times Book Review*, 12 November 2000, p. 29 (review of Francis Jennings, *The Creation of America: Through Revolution to Empire*).
6. See Zeev Sternhell, *The Founding Myths of Israel: Nationalism, Socialism, and the Making of the Jewish State*, trans. David Maisel (Princeton, 1998).
7. For a defense of the new American history, see Gary B. Nash, Charlotte Crabtree and Ross E. Dunn, *History on Trial: National Identity, Culture Wars, and the Teaching of the Past* (New York, 1997).
8. This last is the theme of Yoram Hazony, *The Jewish State: The Struggle for Israel's Soul* (New York, 2000).
9. Quoted in Efraim Karsh, *Fabricating Israeli History: The "New Historians"* (London and Portland, OR, 1997), p. 67.

Left and Right Post-Zionism and the Privatization of Israeli Collective Memory

Daniel Gutwein

Post-Zionism: Left and Right

For the past three decades, Zionist ideology and politics have been the target of a sharp critique by the "post-Zionists."[1] Post-Zionism began as a demand for a revision of historical and sociological academic research in Israel, which, the post-Zionists claimed, has betrayed its scholarly call and formed an unholy alliance with the country's political and social elite. Israeli historians and sociologists, they argue, have not only made Zionist ideology and ethos the premise of their research, but they also serve as court intellectuals, supplying "official versions" and manipulating Israeli collective memory as a means of preserving the hegemony of the Israeli Labor-Zionist establishment.

The roots of the post-Zionist revision are to be found in the works of the "Critical Sociologists" in the 1970s, who emerged against the background of the crises that rocked Israeli society in that decade, particularly the protests by *Mizrahim* (Jews from Muslim countries) against their discrimination by the Labor, mainly Ashkenazi establishment; the shock of the 1973 War, which whittled away at the legitimacy and self-confidence of this establishment; and the political turnabout of 1977, which transferred the reins of power from Labor to a coalition of right-wing and religious parties. The Critical Sociologists argued that by propagating the dominant Zionist ideology, academic sociology in Israel was deliberately avoiding the conflicts within Israeli society, especially that between the Labor establishment — representing the interests of the mainly Ashkenazi middle class, which took advantage of the nation-building project — and groups of "others" like the *Mizrahim* and the Arabs, who were oppressed and excluded by this same process.[2] This critique gained new ground at the end of the 1980s with the opening of archives pertaining to the formative years of the State of Israel, when the Israeli "Whig version" of Zionist–Arab relations came under fierce attack by the "new historians." They argued that, backed by academic research, the official narrative had deliberately blurred Israel's responsibility for the 1948 Palestinian refugee problem, which was the outcome of a premeditated policy of ethnic cleansing, involving mass murder and other atrocities, carried out in the course of the war.[3]

Inspired by the postmodernist school, the post-Zionists gradually expanded their revision to other areas such as culture, education, literature, arts, gender and law, suggesting an overall critique of Zionist ideology and Israeli politics.[4] No less than in its policies towards the Palestinians, the post-Zionists insist, the oppressive nature of Zionism was reproduced by the practices employed by the Labor Ashkenazi ruling elite towards different groups of Jews, before and after 1948. They criticized the idea of the "negation of the diaspora" that lay at the heart of the Zionist ethos, positing the Jewish diasporic life as an ideal type of multicultural existence.[5] The contempt for the "diaspora Jew," they argued, provided the mental background for the Zionist leadership's alleged indifference to the tragedy of European Jewry during the Holocaust,[6] which did not preclude the cynical use of the victims and the survivors to advance the campaign for the Zionist state and to construct a collective memory that would legitimize Israeli aggression and conquest.[7]

After 1948, the post-Zionists furger argue, the Israeli elite discriminated against and excluded different groups of Jews defined by their ethnicity and ideology, most notoriously the *Mizrahim*, who by means of the "melting pot" policy were forced to give up their own culture and adopt the hegemonic one.[8] The emancipation of Israeli society, the post-Zionists conclude, is conditional on its rejection of Zionism, and the annulment of the Jewish character of the State of Israel, turning it into a "state for all its citizens." This concept is based on the multiculturalist recognition of the separate identities of all the "others" in Israeli society, and mainly the Arabs, as a way of struggling against the Zionist-Ashkenazi hegemony.[9]

Whereas "post-Zionism" was initially a left-wing ideology, in the course of the 1990s this term was borrowed to characterize certain sentiments and views among the Israeli right. Among the national-religious right, the principled opposition to the government's peace policies — mainly to the Oslo Accords — coupled with resentment of what they perceived as the continuous erosion of the Jewish and Zionist character of Israeli society, has paradoxically developed in some sectors into a deep estrangement from the Israeli statehood to the point of questioning and even denying one of the foundations of national-religious teachings: the theological justification of Zionism and the sacred nature of its embodiment, the State of Israel. These doubts have strengthened among the national-religious messianic concepts alongside the adoption of stricter religious behavior, which has brought them closer to the Ultra-Orthodox anti-Zionists (*haredim*), an attitude that has been described as "religious-nationalist post-Zionism."[10] At the same time, right-wingers striving to establish an American-style conservative right in Israel began to use arguments of a post-Zionist nature. Their dissociation from the Zionist project moved between ideological rejection of the social radicalism of Zionism and criticism of the collectivist nature of its realization by Labor in Israel.[11]

If initially it seemed that the left and right versions of post-Zionism were opposites, being united only in their criticism of Labor Zionism, gradually it became clear that agreement between them was deeper. Both declared their avowed opposition to mainstream Zionism and emphasized their struggle to undermine its hegemony by exposing the hypocrisy of its underlying ethos. They shared criticism of the basics of Zionist ideology and practice: the "negation of the diaspora"; the Hebrew cultural revolution and the "melting pot" policy; the attitude towards religion and the *haredim*; the stand of the Zionist leadership during the Holocaust; and the way the *Mizrahim* had been absorbed. Their shared opposition to Labor Zionism brought right and left post-Zionism closer together in a way that only several years earlier had appeared impossible: the adoption of the new historiography by spokespersons on the right. The latter began to agree with the new historians that the establishment of the State of Israel had indeed been accompanied by the expulsion of Palestinians and other atrocities as a result of the war. Nevertheless, they insisted that these had been morally justifiable necessary evils and that the State of Israel would not otherwise have come about.

Historical revisionism serves, then, as a meeting point for political extremes on the left and the right. In the name of contradictory ideologies and under the veil of rhetorical confrontation, they, in fact, cooperate in fighting the hegemonic Labor-Zionist ethos and in advancing the post-Zionist agenda, whether in its "Jewish" version on the right or in its "civil" version on the left. The critique and its targets reveal an underlying characteristic common to both left and right post-Zionism: recycling and bringing to the center of public debate views that in the past were voiced by marginal opposition groups on the left and on the right. Claims regarding the colonial nature of Zionism and its ties with imperialism, as well as Israel's responsibility for the refugee problem and the failure of efforts to achieve peace, were prevalent among both the anti-Zionist left and radical left-wing Zionist parties. Likewise, criticism of the Zionist leadership's abandonment of European Jewry during the Holocaust, as well as of the material and cultural absorption of the *Mizrahim*, prevailed among different rightist and religious circles, and had even caused repeated political crises.

In appearing both as critics of the essential foundations of the Zionist ethos and also as spokespersons for its victims, whether *Mizrahim* or Holocaust victims and survivors who are at the center of the Israeli consensus, the left and right post-Zionists have succeeded in becoming one of the axes of public debate in Israel. The synergy between right and left post-Zionism — both seek to discredit established Zionism as well as attacking each other — grants both of them ideological and propagandistic influence that exceeds the value of their separate messages. It further endowed their criticism with a subversive flavor, making it a provocative cultural event and arousing public interest.

This has enabled post-Zionism to redraw the lines delineating political discourse in Israel by crossing the traditional boundaries that distinguish right and left, and to redefine the difference between them.

In an attempt to explain this success, two different manifestations of post-Zionism will be examined below: the "new historiography" from the end of the 1980s and beginning of the 1990s as an expression of left post-Zionism in its formative stages; and the way in which the post-Zionist arguments were adopted by various circles on the right, especially in the journal *Tkhelet* (*Azure*) at the end of the 1990s, as a manifestation of right post-Zionism in its advanced stage.

The New Historiography and the Academic Historiography

At the end of the 1980s and beginning of the 1990s, the new historians launched their offensive with the aim of criticizing and undermining the authority of academic research of the history of Zionism and the State of Israel. Summing up their success, Ilan Pappé wrote in 1994: "When *Matzpen* raised many of the questions that are discussed today by critical post-Zionist scholars, it was a short-lived harmless criticism. There is no doubt that time and political developments also contributed to the change, but essentially it was the transfer of the discussion to the universities that, for the first time, compelled those who were attacked to respond."[12]

Identifying with the stands taken by *Matzpen*, an Israeli anti-Zionist ultra-left-wing organization active in the 1960s and 1970s, Pappé points to the operative conclusion to be drawn from its failure to convince a broader public of its criticism: the struggle against the Zionist narrative cannot be conducted as a political or ideological dispute. Since academic historiography and sociology, as agents of the Zionist establishment, are the bastions of the hegemonic narrative, the struggle has to be transferred to the universities and conducted as an academic debate. In other words, academic research should be used to legitimize, retrieve and restore to the center of public discourse those same stands that had failed in the ideological and political debate. Thus by integrating into the academic establishment, and by posing as a distinct historiographical school, the new historians succeeded in disguising their ideological and propagandistic intentions as something "academic and not necessarily political."[13]

Maintaining that the academic historiography of Zionism was mere propaganda serving the interests of the Israeli establishment, the new historians adopted the technique and tools usually used by historical revisionism: presenting certain scholarly interpretations as "official versions," denying their academic value and "exposing" them as a tool for manipulating public opinion in the service of the hegemonic forces, while presenting theirs as a "corrected version," free of the ideological-political distortions of the official versions. Using revisionist *modus operandi*, the new historians began their crusade against academic historiography by charging it with partisan priorities that subjected scholarly standards to political goals and sacrificed "freedom of opinion and research" on the altar of "Zionist nationalism." They argued that this partisan nature had dire professional implications, leading Israeli academic historiography to reject advanced methods of historical analysis that might expose the Zionist narrative.[14]

However, the development of the academic historiography of Zionism in Israel since the 1960s undermines the validity of both contentions underlying the new historians' demand for revision. After all, the basic assumption of historical research is the constant revision of existing knowledge, which is generated by revealing new previously unknown sources and the re-interpretation of already known sources by new generations of historians, who work in changing political, social and intellectual contexts, equipped with new research methods and analytical perspectives. This dynamic is especially evident in the academic historiography of Zionism, which, since the 1960s, has been marked by the demand for methodological updating and the liberation of historical research from the ideological templates of the Zionist project in general, and the political interests of the different parties and leaders in particular. Although this demand generated fierce opposition from the Zionist "old guard," the latter could no longer arrest the development of academic critical historiography. The very fact that academic historians of Zionism became known in public discourse as "myth breakers" testifies to their success in freeing themselves from the yoke of ideological commitment.[15]

Against this background, the new historians' demand for a revision of the ideological Zionist narrative appeared trivial. Likewise, the "discoveries" of the new historiography were to a great extent nothing but a recycling of arguments that had been raised in the past both by the Zionist opposition parties and the anti-Zionist circles in Israel under the mantle of research and with an expansion of the factual basis.[16] Thus, the new historians created an impossible arena of discussion for historians who did not dispute the legitimacy of the demand for revision and criticism — a demand that academic research had actually led for a generation — but rejected the interpretations that were suggested by the new historians and mainly the repoliticization of historical research. The real significance of the new historiography lay, then, in its *extra*-scholarly ramifications: more than historical research, it is a continuation of the ideological debate whose targets lay in the political, not the scholarly, sphere, a projection of the charge that the new historians themselves made against academic research.

The New Historiography: Between Method and Ideology

The use of the concepts "old historiography" and "new historiography" by the new historians is vague, involving changing and contradictory meanings. In the writings of Benny Morris, who coined these terms, they underwent a complete change as the controversy developed.[17] Originally, Morris distinguished between the new historians and the old historians according to a generational and professional criteria.[18] The "old historians" were those who came from the political or military establishments — the army history department, for example — and their works were no more than memoirs and chronicles, in which history was manipulated to serve political goals, and mainly for justifying Israeli policy in the spirit of Ben-Gurion. The "new historians," by contrast, according to Morris's original definition, were a younger generation of trained academic historians, who based their research on professional analyses of archival material opened in the 1980s and whose studies "significantly shake if not completely destroy" the old historiography. From this generational-professional distinction — which Morris agrees to describe as a distinction between the pre-history and history of research — it follows that the old historiography has practically come to an end, and, since the 1980s, Israeli historiography of the War of Independence is all "new."

Shortly after, though, Morris reversed his definitions, arguing that the age of old historiography was not yet over and that Israeli academic historiography was the arena of a struggle for hegemony waged between the new and the old historiography. According to his new version, the spirit of the retired old historians is preserved in the works of some of the leading figures of the new generation of professional historians, whom he calls "the new-old historians." Among the latter, he particularly attacks Itamar Rabinovich and Anita Shapira, who according to his former generational definition were classified with the new historians. Despite their disciplinary training and against all professional standards, Morris charges, the new-old historians prefer establishment propaganda to historical truth, consciously choosing to adhere to the narrative of the old history and continuing to portray Zionism in "an even rosier light." In their essays, "the Arabs are still strong and we are weak, they are immoral and we are moral," and this unfounded partisan premise brings them to "accuse the Arabs, and them alone, for the continuation of the conflict." This preference, Morris continues, possibly stems from their being "conservative with a partisan commitment toward the State and an almost blind faith in the justice of the Zionist way." Morris, though, prefers to explain their opportunism less as ideology and more as stemming from "motives of career and preserving their positions." The conclusions of the work of Itamar Rabinovich, Morris says, are not of an "honest historian" but rather "of one who thinks politically" and prefers the office of ambassador in the United

States to historical truth. These power relations are reproduced in the universities, where the new-old historians prevail and where "people in academe fear to criticize strong people" like Shapira and Rabinovich; therefore, the "sharp criticism" that their studies deserve is silent, and the hegemony of the old historiography is sustained.[19]

Morris accompanied his conceptual reversal with a modification of the nature of the establishments standing behind the "old" and the "new-old" historiography. Initially the old historiography was fostered by Labor Zionism as a means of securing its hegemony. Since the 1980s, however, the right-wing governments have lost interest in the old historiography, according to Morris, and have actually created conditions for the rise of the new historiography. Thus, the amendment of the Israel Archives Law in 1981 and its relatively liberal implementation made it possible to use previously classified materials; this, Morris states, was the starting point of the new historiography.[20] Likewise, the publishing house of the Ministry of Defense, one of the bastions of the old historiography, has shown "openness and intellectual honesty" by publishing a book that "thoroughly undermines central propagandistic values that have characterized its books from the 1950s to the 1980s."[21]

With the authorities' loss of interest in the old historiography, Morris argues, the universities, where the new-old historians hold senior posts, have become the new establishment encouraging the old historiography. Given the essential differences between the two establishments, however, the career considerations of university professors have replaced the political interests of Labor Zionism in defending and preserving the old historiography. Thus, in Morris's new version academic integrity — or lack of it — has replaced political considerations as the underlying factor informing the difference between the two historiographies. Morris's shift from political considerations to academic integrity and intrigues is problematic from a theoretical point of view. The argument that the old historiography was used by Labor Zionism to manipulate public opinion matches various theories of political and cultural sociology. In contrast, positing the new-old historiography as the consequence of academic careerism devoid of wider political and social contexts seems a simplistic and idiosyncratic interpretation, which works against Morris's own explanation of the rise of the new historiography.

While theoretically problematic, Morris's later definitions of old, new and new-old historians, and of the establishments standing behind them, have a propagandistic advantage. Contrary to the generational-professional interpretation that assumed the end of the old historiography, the later presentation of historical research as an arena for protracted conflicts between rival schools arouses public interest, which has focused on the struggle within the professional community more than on its content. Moreover, the focus of the attack on well-known historians like Shapira and Rabinovich, who combine senior status in the academic establishment with high public profile, added to the controversy a personal, even gossipy, provocative dimension that helped to arouse the interest of the media, thereby turning it into an cultural-political "event."

Pappé attributes to the terms old and new historiography quite different meanings. He describes Israeli historiography as "a combination of positivist methodology and partisan writing," which is backward in comparison not only with the current critical schools but even with nineteenth-century European positivism, which "in the name of scientific accuracy challenged ideological and national commitment." The new historians, accordingly, attempt to free Israeli historiography from its methodological conservatism, ideological bias and Zionist commitment, all of which contradict scholarly standards.[22] Pappé's own definition of the concept of new historiography, however, is not only ambiguous but also contradictory.

In contrast to Morris, whose concept of new historiography is rooted in the narrow context of Israeli historiography, Pappé characterizes the new historiography as an Israeli adaptation of the *nouvelle histoire* — as developed in France and in the English-speaking world — with an emphasis on an interdisciplinary approach, combining history, social sciences and cultural studies. It is difficult to understand, from Pappé's definition, though, what is new in the new historiography; and it certainly does not supply any basis for criticism of Israeli historical research. As Pappé himself admits, since the 1970s, Israeli mainstream historiography — including that of the so-called old historians — has conducted a dialogue with the *Nouvelle Histoire*, as well as with other schools of social history, and adopted the new methods.

As Pappé evolved from new historian to post-Zionist, however, he changed his reasoning. The *Nouvelle Histoire* gave way to postmodernism as the source of inspiration for the new historiography, which, in rather a didactic and simplistic way, has now been presented as an application of postmodern critique to the study of Zionist and Israeli history.[23] If initially for Pappé the new historiography signified methodological innovation and inter-disciplinarity, it later became synonymous with relativism, which acknowledges the legitimacy of every historical narrative. Accordingly, the central traits of the new historians are an awareness of the existence of "earlier positions and hypotheses" influencing their studies and their recognition of the "unavoidable affinity between their actual stand on political questions and their view of the past."

By the claim that every narrative is legitimate and reflects a certain relative truth, the new historiography, Pappé explains, does not strive to replace the Zionist narrative with another, "more correct" narrative; rather, it seeks to undermine the claim of any narrative for the status of scientific truth. The object of Pappé's crude relativism is to emphasize that "the Zionist prism, especially that of the Labor movement ... is not ... the only prism" and to open Zionist history to a multiplicity of narratives, including those of the "others" and of the "losers." In contrast to the impression created by his relativism, however, Pappé posits the new historiography not just as another possible version of the historical events — which implies that it does not have any advantage over the old historiography — but as the true version. He presents his book as "a scholarly, that is historically accurate, account of the war of 1948," and demands to examine the authenticity and credibility of the different narratives.[24] Thus, he undermines his relativist approach and acknowledges that there are accurate accounts and inaccurate ones.

Pappé's objectives, however, apparently extend beyond the academic sphere to the public and political spheres. By undermining "the hegemonic narrative and discourse," especially its Labor-Zionist version, he strives "to expose its control over our lives — whether in Memorial Day ceremonies or in being sent to the battlefield or in deployment as an occupying force in territories that are not ours."[25] And, indeed, while the ambiguous and self-contradictory meaning that Pappé imparts to the new historiography is methodologically and theoretically problematic, it proves to be very useful in the sphere of public debate, enabling him to use postmodern relativism to challenge the academic research and at the same time to posit the new historiography as the politically correct narrative. Thus Pappé, who began his assault on the old historiography with a critique of its partisan, ideological nature, ends up exactly at the same point.

The different meanings that Morris and Pappé impart to the concepts of the old and new historiography stem from a deep methodological dispute between the two. Morris is a positivist who believes in objective historical truth, which the historian must strive to, and can, reveal. He rejects Pappé's relativism, stating that there is "a correct, 'true' narrative, and a distorted, mendacious narrative." In order to arrive at the correct narrative, "not only should the historian not serve political goals in his writing, he cannot take into account the possible political results or effects of his research."[26] In contrast, Pappé argues from his relativistic approach that objective historiography is an illusion and therefore should not be aspired to. In view of his dispute with Morris, he proposes a distinction between "critical historians," like Morris, who are different from the old historians only in their conclusions but not in their methodology, and "the new historians," who arrive at the new conclusions by using up-to-date methodologies.[27]

The methodological differences between Pappé and Morris are closely connected to their ideological disagreements. Both of them think that the new historiography will encourage the struggle for a better society and for peace,[28] but they differ in their attitude to Zionism, a crucial point in the new historiography controversy. Morris defines himself as a Zionist. He thinks that

Zionism is a legitimate national-liberation movement, to the extent that any national-liberation movement is legitimate, and he objects to the definition of Zionism as a sort of colonialism.[29] Pappé, in contrast, condemns Zionism as a colonialist movement, the result of religious illusion and historical falsification, whose oppressive nature is reflected in Israel in the contradiction between Jewish and Zionist ethnocentrism, on the one hand, and liberal and democratic values, on the other.[30]

In Pappé's opinion, Morris is not a new historian. He attacks Morris's stand on Zionism, criticizing his historical positivism, and points to the connection between Morris's Zionist ideology and conservative methodology. Pappé claims that writings may have contributed to shattering several historical myths, but he does not propose an alternative narrative; he only corrects the existing one, without undermining its hegemony.[31] For his part, Morris also attacks Pappé on ideological-methodological grounds. He emphasized that he was the one who actually coined the term "new Historiograph" and complained that it has been "abducted" and distorted by others who, like Pappé, have given it a completely different meaning than Morris' initial intention. Morris further claims that there is no difference between the indoctrination of the old historians, who preserve the myth of 1948, and the historical relativism of Pappé, because "both of them reject objectivity."[32]

The methodological and ideological controversy between Morris and Pappé shows that contrary to all appearances created by the public debate, the new historians do not form a school in any accepted sense. Indeed, the new historiography is neither a historical theory nor a methodology. Its common denominator, it will be argued below, is not a scholarly or an academic factor but lies in the same domain for which the old historiography is faulted: the effort to construct an alternative Israeli collective memory: in this case, to serve the ideological and political agenda of post-Zionism.

The Praxis of the New Historiography

One of the striking characteristics of the new historians is the gap between their far-reaching criticism — which constitutes the core of the new historiography — expressed from public platforms, particularly the press, on the one hand, and the content of their scholarly publications, which are supposed to serve as a basis of this criticism, on the other. For example, Morris's public statements on the place of the transfer of Palestinians in Zionist thinking and Israeli policy contradicts the conclusions of his own studies on the way the refugee problem was created.

As a "new historian," Morris repeatedly argues that the version of the old historiography on the exodus of the Palestinians in 1948 was deliberate, mendacious propaganda that tried to cover up acts of mass expulsion, mass murder, and looting and raping. The deception, he argues, started with Ben-Gurion and the official memory agencies, who knew the truth but suppressed it and intentionally spread the falsehood, which permeated all layers of the society. Moreover, Morris claims that the transfer idea lay at the basis of the Zionist agenda, which strove for the territorial concentration of the Jews in Palestine, and that the Zionist leadership, from Herzl to Ben-Gurion, sought to realize it. The conceptual background and the psychological preparation for the mass expulsion of the Palestinians during the 1948 war and for the prevention of their return after the war was thus created. To support Israel's refusal to permit the refugees' return, the Israeli propaganda machine created the myth, placing the responsibility for the Palestinians' exodus on their leadership — a premise that lies at the foundation of the old historiography and is replicated by the new-old historians.[33]

Morris's studies of the history of Israel's War of Independence and its aftermath, in particular his book *The Birth of the Palestinian Refugee Problem, 1947–1949*[34] — written before the author turned himself into a new historian — actually refutes his new historiography. Many of the facts that Morris uses as a new historian are, indeed, to be found in the book; however, the meanings they assume when fitted into the framework of that research contradict those he later disseminated as a new historian. Morris has made the transition from historical research to the new historiography by omitting two of the book's principal conclusions. First, the refugee problem was basically generated by internal Palestinian causes, foremost among them the weakness of Palestinian society and the psychological and physical crisis in which it was trapped at the beginning of the fighting. Second, the Israeli leadership had no plan whatsoever for the transfer or mass expulsion of Arabs prior to the war, and such a policy was never adopted during it, neither by the government nor by the Israel Defense Forces [IDF].

These two conclusions constitute the framework of Morris's description and analysis of the creation of the refugee problem. This description included documented cases of deliberate expulsions and atrocities, which were the result of local initiatives; but it is clear from the study that, with all their moral severity, these cases were not the result of an overall plan and did not shape the major trends of the process that created the refugee problem. Morris's study is more detailed than previous accounts and, as such, he has shed new light and imparted new insights. Contrary to his claim, though, he does not change the basis of the picture presented by the old historiography; his central conclusions, in fact, strengthen it. In this sense, the principal difference between Morris and his predecessors lies not in the facts but in the intention: the old historians wished to free themselves of the guilt implied in the refugee problem, whereas Morris seeks to blame and condemn those who, in his opinion, bore responsibility for generating the problem.

Morris's new historiography is to a large extent an effort to free himself from the conclusions of his own book. He accomplishes this by blurring the framework that delineates his conclusions, changing the weight and proportions of the various facts, transferring them from the margins to the center and vice versa — all of which allows him freedom of reinterpretation. He replaces the positivist analysis of his book with the moral judgment of the new historiography, and by reiterating selected tendentious facts, he gives them a greater weight than in his original study, while creating the impression that they are but examples confirming a general pattern portrayed in his book. Thus, for example, the expulsion of the Arabs from Lod and Ramle, which from *The Birth of the Palestinian Refugee Problem* may be considered to have been an exceptional event, becomes in Morris's new historiography the test case of the 1948 War.[35]

In order to overcome his book's conclusions, Morris is also prepared to deviate from the firm positivism that he normally preaches and to base his new historiography on psychological evaluations. Since he is unable to prove the claim that there was a transfer plan, he hypothesizes: "I estimate that at the end of 1947, with the beginning of the acts of hostility, a half year before the end of the British Mandate in Palestine, the transfer idea hovered at the back of the minds of the leaders of the Zionist *Yishuv* as a continuation of its presence in the 1930s and 1940s."[36] Using the same method and the same terms, Morris tries to connect Ben-Gurion with the idea of transfer, and he again hypothesizes that even though "a transfer policy was not adopted officially in 1948 and there was no central plan to generate an Arab exodus" and even though "Ben-Gurion did not speak [of it] publicly," the transfer idea was "at the back of his mind."[37]

Another fundamental difference between the new historiography and the studies that supposedly inform them is the presentation of the Israeli establishment as a monolithic body. From Morris's studies it emerges that the Israeli establishment, mainly under Labor Zionist leadership, was split over policies towards the Palestinian issue in general and the refugee problem and its implications in particular. The differences of opinion cut across all Israeli establishments — the political decision-makers, the army and the civil service — and were manifest publicly in inter-party as well as intra-party disputes within Mapai and Mapam, the two parties that constituted the basis of the governing coalition.[38] Unlike the picture of a divided establishment as portrayed in his studies, by dint of the logic behind his new historiography Morris turns the Israeli establishment into a monolith. He glosses over the significance of differences in opinion in order to clear the way for a description of a homogeneous policy, derived from a common Zionist belief that promoted transfer prior to the war, generated it in the course of the war and acted to blur it in constructing Israeli collective memory after the war.

If Morris elides the differences between the various schools within Labor Zionism, Pappé denies the difference between the Zionist left and right altogether, portraying them as merely two facets of the same Zionist monolith that is reflected in an agreed, uniform discourse of blood. This monolithic claim, though, which lies at the basis of his new historiography, contrasts with Pappé's own studies. In referring to Israeli policy towards the Arab world in 1948–56, he states:

> Ostensibly a uniformity of opinions prevailed in those years with regards to the subjects of security policy and the Israeli-Arab conflict. Actually, however, the Israeli leadership was divided in its attitude to the nature of the conflict, its expected duration, its solution, its consequences, and its meanings. These differences of opinion characterized the entire Israeli political spectrum.[39]

Pappé argues further that differences of opinion also split the ruling Mapai party. Following previous studies, he points to the dispute between Ben-Gurion and his foreign minister, Moshe Sharett, which led to "the formulation of two opposing political schools among the senior leadership. One, 'Ben-Gurionist,' promoted a policy of deterrence and retribution; the other, 'Sharettist,' favored a policy of restraint and moderation." Other differences between the two schools were Ben-Gurion's support of the "Hashemite option" while Sharett backed the "Palestinian option"; Ben-Gurion demonstrated "utter pessimism towards the possibility of peace" and worked to integrate Israel into the Western world, whereas Sharett "sought to integrate Israel into the region."[40]

Blurring the division that split the Israeli establishment is vital for sustaining the new historiography's claim to the existence of a homogeneous, official version propagated by the old and new-old historiography. If historiography serves as a tool for political manipulation, as the new historians claim, then the split of the governing elite over central questions of policy had to produce more than a single narrative, something that would deprive the new historiography of one of its principal contentions. As it happened, the Israeli leadership was indeed split during the War of Independence, and the inner struggles gave birth to contrasting narratives of the history of the war, created by rival political and ideological factions which prevented the creation of an official version.

Moreover, one of the achievements of the academic historiography of Zionism and the State of Israel since the 1970s lay in undermining the monolithic appearance of the preceding ideological historiography of the various political parties and organizations. Academic historiography broke down the different establishments into subgroups, exposing the splits over central ideological and political issues between contesting factions as well as within them. This process even led to identifying various "new-old historians" as supporters of certain ideologies, parties, organizations or individual leaders. Thus, for example, Anita Shapira was identified with the heritage of the left-wing, Mapam-oriented Palmah, and Yoav Gelber with the Ben-Gurion line.[41] This has contributed greatly to creating a multifaceted picture, which has made it more difficult to use research as a means of political manipulation. In this sense, the internal contradictions, the ideological, non-critical approach and the monolithic narrative that characterizes the new historiography merely reproduce the partisan narratives for which it criticized the old historiography.

The New Historiography: From Historical Research to Collective Memory

The tension between historical research and collective memory may serve as a suitable paradigm for understanding the new historiography.[42] As is evident from its arguments and *modus operandi*, the principal goals of the new historiography are to be found, not in the area of historical research, but in the construction of an alternative Israeli collective memory focusing on cultivating guilt feelings and self-condemnation. It clearly emerges from Morris's article in which he coined the term "new historiography" that, while speaking about historiography, he means in effect collective memory; that is, the false representation of the past in textbooks, memoirs or the press — the obvious agents of collective memory. Likewise, his criticism of the new-old historians is focused less on their studies — which even in his opinion meet all the standards of historical research — than on the implications of their studies for the collective memory, whose essential assumption can be summarized as: "We are okay, the Arabs are not okay."[43] Morris's focus on collective memory reveals his aspiration to give Israeli society an alternative memory, which, without denying the legitimacy of Zionism, can question its morality.

In Pappé's new historiography, collective memory occupies an even more central place. His relativistic approach elides the difference between historical research and collective memory and turns historiography into a kind of battlefield between opposing narratives striving for hegemony. Pappé claims that Zionism created, "a new collective memory in order to erase other memories," like that of the Arabs or the *Mizrahim*, while using the new collective memory to exclude every rival non-Zionist "other" in Israel and in the Jewish world. By challenging the Zionist collective memory, the new historiography, according to Pappé, is likely to wake Israeli society from the frightful Zionist dream and emancipate it from its nightmare.[44]

Morris and Pappé, then, began the campaign of the new historiography from within historical research and ended up as agents of an alternative collective memory, while trying to blur or even erase altogether the contradiction between research and memory. This may explain how Morris, whose research focused on uncovering the facts pertaining to the birth of the refugee problem, could have contradicted his own findings during his transition to the new historiography, that is to say in his effort to construct a new Israeli collective memory. However, in this endeavor the new historiography has used the same practices of which it accuses the old historiography, a fact which underlines the nature of the new historiography as a partisan ideology.

In its efforts to construct a post-Zionist collective memory, the new historians ascribe great importance to the Israeli memory of 1948, which, in the spirit of the Zionist ethos of "the new Jew," they claim, was turned by the Israeli political and academic establishments into the formative moment of Israeli identity. Accordingly, in order to construct a morally stainless Israeli collective memory, the Palestinians' past and their suffering were excluded from the victorious Israeli narrative of 1948, as was the alleged indifference of the Zionist leadership to the destruction of European Jewry during the Holocaust. Since the new historians perceive the Palestinian as the ultimate "other" that marks the boundaries of the Israeli identity, it was only natural that they would make the refugee question the nub of their revision.

The Israeli collective memory of 1948, however, does not confirm the post-Zionist criticism; in fact, in order to justify their revision, the new historians invented a phantom, imagined version of an official Israeli collective memory, which was cultivated, so it is claimed, by the political and academic establishments. This fictitious version ranged from the grotesque and righteous to the vulgar and demonic and focused on the contrast between "the good Israelis" and the "bad Arabs." This simplistic and untenable version of the memory of the war — easy to ridicule and criticize — was intended to blur the political and moral complexity of the prevailing Israeli memory of the War of Independence and the refugee problem, a memory that undermines the core of the claims of the new historiography.

Morris's psychological interpretation, that the veterans of 1948 could only remember the war through the nostalgia of "their finest hour," which left no place for the dark side,[45] contrasted with the way this memory was actually constructed. In the course of the war itself — as emerges from Morris's own studies — voices condemning acts of violence against citizens were raised in different quarters of the political and military establishments and acted to stop them. These voices pointed to the harsh consequences of the growing refugee problem and urged the government to take practical measures to put an end to the human suffering and the political damage that would ensue. These voices were particularly loud on the Zionist left, which was not only a senior partner in the Labor government coalition but exerted great influence on both intellectual circles and the army. In fact, the left played a dominant role in constructing the Israeli collective memory of 1948 both during and in particular after the war.[46]

The complex way in which the Israeli memory of 1948 coped with the human and moral consequences of the war is reflected, for example, in the writings of two of its most important agents: the writer Yizhar Smilansky (alias S. Yizhar) and the poet Nathan Alterman. In his short stories, "Hirbet Hizah" and "Ha-shavu'i" (The Prisoner), stories that were included in the school curriculum and became cornerstones of the Israeli memory of the war, Yizhar clearly portrayed the injuries inflicted on innocent Arabs by Israeli soldiers in the course of the war, pointing to their difficult moral implications.[47] Alterman, in one of his popular political newspaper columns, attacked the harming of the Arab civilian population during the conquest of Lod (Lydda) and the indifference of Israeli public opinion to these acts. Alterman's reproach did not remain unnoticed: Ben-Gurion praised this column in a letter to Alterman and read it at a meeting of the Provisional State Council. He also had it distributed among IDF soldiers along with his own letter to Alterman.[48] Yizhar and Alterman were not only two of the leading literary figures in Israel, they were also the closest to any possible definition of "establishment artists." The two were close to Ben-Gurion and accompanied him through every political twist and turn. Yizhar was a Mapai member of the Knesset, and Alterman — the nation's leading poet, according to Morris — was described as Ben-Gurion's "court poet." In the words of Moshe Dayan, "Alterman with his special Altermanism was the one who educated the people to Ben-Gurionism."[49]

Grappling with the complex moral questions pertaining to the human aspect of the war played a central role in constructing the Israeli collective memory of 1948. The accepted version did, indeed, blame the Arab leaders for the creation of the refugee problem by encouraging the exodus of the Palestinians with the promise of a quick return after an anticipated victory while rejecting the urgings of the local Jewish leadership to remain, as in the cases of Haifa and Tiberias. However, there was also the recognition that a key factor in hastening the refugee flight was the massacre of Palestinians in the village of Deir Yassin. The fact that the massacre was carried out by paramilitary right-wing opposition organizations made it easier for the Israeli hegemonic collective memory to acknowledge a certain Jewish responsibility for the Arab exodus, while exempting the Labor-Zionist leadership from any guilt.

Moreover, the struggle between the ruling Labor Zionism and the right-wing opposition transformed the condemnation of the right for the atrocities in the Deir Yassin affair into a propaganda asset that promised clear political profit. By keeping the affair alive in the Israeli collective memory, the party conflict prevented any attempt to blur the question of Jewish responsibility for the refugee problem and encouraged scholarly and political debate of its causes. In response to the condemnation of the Deir Yassin affair by the Israeli, mainly Labor, establishment, the right-wing opposition charged the left with responsibility for "Deir Yassins" of its own, a charge that reflected a certain degree of recognition that acts of expulsion were morally wrong. The presence of the Deir Yassin affair in Israeli political discourse has constantly raised the question of Jewish responsibility for the refugee problem, and thus turned it into an integral part of the Israeli collective memory of the War of Independence.[50]

In contrast to what the new historians claim, and unlike what one may have reasonably expected, the Israeli establishment did not adopt a strategy of repressing the memory of the refugee issue; it was not excluded from the hegemonic memory of 1948, and the principal moral questions involved were not avoided but became part of Israel's political discourse. The reasons for this "unnatural" development should be sought in the inter-party struggle of the 1950s and 1960s, which placed the memory of 1948 at the center of two different ideological disputes. One was the struggle between right and left, in which the hegemonic Labor Zionism made political capital from blaming the right-wing opposition for atrocities that occurred during the war. The second was the struggle between "doves" and "hawks" within Labor Zionism — particularly between Mapai and Mapam, but even within Mapai — in which the "doves" turned the status of the Arab citizens in Israel and a solution to the refugee problem into major issues in their struggle for peace. It appears, therefore, that in contrast to the simplistic and superficial description offered by the new historians, the Israeli hegemonic memory of 1948, mainly cultivated by Labor Zionism, was characterized by a dialectical attitude towards the refugee question: the political and moral questions pertaining to it were placed on the memory map; however, the responsibility for it was cast on the "other," whether the Palestinians themselves or Jewish right-wing rivals.

What made it easier to include the refugee issue in the hegemonic memory was the declared Israeli readiness to solve it. This policy, though, did not have an immediate practical implication; it was conditional on an overall solution to the Israeli–Arab conflict and was therefore postponed to an indefinite future. In this context the hegemonic memory of 1948 used a practice that may be defined as "conditional justification": it acknowledged the refugee problem, but without accepting blame or responsibility for its creation; it expressed a principled willingness to solve it, but only in the framework of an overall Israeli–Arab settlement. This practice politicized the refugee question, blurring its moral, human aspects. Conditional justification influenced the strategy that informed the construction of Israeli memory: once the refugee question ceased to be a source of guilt and became solvable as part of an expected Israeli–Arab peace, it could easily be incorporated into the Israeli hegemonic collective memory.

By contrast, the respective memories of the Israeli radical left and right — which had a similar content but contrasting political objectives — were constructed through an opposing practice, that of guilt and accusation. The radical left argued that the refugees were expelled as part of a "grand plan" of ethnic cleansing and that the expulsion attested to the immorality and illegitimacy of Zionism. Contrary to the politicization of the refugee question in the hegemonic memory, the radical left — and the new historians in their wake — turned it into a moral issue, an original sin that was a source of feelings of guilt.[51] The right, too, emphasized Israeli responsibility for the expulsion of the refugees, but claimed that, for national security reasons, it had not been possible to act otherwise. It contended that the whole Zionist project from the very beginning would not have been possible without the dispossession of the Arabs, and that this existential necessity gave it moral justification. Hence, any political effort to solve the refugee problem would have undermined the foundations of Zionism.[52]

The "discoveries" of the new historiography, it appears, are nothing else but a recycling of arguments that have been reiterated in the Israeli political debate over the last 50 years by opposition circles, Zionist and non-Zionist, merely updating the factual base and masquerading as scholarly research. Moreover, in some of their attempts to construct an alternative Israeli collective memory of 1948, the new historians take pains to present a one-dimensional, simplistic and vulgar version of the hegemonic collective memory that is easy to demonize, ridicule, attack and refute. Thus, they obfuscate the real nature of the "accepted version," which has politicized the refugee problem and its solution, thus enabling the incorporation of this problem, with all its human and moral dilemmas, into the hegemonic memory.

Right Post-Zionism

While left post-Zionism created a basis for undermining the moral foundations of Zionism, various circles on the right seemed willing to adopt this criticism, but setting it within a different value system. This meeting of the extremes occurred in the 1990s in the course of the struggle by the right against the Israeli withdrawal from the West Bank and Gaza Strip based on the Oslo Accords. Various rightist circles started to use the new historiography's claim regarding the dispossessing nature of Zionism as a moral and historical basis for opposing any withdrawal, while developing an alternative ideology that may be termed "right post-Zionism."[53] The right post-Zionists claim that those same arguments that are used to justify the dismantling of Jewish settlements in the West Bank and Gaza can be used to negate the legitimacy of the Zionist project as a whole.

POST-ZIONISM AND THE PRIVATIZATION OF ISRAELI MEMORY 27

In a column entitled "Who's Afraid of the Truth?" published in the most popular Israeli Hebrew daily, *Yediot Aharanot*, in late 1999, Emunah Eilon, a religious-nationalist publicist who represents the hard line among the settlers, came to the defense of the new historians. She argued that "the official Mapai version" of the history of Israel may be nicer and friendlier, but "the version of the new historians is the true version." Referring to the "difficult, even shocking discoveries" that the new historians "lay at the doorstep of the Israeli entity," she writes:

> Even the guardians of the walls of Zionism, who demand to remove the new historians to outside the consensus ... do not try to argue that their discoveries are nothing but wicked and anti-Semitic false facts. The claims of those who object to the new historians ... are not understandable. ... If the country is ours ... we have no choice but to fight for it when necessary and to chase away anyone who needs to be expelled, and we have no choice but to acknowledge the tragedy that we have caused others. ... In any event, there is nothing there to undermine our faith in the justness of our way and our certainty in our right to the Land.[54]

The new historiography integrates well, then, with Eilon's outlook, according to which "the Israeli entity" was established through conquest, dispossession and expulsion and might use these practices again in the future in order to survive. Thus like the new historians, Eilon, too, transforms the debate about the past into a discussion of the morality of future policies and practices.

Acceptance of the new historiography, rejection of the "official Mapai version" and criticism of the "guardians of Zionism" are repeatedly expressed in the right-wing journal *Tkhelet* (*Azure*), which appears in both Hebrew and English editions. *Azure* is published by the Shalem Center, a research institute set up by Ron Lauder, a right-wing American Jewish philanthropist and supporter of Binyamin Netanyahu, which offers an Israeli version of the "New Conservatism" developed by Judeo-conservatives in the US that combines American-like competitive capitalism, Jewish religious tradition and Israeli hawkish foreign policy.

In an editorial named "Making History," Daniel Polisar, the editor of *Azure*, adopts an ambivalent attitude towards the new historians: on the one hand, he warns against their penetration into the academic, cultural and educational establishments of Israel, arguing that "the assault on the legacy of Zionism poses a grave threat to Israel's future," for "no nation can retain its basic vitality if its entire historical narrative comes to be seen in the public mind as a long series of moral failings." On the other hand, he accepts the facts on which the new historians base their moral condemnation of Zionism. He attacks the mainstream historians who question the reliability of the new historians and their findings, arguing that it is not the facts used by the new historians that need to be questioned but rather their perspective and interpretations. Therefore, he suggests adopting a "Jewish-nationalist" perspective that will judge the "problematic chapters" and the "skeletons" that will continue to emerge from the Zionist closet in the light of moral criteria that give priority to the interests of the nation and the state over injustice and human suffering, of Jews and Arabs alike.

Polisar adopts, then, the factual basis offered by the new historians, but disputes their moral judgment of Zionist history: the policy they condemn as immoral and as reflecting the oppressive nature of Zionism, he justifies as an existential necessity morally justified by its service to Jewish and Israeli interests. Polisar, like Eilon, focuses his attack on "Israel's mainstream cultural leadership," who lack an appropriate historical perspective and whose response to the moral challenge posed by the new historians has been "less than inspiring." This failure, he concludes, might have implications that extend beyond the cultural area, for "the future of the Jewish state" may be dependent on the vindication of the "nation's past."[55]

The support for the new historiography by post-Zionists on both the left and the right may be explained in ideological terms by its contribution to undermining "the morality of partition" (that is, the partition of pre-1948 Mandatory Palestine into Jewish and Arab nation-states), a principle that is historically fundamental to the policy of Labor Zionism and bases the justice of Zionist policy in the conflict with the Arabs on its willingness to compromise and on its use of force only as a last resort in face of Arab rejectionist aggression. Left post-Zionism repudiates the morality of partition, advocating instead a different kind of binational solution that denies the legitimacy of Israel as a Jewish nation-state. Right post-Zionism repudiates it, advocating the principle of "Greater Israel," which rejects the idea of a Palestinian nation-state alongside Israel. Presenting Zionism as tainted by the expulsion and dispossession of Palestinians enables both left and right post-Zionism to claim that the policy of partition has historically failed to solve the Israeli–Arab conflict. Moreover, both claim that Zionism can be realized only by military force and not through political agreement — according to left post-Zionism because of the colonial dispossessing nature of Zionism, which exposes its immorality, and according to right post-Zionism because of Palestinian rejectionism, which justifies the use of force.

Polisar's ambivalence towards the new historiography characterizes *Azure*'s attitude towards post-Zionism. On the one hand, *Azure* presents itself as the ultimate critic of post-Zionism and warns against its growing influence. Positing post-Zionism as a reflection of the deep-seated value crisis in Israeli society, *Azure* repeatedly attacks the failure of the mainstream's "hollow Zionism" to deal with it;[56] it emphasizes the Jewish-conservative approach as the only answer to the crisis of Israeli society in general and to the challenge of post-Zionism in particular. On the other hand, these very arguments raise doubts whether *Azure* indeed offers an antithesis to post-Zionism, as it seeks to portray itself, or whether this is yet another example of a meeting between political extremes, which in the name of competing ideologies and under the guise of rhetorical polarization in effect cooperate and sustain each other.

The critique of "Israel's mainstream cultural leadership"[57] and of its failure to confront left post-Zionism reveals *Azure*'s doubt whether Zionism can constitute a framework for "the Jewish state." Assaf Sagiv, *Azure*'s deputy editor, almost goes as far as proclaiming "the end of Zionism." Attacking the spread of the "Dionysian youth culture," which reflects and reinforces the dissolution of Israeli society, he argues that a Dionysian ecstatic revival has filled the ideological vacuum "left by the demise of the old Zionism" and that it "has been fueled by a mistrust felt by many youth toward anything reminiscent of the grandiose slogans and utopian promises of an earlier day."[58] Sagiv emphasizes that in Israel, which "adopted the modern cult of youth," the youth were the first to enlist in the service of the Zionist revolution, while today they are also the first "to herald its demise."[59] He concludes that the Dionysian outburst originates in the failure of Israeli society "to provide its young with a viable alternative ethos," and that in order to nurture "a countervailing cultural force," Israel needs a "new faith."[60]

Azure's attack on Zionism continued in a critique of one of its most important cultural manifestations: modern Hebrew literature. In his article "Towards a Hebrew Literature," Assaf Inbari differentiates "Hebrew literature" from "literature in Hebrew." He states that "almost none of the literature written in the Hebrew language in the twentieth century retained the Hebrew poetics." For him, Hebrew literature in its various genres, which was intertwined in the fabric of Jewish religious life down through the generations, is "historical, national, deed-based narrative prose." On the other hand, modern Hebrew literature — the child of the Zionist revolution — has broken this continuity and "is not historical but perceives time as immersed in the present; it is not national, but individualistic in content."

The "only significant exception" to this rule, Inbari maintains, is S. Y. Agnon, who was "the only author writing in the Hebrew language in the twentieth century who produced anything that can properly be called 'Hebrew' literature." It is not Agnon, however, Inbari continues, but Y. H. Brenner, whose "poetics can be understood as the precise opposite of those of the Hebrew narrative tradition," who is "the most widely emulated" model of Israeli authors. Current Hebrew literature, Inbari believes, is no more than "a shallow reflection" of prevailing trends in Western culture, and thus "we have consigned ourselves to self-destruction." He concludes by calling upon "those who hold Jewish cultural identity dear" to renew links "with the Hebrew literary heritage," which is the pre-Zionist one.[61] Inbari adds, then, a cultural-historical dimension to Sagiv's criticism of Zionism: the failure of Zionism to deal with the present crisis of Israeli society is rooted in its core, in particular in its rupture of continuity with the Jewish past.

Yoram Hazony, president of the Shalem Center, proffers an overall explanation for the failure of Zionism and a basis for a "new faith." In his article "'The Jewish State' at 100," he identifies the principal cause of the failure of Zionism in its retreat from the original Herzlian vision, which combined conservatism, idealism, private enterprise and Jewish religion. After Herzl's premature death, Hazony explains, his opponents took over, and Zionism was realized by the Labor movement, which under the influence of Russian Marxism combined materialism, socialism and statism. In contrast to Herzl's idealism, it placed its emphasis on "practical work" — building farms and factories — as a means of creating a "new Jew." The State of Israel, as born in 1948, "reflected Labor's priorities, not Herzl's — and still [it] does." The Labor movement under Ben-Gurion's leadership advanced its materialistic agenda, using "the constant threat of imminent war" to create a sense of collective mission. When finally the military tension eased, Labor Zionism, like Soviet Communism, collapsed, leaving an ideological vacuum. The waning of Zionism began after Ben-Gurion's retirement in 1963, which was perceived by his rivals as an opportunity to replace the Zionist mission with the desire for "normality," manifested by "peace abroad and personal self-fulfillment at home" — the origins of post-Zionism.[62] Hazony's interpretation enables him to appear, on the one hand, as the guardian of "true" idealistic Zionist ideology and, on the other hand, as the most pointed critic of historical Zionism, all of whose practical, "materialistic" manifestations he negates.

After the degeneration of Labor Zionism, Hazony continues, "the only Zionist idea with any kick left in it was the yeshiva nationalism ... and the religious-nationalist leadership," which emerged after 1967, as the dominant power of the Israeli right. "Yeshiva nationalism," however, failed to delineate a new agenda and became "eerily reminiscent of Ben-Gurionism" and its political message and methods. No wonder that under its hegemony the Israeli right has turned into a "new Mapai." Yeshiva nationalism, according to Hazony, did not transcend the Labor paradigm and did not constitute a real alternative to Labor Zionism. Absurdly "the materialistic concerns" that have been at the heart of Labor — Jewish settlement, Jewish immigration, military service, and even farming — remained virtually unchanged."[63] In order to revive the Israeli right, Hazony and the Shalem Center promote Jewish-American neoconservatism as a real alternative that will replace the one offered by yeshiva nationalism. Hazony emphasizes that "the crucial war is not being waged over the territories of Judea and Samaria and the Oslo Accord, but between conservatism and liberalism."[64] Thus, he turns the territorial and strategic emphases of the national-rightist agenda into values that draw their justification from the neo-conservative *Weltanschauung*.

Hazony's critical analysis of the Zionist project certainly reflects a prevailing sentiment among the right, even if it is not the hegemonic one. In his article, "In Praise of Post-Zionism," in the settlers' journal *Nekudah*, Yair Shapira offers a similar analysis. He rejects the idea that gained a certain popularity in national-religious circles after Yitzhak Rabin's assassination, that they had to come to terms with the mainstream of Labor Zionism in order to fight the spread of post-Zionism together. By contrast, Shapira calls on the disciples of Rabbi Kook — yeshiva nationalism, in Hazony's term — to draw closer to the post-Zionists "in order to save their souls from the affliction of the guardians of the corpse of historical Zionism," that is, Labor Zionism. The affinity of yeshiva nationalism and post-Zionism is based, according to Shapira, on their mutual opposition to Zionist materialism and to the desire to be normal "like all other nations." Against Zionist materialism and normality, Shapira emphasizes, Judaism is characterized by spiritualism, particularism and alienness. The Jewish people developed in the diaspora, where its culture and values were created, and therefore he rejects the Zionist negation of the diaspora. He stresses that the only way for the Jews in Israel to retain their Jewish particularism is, paradoxically, by rejecting the developing normality and nurturing the sense of being strangers even there. In Israel, the Jewish people has "to continue to cling to its trait as a wandering people ... to continue to be in exile in its redemption." In contrast to the classic Zionist stand, which holds that it is not enough to take the Jews out of the diaspora, but that the diaspora mentality has to be taken out of the Jews, Shapira believes that while Jewish continuity indeed necessitates taking the Jews out of the diaspora, diasporic alienness should not be taken away from the Jews.[65] Establishing the diaspora as a positive situation is essential to the post-Zionist argumentation, which presents diaspora Jewry as the ultimate "other," preceding the postmodern condition.[66]

Hazony, like Shapira, shows empathy with post-Zionism as a negation of materialist, Ben-Gurionist Zionism. He even argues that post-Zionism and yeshiva nationalism are closer, each in its own way, to the spirit of the ideas of Herzl than is Labor Zionism:

> Far from being a sign of advancing materialism, as is often claimed among Zionist diehards, the turn towards Post-Zionist values in Israel after Ben-Gurion was precisely the opposite: It presented the search for something higher on the part of many intelligent, very spiritual Jews, for whom trying to persist on the inspiration of Labor Israel's actually rather mediocre physicality meant suffocation. ... Among today's Post-Zionists, there are competing conceptions as to what must be done to satisfy the longings of many Israelis to freedom, creativity,

intellectualism, constitutionalism, internationalism, and a touch of universalism — all things which Labor Zionism, in its tribalism, provincialism and materialism, had never been able to provide.[67]

Hazony continues:

> Virtually alone on the Israeli political landscape, Post-Zionists and others on the New Left have made conscientious, if often mistaken, efforts to make Israel a country in which the needs of the individual can find satisfaction — while cultural apolitical figures identified with Jewish nationalism have consistently opposed these efforts, believing that it is the introduction of "American" norms which has caused the destruction of the collective Jewish-national identity. But the nationalists have tragically misunderstood the revolution they were witnessing: Post-Zionism is not a consequence of increasing individual freedom; it is a reaction to decades of intentional suffocation of the individual by state socialism. That is, Post-Zionism is caused not by freedom, but by bondage. It is the abuse of the individual by the Labor Zionist state, which has brought about the disgust for the Jewish national idea.[68]

Hazony accepts, then, the core of the post-Zionists' criticism: Zionism as realized — by left, right and the religious — involved collectivism and oppression of individualism; the collective nature of Zionism, in all its various forms, left no outlet for Israelis of conscience, thus encouraging in reaction the development of post-Zionism. Nevertheless, unlike the post-Zionists, Hazony does not negate Zionism in principle, because of its collectivist and oppressive nature, but presents an alternative model of an individualistic Zionism. In contrast to Labor Zionism — and its yeshiva nationalism version — which in his interpretation was based on the state, he presents what might be called "market Zionism," a capitalistic society built on an individualistic ethos and free market, with minimum state regulation. Like the post-Zionists, Hazony's market Zionism reproaches historical Zionism; unlike them, he tries to enlist the term "Zionism" into the service of an opposing ideology rooted in the Israeli right. In order to impart historical legitimization to his market Zionism, Hazony turns it into Herzl's "true vision." Employing an idiosyncratic interpretation, Hazony distorts Herzl's Zionism, forcing it into the contours of American Jewish neoconservatism.[69] He transforms Herzl from a radical who believed in social justice and public regulation of the economy and society into a conservative who combines free-market capitalism and Jewish religiosity in the spirit of the Judeo-conservatives in the US.[70]

Azure promotes the neoconservative ideology as a model for the Israeli right. In his article "On the political stupidity of the Jews," Irving Kristol, one of the leading Judeo-conservatives, rejects Israeli Zionist mainstream political thought because its concepts derive from "romantic nationalism" in Central and Eastern Europe and "from the European Left." In contrast he proposes "Western political conservatism" as a basis for Israeli political thought. Reconciling Adam Smith with Edmund Burke, the ideologues of a free-market and a conservative society, Kristol emphasizes that Western conservatism perceives tradition and religion as indispensable for the orderly function of a free-market economy, and he urges Israelis to adopt this ideological combination. Like another ideologue of the free-market economy, Friedrich Hayek — whose thinking the Shalem Center and *Azure* work to propagate in Israel — Kristol criticizes the "universalist utopianism that characterized the Enlightenment," which strove to construct society in accordance with a universally valid program.[71]

In contrast to Hazony's and *Azure*'s stand, however, revolutionary radicalism, offspring of the "universalist utopianism that characterized the Enlightenment," is the conceptual basis of Herzlian Zionism. As expressed in his writings, in *Altneuland* in particular, Herzl perceived Zionism as "social engineering" in the spirit of utopian socialism, which by planned and regulated economy aspires to construct "a new society" that will constitute an alternative to capitalism with its failures and evils.[72] Zionism, in Herzl's view, was a rebellion against traditional Jewish society — characterized by the rule of the rabbis and the wealthy, middleman economics, fear of the non-Jew, and messianism — in an effort to modernize, normalize and politicize Jewish existence. In place of the traditional religious ethos, Herzl's Zionism offered the Jews radical, social utopianism, namely a conscious construction of their economics, society and culture, as well as reconciliation with the Gentile world.[73] *Azure* and Hazony, in contrast, come out against the Zionist radical-utopian ethos and, instead, advance a conservative ethos that combines competitive capitalism with Jewish traditionalism.

On the face of it, *Azure*'s right post-Zionism is focused mainly on criticizing the way that Zionism was realized in Israel; in a deeper sense, however, it is based on a principled rejection of the essential foundations of the prevalent Zionist idea: rebellion against the Jewish past, the politicization of the Jews, the creation of a model welfare state, the separation of Jewish nationalism and religion, the normalization of Jewish relations with the non-Jewish world, and the secularization of Hebrew culture. Right post-Zionism acknowledges only the Zionist principle of Jewish sovereignty, while working to neutralize the effect of its social-radicalism on Israeli society, in order to adapt it to the agenda of the "new conservatism."

Left and right post-Zionism do, though, share a common ground: both reject Zionism as a basis for Israeli collective identity, whether for "civil" reasons on the left or for "Jewish" reasons on the right. Both are of the opinion that the "old" Zionism — Labor Zionism and national-(religious) Zionism alike — is in the process of dissolution, losing its hegemony as the organizing idea of the Israeli public sphere. Against the background of their agreement on "the end of Zionism," the post-Zionists disagree on a worthy substitute: the left post-Zionists perceive the dissolution of Zionism with its oppressive nature as an emancipatory process and, therefore, reject its replacement with any other organizing project. Right post-Zionists, in contrast, consider the withering of Zionism an unavoidable consequence of its limited Jewish horizon and of its historical subordination to the hegemony of the left; they point to the need for "a new faith," whose basis is to be supplied by neoconservatism grounded on a commitment to Jewish heritage.

Right and left post-Zionism, each in its own way, struggle against the radical-collectivist ethos of Zionism, which serves as a source of legitimization for the regulation of the economy, society and culture in constructing a "new society," a "new human being" and a "new Jew." Right and left post-Zionism are inspired by opposing intellectual traditions and define themselves by means of rival ideologies; at the same time, however, in the tradition of the encounter between political extremes that sustain each other — like that between the right and postmodernism in general — they are potential political partners. Both oppose the project of Enlightenment, which they view as totalitarian and oppressive, although the left adopts the postmodern criticism of the Enlightenment, whereas the right attacks it in arguments taken from conservative thinking. Both make use of the category of "the Jew" in order to dismantle Israeli collective identity as defined by "the Zionist." The left sees the dissolution of Zionist collectivism as the first step in transforming Israel from an "ethno-democracy" and even a Jewish "ethnocracy" into a multicultural, universalist democracy; whereas the right uses "the Jew" to replace Zionism with an alternative "more Jewish" collective identity.

Both ideologies employ arguments from the arsenal of the politics of identity to undermine the hegemony of Labor Zionism and its offspring: left post-Zionism supports the struggles for the recognition of the "others" of Israeli society and attacks what it perceives as the primordial Jewish nature of Zionism; right post-Zionism criticizes the "non-Jewish" nature of Israeli politics and culture, and in adopting Samuel P. Huntington's paradigm of the "clash of civilizations"[74] encourages Jewish primordialism as the basis for its "new faith." Both view the collectivism that characterizes Zionism as a source of oppression and prefer free-market capitalism to the regulating force of the state. Whereas right post-Zionism supports capitalism, which it presents as a kind of "natural law," left post-Zionism opposes state intervention and capitalism alike; however, it supports privatization as an emancipatory step, since it perceives the state's power of coercion to be a greater menace than that of a capitalist free market.

Post-Zionism and the Privatization of Israeli Collective Memory

Left and right post-Zionism repeatedly present themselves as an opposition to the hegemonic Zionist establishment in Israel and as a challenge and alternative to its values. Most commentators have accepted this claim in discussing the factors that account for the rise of post-Zionism — mainly the left version — and its success in redelineating the contours of Israeli discourse. A closer look at the way in which post-Zionism acquired its central public standing, however, shows that this oppositionist stance is fictitious, no more than a means to arousing public interest. In fact, the ascendancy of Post-Zionism is due to cooperating with parties found at the very heart of the establishment. Overcoming the oppositionist appearance of post-Zionism and examining its relationship with the Israeli establishment are, then, preconditions for analyzing the factors that enabled its ascendancy.

The debate over the new historiography and critical sociology began as a dispute within Israeli academe, which has since continued to be the principal arena for discussing various issues pertaining to the post-Zionist agenda. Contrary to the myth cultivated by the post-Zionists, who present themselves as an opposition to the academic establishment, they were, in fact co-opted by it. As part of the acceptance of postmodernist concepts in universities and as part of the normal succession of generations, researchers with post-Zionist views gradually began to occupy a central place in the academic establishment and to define a new orthodoxy.[75] This, paradoxically, may suggest the possibility that Post-Zionism was in effect assisting establishment interests.

An important role in propagating post-Zionist ideas has been played by the Van Leer Institute in Jerusalem, a semi-governmental institution that serves as one of the main channels for the flow of ideas from academe to the public at large and has a dominant role in setting Israel's intellectual agenda.[76] Yehuda Elkana, who was a professor at Tel Aviv University and headed the Van Leer Institute during the emergence of post-Zionism, delineated its ideas back in 1988.[77] During Elkana's term as director, the Van Leer Institute supplied a range of forums for the dissemination of post-Zionist ideas which were presented as the application of the postmodern critique to Israeli reality. The most prominent of these forums was the journal *Theory and Criticism*, published jointly by the Van Leer Institute and the Ha-Kibbutz Ha-Meuhad Publishing House. The latter, one of the leading publishers in Israel, is identified with the Labor-Zionist establishment. Under the auspices of these two agents of the Israeli establishment, *Theory and Criticism* became the leading forum in crystallizing the post-Zionist ideology.

Another agent that played a crucial role in the wide dissemination and rapid acceptance of post-Zionism was the Hebrew daily, *Ha'aretz*, which constitutes the unofficial forum for the business, professional and cultural establishments in Israel. *Ha'aretz* opened its columns to post-Zionist ideas and gave them thorough and lengthy exposure.[78] As a result of what can be seen as editorial policy, the various sections of the newspaper became a forum for protracted polemics on post-Zionist criticism, thereby positioning it at the center of public debate. The status of *Ha'aretz* in the Israeli media endowed post-Zionist criticism with the establishment's seal of approval, legitimacy and mantle of dignity, which eased its acceptance by significant sectors of the Israeli middle class. Following *Ha'aretz*, other media, from TV through the popular dailies to the local press, soon made the post-Zionist debate the focus of cultural and political discussion.[79]

Right post-Zionism, too, has a close connection with the establishment. The Shalem Center is intimately connected with the former prime minister Binyamin Netanyahu's "ideological-financial infrastructure." Netanyahu himself had close relations with Hazony, and high-ranking officials in his administration had been involved in the various activities of the Shalem Center prior to their governmental appointments. These ties continued after Netanyahu took over, and the Center's ideas on strategic as well as economic issues were embraced by his administration and individual ministers, on both a formal and an informal level.[80] At the same time, the permanent membership of anti-Zionist, ultra-Orthodox parties in the coalition and in the government transformed Right-wing criticism of Zionism — now voiced by ministers, Knesset members and state officials — from an opposition stand into a legitimate establishment position.

There is, then, an intriguing gap between the critical rhetoric employed by the post-Zionists and the current oppositionist image they acquired, on the one hand, and the fact that they have acted from within and through the strongholds and agencies of the Israeli establishment to the point at which post-Zionism may be seen as an offspring of this establishment, on the other. The post-Zionists fostered this oppositionist image by attacking Labor Zionism, which was a central agent of the Zionist ethos and the hub of the Israeli establishment until the mid-1970s. Since then, however, the hegemony of Labor Zionism has declined, to be taken over by a new neoliberal establishment, which challenged the earlier collective values and created far-reaching changes in economic, social, political and cultural power relations in Israel. One of the main goals of this neoliberal policy was the privatization of the public sector of the economy and of social services, which culminated in the gradual dissolution of the universal welfare state, an increase in class differences overlapping ethnic lines, and increased political, social and cultural fragmentation and sectorialization. While attacking the declining Labor Zionism, the spread of post-Zionism came about, in fact, in the context of the rise of neoliberalism, sectorialization and privatization in Israel and served as an agent in promoting them.

Although the privatization project, with its neoliberal ideology and rhetoric, was part of a global trend, in Israel it has encountered special difficulty: the Zionist ethos and the Israeli collective memory, which served as a sort of "secular religion," had a strong collective basis that contrasted the notion of privatization. The basic idea of Zionism was to create a new Jewish national collectivity based on social solidarity, which had clear socialist inclinations in its hegemonic Herzlian and Labor versions. The Zionist collectivist ethos was manifested in the nation-building project and the melting-pot ideology. This ethos became a real force in Israeli life through state regulation of the economy, the dominant role of the public sector, the social services provided by the welfare state, and a high degree of equality in income distribution. Since the 1980s, though, in its efforts to advance the privatization project — and mainly to dissolve the welfare state — the emerging neoliberal elite found the secular religion of social solidarity, encapsulated in the Zionist ethos and Israeli collective memory, as one of its main obstacles. The way to override this obstacle was to undermine the Zionist ethos by creating an alternative, post-Zionist collective memory.

Against the background of the struggle waged by the new elite to advance its neoliberal agenda and in particular the privatization of the services of the welfare state, post-Zionism revealed itself as an effective agent for deconstructing the collective mainstream and the Labor Zionist ethos. Right post-Zionism advanced this agenda very clearly. Its attack on the Zionist mainstream is focused on a denial of an essential element of the Zionist idea: its social radicalism, namely, its striving to establish "a new society" based on non-capitalist economic and social foundations. Right post-Zionism sharply criticizes the socialist tendencies of historical Zionism and presents neoconservatism as an alternative ethos to the collectivism that brought about the decline of Labor Zionism and yeshiva nationalism. As a substitute for Labor Zionism, right post-Zionism offered market Zionism, which combined ethnic and religious particularism along with a privatized economy and society. Left post-Zionism advances the privatization project, employing the whole arsenal of postmodern criticism: it attacks the clear modernist and social-democratic nature of Zionism and presents it as an oppressive force, the emancipation from which can be achieved only by the dissolution of its collectivist structure and by the privatization of Israeli identity.

The new historiography fits into the privatization project of left and right post-Zionism through the privatization of its collective memory. As, contrary to the appearance, the goal of the new historiography is not historical research but the construction of an alternative Israeli collective memory, it strives to delegitimize the Zionist narrative, which serves as a mental block to privatization, and to proffer a privatized memory instead. Methodologically, the privatization of Israeli memory is carried out through attempting, in the tradition of postmodern relativism, to replace the hegemonic collective memory with a number of conflicting and competing narratives and memories. This trend is a reflection of the process of splintering society into a multiplicity of contesting identity groups and alienated individuals, and reproducing them as such. Moreover, undermining the professionalism and reliability of academic historiography integrates well into the privatization ethos. The relativization that informs the attack of the new historiography transforms historical research from a scholarly discipline into a kind of consumer commodity, modeled to suit the changing taste of the prevailing fashion and its clients.

Ideologically, the privatization of Israeli memory is carried out by challenging the morality of Zionism, whose justice constitutes one of the basic assumptions of Israeli collective memory. Employing a variety of accusations — such as the abandonment of European Jewry during the Holocaust, the expulsion of the Palestinians in 1948, the oppression of *Mizrahim* etc. — post-Zionism strives to make Zionist history loathsome and abhorrent in order to present Israeli collective memory as preserving, even glorifying, injustice and atrocities towards Jews and Arabs alike. Similarly, positing the Zionist establishments as immoral and oppressive by their very nature is intended to delegitimize the Israeli collective they lead. The only choice left for moral Israelis is to dissociate themselves from the collective that is defined by such a memory and to privatize themselves. Thus the privatized memory serves as an antithesis to any form of Israeli collectivity and social solidarity, obviating the crystallization of an Israeli collective identity and calling for the dismantling of the existing one.

The alternative collective memory constructed by the post-Zionists is a kind of purification rite, absolving the individual Israeli from responsibility for the group guilt through the privatization of memory. The starting point of the alternative memory constructed by the new historiography, like its empathy, is Jews as individuals alienated from the Israeli collective and hostile to the "new Jew," which is the cornerstone of Zionist ideology. In the same way, the heroes of the new historiography are the "victims" of Zionism, be they diaspora Jews, Holocaust survivors, *Mizrahim* or Palestinians, whose victimization is proof of the immorality of Zionism. Challenging the hegemonic Israeli memory, the new historians strive to construct a new collective memory that is focused on the individual Jew who struggles to preserve his or her individualism, a struggle that fits and sustains the neoliberal privatization revolution.

Contextualizing post-Zionism shows it to be a false critique. It is not an application of critical theories to Israeli reality, as it claims to be, but a neoliberal ideology, masquerading in angry rhetoric that works through the channels of the establishment to advance and reaffirm the privatization of Israeli Society.

POST-ZIONISM AND THE PRIVATIZATION OF ISRAELI MEMORY 39

NOTES

1 On the debate over post-Zionism see Pinchas Ginossar and Avi Bareli (eds.), *Tziyonut — Pulmus ben zmanenu: Gishot mehkariyot ve-ideologiyot* (Zionism — A Contemporary Controversy: Research Trends and Ideological Approaches) (Sede-Boker, 1996); Yehiam Weitz (ed.), *Bein hazon le-reviziyah: Meah shnot historiografiyah tziyonit* (From Vision to Revision: A Hundred Years of Historiography of Zionism) (Jerusalem, 1977); Dan Michman (ed.), *Post-Tziyonut ve-shoah: Ha-pulmus ha-tziburi ha-yisre'eli be-noseh ha-"post-tziyonut" bashanim 1993–1996, u-mekomah shel sugiyat ha-shoah bo* (Post-Zionism and the Holocaust: The Role of the Holocaust in the Public Debate on Post-Zionism in Israel, 1993–1996) (Ramat Gan, 1997); Yair Sheleg, "Tziyonut: Ha-krav al ha-rating" (Zionism: The Battle for Rating), *Kol ha-ir*, 6 October 1995; Dan Margalit, "Al tziyonut, post-tziyonut ve-anti-tziyonut: Diyun be-hishtatfut historiyonim" (On Zionism, Post-Zionism and Anti-Zionism: A Historians' Discussion), *Ha'aretz*, 15 October 1995; special issue of *History & Memory*, Vol. 7, No. 1 (1995), *Israeli Historiography Revisited*.
2 On the "Critical Sociologists" see Uri Ram (ed.), *Ha-hevrah ha-yisre'elit: Hebetim bikortiim* (Israeli Society: Critical Perspectives) (Tel-Aviv, 1993), and *The Changing Agenda of Israeli Sociology: Theory, Ideology, and Identity* (New York, 1994).
3 Benny Morris, *1948 and After: Israel and the Palestinians* (Oxford, 1990), pp. 27–34; Ilan Pappé, "Ha-historiyah ha-hadashah shel ha-tziyonut: Ha-imut ha-akademi veha-pumbi" (The New History of Zionism: The Academic and Public Debate), *Kivunim*, Vol. 8 (1995), pp. 39–47.
4 The various aspects of the post-Zionist critique are represented in *Teoriyah u-Vikoret* (Theory and Criticism), a journal that serves as the main forum for post-Zionist thinking.
5 Amnon Raz-Krakotzkin, "Galut mitokh ribonut: Le-vikoret 'shlilat ha-galut' ba-tarbut ha-yisre'elit" (Exile within Sovereignty: Towards a Critique of the "Negation of Exile" in Israeli culture), *Teoriyah u-Vikoret*, No. 4 (1993), pp. 23–55, No. 5 (1994), pp. 113–32; Daniel Boyarin and Jonathan Boyarin, "Ein moledet le-Yisrael: Al ha-makom shel ha-Yehudim" (The People of Israel Have No Motherland: On the Place of the Jews), ibid., No. 5 (1994), pp. 79–103; Yoav Peled, "Galut de luks: Al ha-rehabilitatziyah shel ha-galut etzel Boyarin ve-Raz-Krakotzkin" (Deluxe Diaspora: On the Rehabilitation of the Concept of Diaspora in Boyarin and Raz-Krakotzkin), ibid., pp. 133–9.
6 Tom Segev, *The Seventh Million: The Israelis and the Holocaust*, trans. Haim Watzman (New York, 1993); S. B. Beit-Zvi, *Ha-tziyonut ha-post-ugandit be-mashber ha-shoah* (Post-Ugandian Zionism in the Crucible of the Holocaust) (Tel Aviv, 1977); Moshe Zukermann, *Shoah ba-heder ha-atum: "Ha-shoah" ba-itunut ha-yisre'elit bi-tkufat milhemet ha-mifratz* (Shoah in the Sealed Room: "The Shoah" in the Israeli Press during the Gulf War) (Tel Aviv, 1993).
7 Yosef Grodzinsky, *Homer enoshi tov: Yehudim mul tziyonim, 1945–1951* (Good Human Material: Jews vs. Zionists, 1945–1951) (Or-Yehuda, 1998); Idith Zertal, *From Catastrophe to Power: Holocaust Survivors and the Emergence of Israel* (Berkeley, 1999). For a critical discussion of the construction of the collective memory of the Holocaust in Israel and relevant bibliography, see Daniel Gutwein, "Hafratat ha-shoah: Politikah, zikaron ve-historiyah" (The Privatization of the Holocaust: Politics, Memory and Historiography), *Dapim le-Heker ha-Shoah*, Vol. 15 (1998), pp. 7–52.
8 Tom Segev, *1949 — Ha-Yisre'elim ha-rishonim* (1949 — The First Israelis) (Jerusalem [N.D]), pp. 105–243.
9 Baruch Kimmerling, *Ketz shilton ha-Ahosalim* (The End of the Ashkenazi Hegemony) (Jerusalem, 2001).
10 Israel Harel, "Likrat post-tziyonut datit-le'umit" (Towards Religious-National Post-Zionism), *Ha'aretz*, 3 October 1995.
11 Daniel Gutwein, "Post-tziyonut yemanit" (Right Post-Zionism), *Ha'aretz*, book section, 18 October 2000, pp. 10, 13.
12 Ilan Pappé, "Hashpa'at ha-ideologiyah ha-tziyonit al ha-historigrafiyah ha-yisre'elit" (The Influence of Zionist Ideology on Israeli Historiography), *Davar*, 15 May 1994.
13 Ibid.
14 Ilan Pappé, "Shi'ur be-historiyah hadashah" (A Lesson in New History), *Ha'aretz*, weekend

supplement, 24 June 1994, "Bi-gnut ha-ziyuf ha-histori" (In Condemnation of Historical Forgery), *Kol ha'ir*, 6 October 1995, and "Hashpa'at ha-ideologiyah ha-tziyonit."
15 For example: Anita Shapira, *Ma'avak nekhzav: Avodah ivrit, 1929–1939* (Futile Struggle: The Jewish Labor Controversy, 1929–1939) (Tel-Aviv, 1977); Nakdimon Rogel, *Tel-Hai: Hazit bli oref* (Tel-Hai: A Front without Rear) (Tel Aviv, 1979); Moshe Samet, *Moshe Montefiore, ha-ish veha-agadah* (Moses Montefiore, Reality and Myth) (Jerusalem, 1989).
16 For example, Israel Beer, *Bitahon Yisrael: Etmol, ha-yom ve-mahar* (Israel's Security: Yesterday, Today and Tomorrow) (Tel Aviv, 1966); Simha Flapan, *The Birth of Israel: Myth and Realities* (London, 1987); cf. Benny Morris, *1948 and After*, pp. 8–9; Moshe Sneh, *Sikumim ba-she'elah ha-le'umit le-or ha-marksizm veha-leninizm* (Summations of the National Question in Marxist-Leninist Perspective) (Tel Aviv, 1954), pp. 85–123; Tamar Gozhansky, *Hitpathut ha-kapitalizm be-Palestinah* (Formation of Capitalism in Palestine) (Tel Aviv, 1986), pp. 43–87; A. Israeli, *Shalom shalom — ve-ein shalom: Yisrael–arav, 1948–1961* (Peace, Peace — and No Peace: Israeli–Arab Relations, 1948–1961) (Jerusalem, 1961).
17 Benny Morris, "The New Historiography: Israel Confronts its Past," *Tikkun*, Vol. 3, No. 6 (November–December 1988), pp. 19–23, 99–102.
18 Benny Morris, *1948 and After*, pp. 4–7, 27–8.
19 Ibid., pp. 8, 40–41; Benny Morris, "Historiyah obyektivit" (Objective History), *Ha'aretz*, weekend supplement, 1 July 1994. See also interviews with Morris in *Yediot Aharonot*, 16 December 1994, and *Maariv*, 21 January 1996.
20 Benny Morris, *1948 and After*, p. 7.
21 Benny Morris, review of A. Ilan, *Embargo: Utzmah ve-hakhra'ah be-milhemet tashah* (Embargo: Power and Victory in the 1948 War), *Yediot Aharonot*, 15 September 1995.
22 Ilan Pappé, "Ha-historiyah ha-hadashah shel milhemet 1948" (The New History of the 1948 War), *Teoriyah u-Vikoret*, Vol. 3 (1993) pp. 99–114; "Seder yom hadash la-historiyah ha-hadashah" (New Agenda for the New History), ibid., No. 8 (1996), pp. 123–37; and "Shi'ur be-historiyah hadashah."
23 Ilan Pappé, "Ha-historiyah ha-hadashah shel milhemet tashah"; "Ha-tziyonut ke-parshanut shel ha-metzi'ut" (Zionism as a Hermeneutics of Reality), *Yediot Aharonot*, 26 May 1995; "Bi-gnut ha-ziyuf ha-histori"; "Tahalikh hitbagrut ko'ev" (A Painful Growing-Up Process), *Ha'aretz*, 11 August 1995; Yair Sheleg, "Tziyonut: Ha-krav al ha-rating."
24 Ilan Pappé, *The Making of the Arab–Israeli Conflict, 1947–1951* (London and New York, 1992), p. xi, and "Ha-historiyah ha-hadashah shel milhemet tashah," pp. 102, 110.
25 Ilan Pappé, "Ha-tziyonut ke-parshanut shel ha-metzi'ut."
26 Benny Morris, "Historiyah obyektivit"; interview with Morris, *Yediot Aharonot*, 16 December 1994, and *Maariv*, 21 January 1996.
27 Ilan Pappé, "Hashpa'at ha-ideologiyah ha-tziyonit," and "Ha-historiyah ha-hadashah shel milhemet tashah," pp. 99–100.
28 Benny Morris, "The New Historiography," p. 102; Ilan Pappé, "Ha-historiyah ha-hadashah shel ha-tziyonut," p. 45, and "Ha-tziyonut ke-parshanut ha-metzi'ut."
29 Yair Sheleg, "Tziyonut: Ha-krav al ha-rating"; Margalit, "Al tziyonut, post-tziyonut ve-anti-tziyonut"; interviews with Morris, *Yediot Aharonot*, 16 December 1994, *Maariv*, 21 January 1996, *Svivot*, Vol. 28–29 (April 1992); cf. interview in *Yediot Aharonot*, 23 November 2001.
30 Ilan Pappé, "Ha-tziyonut ke-parshanut shel ha-metzi'ut," "Bi-gnut ha-ziyuf ha-histori," "Shi'ur be-historiyah hadashah"; cf. interview with Ilan Pappé, *Anashim*, 30 April 2001.
31 Ilan Pappé, "Be-sherut ha-moledet" (In the Service of the Motherland), *Ha'aretz*, 30 June 1995, and "Hashpa'at ha-ideologiyah ha-tziyonit."
32 Yair Sheleg, "Tziyonut: Ha-krav al ha-rating"; interviews with Morris, , *Yediot Aharonot*, 16 December 1994, and *Maariv*, 21 January 1996.
33 See note 29. Benny Morris, "He'arot al ha-historiografiyah ha-tziyonit ve-ra'eyon ha-transfer ba-shanim 1937–1944" (Notes on Zionist Historiography and the Transfer Idea, 1937–1944") in Yehiam Weitz (ed.), *Bein hazon le-reviziyah*, pp. 195–208.
34 Benny Morris, *The Birth of the Palestinian Refugee Problem, 1947–1949* (Cambridge, 1987).
35 Benny Morris, *1948 and After*, pp. 1–5.
36 Interview with Benny Morris, *Svivot*, Vol. 28–29 (April 1992).
37 Interview with Morris, *Yediot Aharonot*, 16 December 1994.

38 Morris, *Leidatah shel be'ayat ha-plitim ha-falastinim, 1947–1949* (The Birth of the Palestinian Refugee Problem), Hebrew enlarged edition (Tel Aviv, 1991), pp. 153–4, 163–44, 198–200, 203–4, 209–10, 222–3, 227–9, 278–9, 306, 317–19, 390, 428–58.
39 Ilan Pappé, "Moshe Sharett, David Ben-Gurion ve-'ha-optziyah ha-falastinit', 1948–1956 (Moshe Sharett, David Ben-Gurion and the 'Palestinian Option', 1948–1956), *Ha-Tziyonut*, Vol. 11 (1986), p. 361.
40 Ibid., pp. 362–79; Ilan Pappé, "Ve'idat Lausanne ve-nitzanim rishonim la-mahloket al mediniyut ha-hutz ha-yisre'elit" (The Lausanne Conference and the First Signs of Controversy over Israeli Foreign Policy), *Iyunim Bitkumat Israel*, Vol. 1 (1991), pp. 241–61.
41 See for example the controversy between Shapira and Gelber: Anita Shapira, *Me-piturei ha-ramatkal ad peruk ha-Palmah: Sugiyot ba-ma'avak al ha-hanhagah ha-bithonit, 1948* (The Army Controversy, 1948: Ben-Gurion's Struggle for Control) (Tel Aviv, 1985); Yoav Gelber, *Lamah pirku et ha-Palmah* (Why the Palmakh Was Disbanded) (Tel Aviv, 1986).
42 On collective memory, see for example, Maurice Halbwachs, *On Collective Memory* (Chicago and London, 1992); Iwona Irwin-Zarecka, *Frames of Remembrance: The Dynamics of Collective Memory* (Cambridge MA, and London, 1994); Yael Zerubavel, *Recovered Roots: Collective Memory and the Making of Israeli National Tradition* (Chicago and London, 1995); Robert Wistrich and David Ohana (eds.), *The Shaping of Israeli Identity: Myth, Memory and Trauma* (London, 1995).
43 Benny Morris, "The New Historiography," and interview, *Yediot Aharonot*, 16 December 1994.
44 Ilan Pappé, "Shi'ur be-historiyah hadashah" and "Ha-historiyah ha-hadashah shel milhemet tashah," p. 112.
45 Interview with Benny Morris, *Yediot Aharonot*, 16 December 1994.
46 See note 38. On the complex way in which the memory of 1948 was constructed, see also Anita Shapira, "Historiografiyah ve-zikaron: Mikreh Latrun tashah" (Historiography and Memory: The Case of Latrun, 1948), *Alpayim*, Vol. 10 (1994), pp. 9–41.
47 S. Yizhar, *Sipur Hirbet Hizah* (The Story of Hirbet Hizah) (Tel Aviv, 1949). Cf. Anita Shapira, "Hirbet Hizah: Between Remembrance and Forgetting," *Jewish Social Studies*, Vol. 7, No. 1 (Fall 2000), pp. 1–62.
48 Morris, *The Birth of the Palestinian Refugee Problem*, pp. 233–4.
49 Michael Keren, *Ben-Gurion veha-intelektu'alim* (Ben-Gurion and the Intellectuals) (Sede-Boker, 1988), pp. 123–31, 136; Benny Morris, *The Birth of the Palestinian Refugee Problem*, pp. 233–4.
50 Morris, *The Birth of the Palestinian Refugee Problem*, pp. 113–15; A. Israeli, *Shalom shalom — ve-ein shalom*, pp. 69–72.
51 A. Israeli, *Shalom shalom — ve-ein shalom*, pp. 28–88; Amnon Raz-Krakotzkin, "Hizakhrut ke-praksis tarbuti" (Remembering as Cultural Praxis), *Davar*, 26 July 1991; Baruch Kimmerling, "Al-Nakba" (The Palestinian Disaster of 1948), in Adi Ophir, *Hamishim le-arba'im u-shmoneh: Momentim bikortiim be-toldot Medinat Yisrael* (Fifty since Forty-Eight: Critical Moments in the History of the State of Israel) (Jerusalem, 1999), pp. 33–7.
52 See following section.
53 Harel, "Likrat post-tziyonut dati‑le'umit"; Yair Sheleg, *Ha-dati'im ha-hadashim: Mabat akhshavi al ha-hevrah ha-datit be-Yisrael* (The New Religious Jews: Recent Developments among Observant Jews In Israel) (Jerusalem, 2000), pp. 42–6; Israel Harel, "Esrim shanah le-Gush Emunim" (Gush Emunim at Twenty), *Nekudah*, No. 187 (July 1995), pp. 14–23; David Hanushka, "Netzah Yisrael eino mutneh ba-tziyonut" (The Glory of Israel Is Not Conditional on Zionism), *Nekudah*, No. 188 (September 1995), pp. 28–30.
54 Emunah Eilon, "Mi mefakhed meha-emet?" (Who's Afraid of the Truth?), *Yediot Aharonot*, 29 September 1999.
55 Daniel Polisar, "Making History," *Azure*, No. 9 (2000), pp. 14–22.
56 Ophir Haivry, "The Knesset Divided against Itself," *Azure*, No. 8 (1999), p.12.
57 Daniel Polisar, "Making History," p.19.
58 Assaf Sagiv, "Dionysus in Zion," *Azure*, No. 9 (2000), pp. 173–4.
59 Assaf Sagiv, "Dionysus be-Tziyon" (Dionysus in Zion), *Tkhelet*, Vol. 9 (2000), p. 121 (the English and Hebrew versions differ slightly).
60 Assaf Sagiv, "Dionysus in Zion," pp. 173–4.

61 Assaf Inbari, "Towards a Hebrew Literature," *Azure*, No. 9 (2000), pp. 127, 128, 131, 140.
62 Yoram Hazony, "'The Jewish State' at 100," *Azure*, No. 2 (1997), pp. 21–22, 24 26, 27.
63 Ibid, p. 30.
64 In Nadav Haetzni, "Makhon Shalem: Ha-anashim she-hoshvim bishvil Netanyahu" (The Shalem Institute: The People Who Think for Netanyahu,), *Maariv*, 18 June 1996.
65 Yair Shapira, "Be-shevah ha-post-tziyonut" (In Praise of Post-Zionism), *Nekudah*, No. 204 (April 1997), pp. 42–3.
66 Amon Raz-Krakotzkin, "Galut mitokh ribonut"; Daniel Boyarin and Jonathan Boyarin "Ein moledet le-Yisrael."
67 Yoram Hazony, "'The Jewish State' at 100," pp. 27–8.
68 Ibid., pp. 36–7.
69 Ibid., pp. 21–4, 35–7.
70 Joseph Adler, *The Herzl Paradox: Political, Social and Economic Theories of a Realist* (New York, 1962); U. Zilbersheid, "Hazono ha-hevrati-kalkali shel Herzl" ("Herzl's Social and Economic Vision), *Iyunim Bitkumat Israel*, Vol. 10 (2000) pp. 614–40.
71 Irving Kristol, "On the Political Stupidity of the Jews," *Azure*, No. 8 (1999), pp. 49, 51–4, 62–3.
72 See note 68 above; Theodore Herzl, *Altneuland: Old New Land* (Haifa, 1960).
73 Daniel Gutwein, "Utopiyah ve-hagshamah: Antishemiyut ve-shinu'i atzmi 'ke-'ko'ah meni'a' ba-hagut ha-tziyonit ha-mukdemet shel Herzl" (Utopia and Realization: Anti-Semitism and Self-Transformation as a 'Driving Force' in Herzl's Early Zionist Thought), *Ha-Tziyonut*, No. 19 (1995), pp. 7–29.
74 Samuel Huntington, "Hitnagshut ha-tzivilizatziyot?" (The Clash of Civilizations?), *Azure*, No. 9 (2000), pp. 129–57.
75 Neri Livneh, "Aliyatah u-nefilatah shel ha-post-tziyonut" (The Rise and Fall of Post-Zionism), *Ha'aretz*, weekend supplement, 29 September 2001.
76 The status of the Van Leer Institute is defined in a special law, "Law of the Israeli Center for the Advance of Human Culture, 1958."
77 Yehuda Elkana, "Bi-zkhut ha-shikhehah" (In Defense of Forgetting), *Ha'aretz*, 2 February 1988.
78 Alon Kadish, "'Ha-historiyah' ve/o historiyah" ("The History" and/or History), *Davar Rishon*, 8 December 1988. After describing the role that *Ha'aretz* played in propagating the new historiography, he notes that these ideas suit the self-image of *Ha'aretz* as it is fostered by its leading columnists.
79 See, for example, Daniel Gutwein, "Hafratat ha-shoah," pp. 28, 49.
80 Nadav Haetzni, "Makhon Shalem."

Historiosophical Foundations of the Historical Strife in Israel[*]

Uri Ram

Since the 1990s Israeli collective identity and historical consciousness are much more heterogeneous and conflictual than ever before. Zionism, modern Jewish nationalism, emerged in Eastern Europe in the last third of the nineteenth century. It arose in the midst of a major shift in Jewish identity and an enormous wave of Jewish mobility and migration. In its first decades Zionism was a minority trend. It remained on the margins of this shift. Only a trickle of the Jews emigrating from Eastern Europe made their way to Palestine, and those who stayed there established the nucleus of the new Israeli society. The Holocaust of European Jewry, the emergence of a prosperous and influential Jewish community in the United States and the establishment of the State of Israel in 1948, all marked a new and different phase in modern Jewish and Israeli history. Today, at the beginning of the twenty-first century, the old nineteenth-century nationalist paradigm has already passed its peak. Two new major paradigms struggle, sometimes very ferociously, over the hearts and minds of Israeli Jews: a Jewish ethno-nationalist paradigm, and an Israeli civic-liberal paradigm. It is as if the hyphenated Israeli-Jewish identity is breaking apart, and the "civic Israelis" and "ethnic Jews" are drifting in opposite directions. On the one hand, Israeli political culture is fast becoming ever more universalistic and globalist; on the other hand, Jewish political culture in Israel is becoming ever more particularistic and localist. These two trends will be referred to below as post-Zionism and neo-Zionism respectively. This struggle between three different paradigms of collective identity — the historic, the ethnic and the civic — underlies the historical strife that erupted in Israel in the 1990s. In question are the spatial and temporal dimensions of the collectivity, the boundaries of its membership, and hence, its historical meta-narrative.

Thus the current political-cultural rivalry in Israel is a matter not of routine party politics but rather of profound issues of identity, memory and constitution. Usually this rivalry takes the form of "culture wars," but at times it is in danger of escalating into a barely contained civil war, as was revealed by the assassination of Prime Minister Yitzhak Rabin in 1995. In what follows I shall focus mainly upon two dimensions of this unfolding war: the conflicting perceptions of time and space, and the ways they affect the perceptions of the boundaries of the collectivity, either in an inclusionary manner (the "post") or in an exclusionary manner (the "neo"). In these terms, one may say that the temporal horizon of post-Zionism is the present and near future, while the temporal horizon of neo-Zionism is the ancient past and the messianic future. For the neo-Zionists, the present does not have a meaning in and for itself but is rather considered as merely a recent link, and not the most important one, in an endless chain. In temporal terms, then, the battle is waged between contending commitments to past, present and future. There is also a spatial dimension to the battle of identity. Post-Zionism aspires to "territorial nationalism," that is to say, civility defined by common life within specified territorial boundaries under a common regime. Neo-Zionism, in distinction, aspires to "ethnic nationalism," defined by an assumed common ancestry or assumed primordial familiarity.[1] Thus, the normative horizon of post-Zionism is civil-constitutional "Israeli citizenship," while the normative horizon of neo-Zionism is the ethno-communal "Jewish people" in Israel (and outside). Hence, for post-Zionism, the relevant spatial realm is the unconsecrated "State of Israel," while for neo-Zionism it is the consecrated *Eretz Yisrael*, the biblical Land of Israel.

This study examines the temporal and spatial dimensions of these contesting collective identities — the national, the ethnic and the civic — their contrasting calendars and maps, their notions of the collectivity's boundaries, and their conflicting historical meta-narratives. In each case I shall discuss emblematic manifestations of these different trends.

Historical Nationalism

The Zionist immigrants who started to arrive in Palestine from 1881 constructed a cultural barrier between themselves and their (mostly) East European Jewish communities of origin. They rebelled against rabbinic Judaism and against their own *shtetl* (Jewish small town) parents, and constituted their own identity in contradistinction to diaspora Jews: they discarded Jewish religious observance, the East European-Jewish "jargon" (Yiddish) and revived the Hebrew language. They labeled themselves "Hebrews" (*ivrim*), rather than Jews (for example, the term that is usually translated into English as "the pre-state Jewish community" was called in Hebrew "the Hebrew settlement": *ha-yishuv ha-ivri*). They even imagined themselves as young Hebrews, compared to their old-Jewish parents. They did not simply forget the Jewish past; on the contrary, they made a deliberate effort to be released from its burden. In material terms, they also abandoned the typical occupations of European Jewry and underwent what one of their ideological guides, the Marxist-Zionist theoretician Dov Ber Borchov, termed productivization and proletarization. This self-reconstruction of their collective identity was functional, even necessary to the tasks ahead of them: the conquest of land and labor and the construction of the organizational and economic infrastructure of a new society. Of course, not everybody was equally immersed in the new identity, but this was the parlance of the vanguard, that is the Labor movement's pioneers, and it shaped the dominant political culture of the time.

One literary protagonist called Yudke, from the story "The Sermon" by Haim Hazaz, gave emblematic expression to the historical consciousness of the Hebrews: "I object to Jewish history," he proclaimed, "I object to it. I mean, I don't accept it ... I don't respect it!" What Yudke objected to was "edicts, vilifications, persecutions and martyrdom, and yet again, edicts, vilifications, persecutions and martyrdom, over and over and over again...." What Yudke was willing to remember was "[g]reat deeds and stories, heroes, bold-hearted and bold-spirited fighters and conquerors. In a word, a world full of heroism."[2] In very loaded words Yudke literally kicks history off the field: "Guys, we don't have a history! Since the day we were expelled from our country we have been a people with no history. You are dismissed, go play football." The implication is that the Jewish, or rather Hebrew, spirit and identity are linked to *Eretz Yisrael*, not to diasporic Judaism. Zionism leaps over two millennia of diaspora and connects the ancient biblical era directly with current Zionist times. David Ben-Gurion related to the Zionist state as the "Third Temple." This was the structure of Zionist memory and forgetfulness in a nutshell. In Yudke's conclusion, Zionism is not a continuation of Judaism but a rebellion against it:

> Zionism starts from where Judaism is destroyed. ... Zionism is not a continuation, not a remedy. That's nonsense! It means dislocation and destruction, it is the opposite of what used to be ... it's the end ... it's hardly a part of the people, it's an absolutely non-popular movement. ... It's a nucleus of a different people ... the Land of Israel is no longer Judaism. Even now, and even more so in the future ... [Zionism] is not a continuation, it is different, unique in itself, almost not a Jewish matter, almost entirely un-Jewish.[3]

In retrospect it seems that Yudke was too hasty in concluding that "the Land of Israel is no longer Judaism." Today, given the territorial fetishism of most religious Jews in Israel, it seems that for them Judaism is nothing but "the Land of Israel." Yet Yudke did express the mainstream ethos of secular Zionism of his time, which conceived of Zionism as a revolt against Jewish history and culture rather than their offshoot.

The Hebrew culture that was created in Palestine before the establishment of the state was a far cry from the Jewish culture elsewhere. Jews immigrating to Palestine were rapidly resocialized into it, and their "Sabra" offspring contrived a native ethos founded on the triad of settlement, communality and soldiering. They spoke only Hebrew and were ignorant of Jewish religious law, *Halakhah*; they were oblivious of the culture of their parents, let alone their grandparents. Regarding the diaspora, theirs was a culture of pure amnesia. They forgot the diasporic Talmud and remembered the biblical stories;[4] they forgot Jewish names and chose new Hebrew names for their offspring;[5] they forgot the rabbis of Yavneh and remembered the rebellion of Bar Kokhba;[6] they forgot the Holocaust but recalled the heroic ghetto rebellions (Holocaust memorial day is officially called the "Memorial Day for the Holocaust and Heroism," thus emphasizing the underground anti-Nazi groups whose resistance activities accorded with the Zionist ethos).[7] This admixture of memory and forgetfulness constituted the Israeli national ethos, as it grew out of Zionist culture during the pre-state era, and shaped three to four Israeli generations: the "pioneers," the Hebrews, the "Sabras," and the Israelis.[8] The following excerpt from memoirs of the writer Yoram Kaniuk expresses the cultural wall that was erected in Palestine between Jews and Israelis:

> I was born in Tel Aviv ... I was taught that we were born from the sea ... we learnt that we did not have a history ... we called ourselves Hebrews, *Eretz Yisraelim* (people of the Land of Israel), not Jews. Our teachers proudly called us Sabras. In our view, and in the view of our teachers who had immigrated from Eastern Europe, Jews were ridiculous figures from the stories of Mendele the Book Seller and Peretz ... there were "Jews," and on the other side there were us.[9]

It is not by chance that one of Kaniuk's books is called *The Last Jew* (1982).

One group of young intellectuals took this ethos to its extreme. They called themselves "the Hebrew Youth" and were called by others "Cannanites," to indicate the ancient pre-Jewish anchorage of their imagined identity. In their view, the new Hebrew people emerging in Israel descended from the Ancient Hebrews, not from the diaspora Jews. Diaspora Jewry represented a distortion of the original Hebrew culture. From being an independent nation planted in its homeland, the Hebrews had become a dispersed and repressed people. The Hebrews had been a people of toil and battle, while the Jews had turned into a people of prayer and commerce. Yonathan Ratosh, the leading spirit of the Cannanites put this view most succinctly: "The old entanglement of Judaism cannot be untied — it can only be cut;"[10] two millennia of Jewish history were to be overcome in order to restore the golden age of youth and vitality. This marginal movement of intellectuals would not have deserved the attention it has received had it not provided an explicit and lucid expression of the implicit and ambiguous trends of mainstream Zionism. Thus, for example, much ink has been spilt by the "new historians" in recent years over the emotional and cultural alienation between Israelis and Holocaust survivors in the early years of the state, which was a most tragic expression of the cultural barrier discussed here.[11]

National Transformations

The catastrophic events of the Holocaust and the absorption of Holocaust survivors in Israel after 1945 were indeed a watershed in Israeli national identity. They contributed to the gradual "Judaization" of Israeli culture from the 1950s, that is to say, a gradual return of the imaginary internal "repressed." This was only one factor though. During the 1950s yet another demographic change made the former "Hebrew project" grind to a halt: the arrival in Israel of a massive wave of Jewish immigrants from Muslim countries. In a very short period, from 1949 to 1952, the ethnic complexion of Israel was radically transformed. The Hebrew settlers lost their exclusivity. The new immigrants from Europe, the Middle East and North Africa had not been educated in a Zionist hothouse. They brought with them to their new country collective identities rich with a variety of components, including Jewish and other traditions. Very little, if any, of this was steeped with Zionism, let alone Hebrewism. In order to draw them quickly into the new national fold, the young state and the old elite turned, somewhat reluctantly, towards the wider common denominator of all Jewish groups, namely Jewish tradition. And so, while the new immigrants were absorbed into Israel, their presence contributed to the emergence of a new blend between Hebrewism and Judaism. Thus, Israeli civil religion turned, as Charles Liebman and Eliezer Don-Yehiya have aptly analyzed, from a "rejection" of Jewish tradition to a "selective adoption" of appropriate elements from it.[12] The 1961 Eichmann trial was a benchmark in the destruction of the cultural wall between Israeli identity and Jewish history.[13]

The redefinition of Israel as "Jewish" should also be understood within the context of the Israeli–Arab conflict, which reached a climax in the 1948 war. For Israel the war resembled a war of independence, but for Palestinian Arabs it was a war of destruction. Some 400 Palestinian villages were destroyed and some 700,000 Palestinians went into exile.[14] In fact, and despite the distinction drawn between Hebrew and Jewish identities, the Hebrews could never have relinquished Judaism in its entirety. Productivization and proletarization were inextricably tied to another process — the colonization of Palestine. Jewish tradition — the religious and historical yearning for *Eretz Yisrael* — supplied the legitimization needed for their project of colonization, and a definition of the group's boundaries. In these circumstances "Jewish" would come to mean more than anything else "non-Arab." The justification for immigrating to a foreign country, the acquisition of land and the deportation of part of its Arab inhabitants necessitated an appeal to the Bible and Jewish continuity and solidarity even on the part of secular Jews.[15] Gradually, between the late 1940s and early 1970s Israeli-Jewish identity came to be founded upon two major pillars: the Holocaust and the Israeli–Arab wars; "Jewishness" was now a memory of the disaster that fueled the determination in the battlefield.[16]

Thus in Israel a novel meaning was added to being Jewish — that of being a "non-Arab." This added yet another layer of collective memory and forgetfulness to the multifaceted Israeli collective identify. The liberal and left conscience of Israel started to anxiously recollect Palestinian suffering. S. Yizhar published an insightful story about an Israeli soldier who participated in the expulsion of Arab villagers; A. B. Yehoshua published an account relating to the ruins of Arab villages underneath woods planted by Israelis; David Grossman reported on the "present absentees," a particularly Orwellian term, referring to the Arab inhabitants of Israel whom the state recognizes de facto but refuses to recognize de jure as citizens.[17] Yet mainstream culture turned its back on the Palestinian issue and was only willing to view it through the sight of the gun.[18]

The memory of the Palestinians and their 1948 disaster was eradicated not only from canonical texts of history and school textbooks, but the landscape itself was de-Arabized: remnants of Arab villages were either given to Jewish immigrants or destroyed, and their lands dispersed among Jewish settlements.[19] Typical of the process of Israeli national forgetfulness, but also its belated recollection, is the articulation in Israeli art of the Arab village of Tsuba near Jerusalem. As art curator Tali Tamir put it, Tsuba lies at the heart of a prolonged paradox of seeing and blindness.[20] The remnants of the houses in Tsuba are now covered by thick forest. Public authorities have marked the area with signposts relating to the landscape, the liberation of the area during the War of Independence, and its archaeological sites. No Palestinian village is mentioned. Since the 1970s Tsuba has attained a special status in the history of Israeli art. The watercolor paintings of the village by Yosef Zaritsky are recognized as emblematic of the "concept of Israeli landscape": "an embodiment of the dazzling Eretz-Israeli light, an exposed and unmediated encounter with nature, an open surveillance of the seasons of the year, light and shade, sunrise and sunset. ..."[21] Zaritsky's paintings are abstract and lyrical, sensitive to areas, tempos and patches of color, but blind to details, especially disturbing details such as remnants of deserted houses.

During the early 1990s another painter was absorbed by Tsuba, Larry Abramson. Abramson was dazzled by the duplicity of the view in front of him: the Israeli planted forest on top; the ruins of the Palestinian village underneath. His paintings aimed to offset those of his predecessor and to expose the painful genealogy of the area. The paintings, like the site itself, are multilayered and vague: as each landscape painting reached completion, with thick layers of oil paints on canvas, Abramson pressed a sheet of newspaper onto it. He then peeled it away, taking with it the upper layers of paint. He was left with two parallel products: the peeled painting, damaged and impaired, but still bearing the picture of the village, and the sheet of newspaper bearing the reversed mirror-image, the stripped-off layer, the traces of the painting. As Tamir comments:

> The mechanical abstraction that Abramson obtained by means of the application, and the peeling of the newspaper is an abstraction without glorification. ... The illuminated radiance in Zaritsky's watercolors is replaced here by a murky and muddy coloration, gray-brown in hue, spotted with patches of olive-green. ... In the final state the paintings themselves have turned into something like remains of paintings.[22]

This state is metaphoric, of course, of the remains of the abandoned villages; they are seen and not seen. For Abramson, unlike Zaritsky, the Israeli landscape cannot be innocent. By exposing the "double map" Abramson re-collects the memory of the repressed, perhaps hoping to re-include them in the collectivity, at least symbolically.

The de-Arabization of the land, the obliteration of the Arab memory and the escalation of the Israeli–Arab conflict in general generated yet another painful consequence. While Jewish immigrants from Europe were expected and encouraged to forget their pasts and traditions while assimilating to the new Hebrew (or Israeli) culture, Jewish immigrants from the Middle East and North Africa were forced to forget their very identity. The Jews from Europe were "non-Arabs" from the outset; yet the identity of Jews from the Muslim societies was partly Arab. To be an Arab in the Jewish state would have meant to be an enemy. In order to be entirely dissociated from the enemy, these Jews were redefined as *Edot ha-mizrah* (Oriental communities). They had to discard anything Arab about them: names, languages, music, literature, family patterns, life-style. Anything "contaminated" with Arabism had to be concealed.[23]

This was the gist of the paradigm of Zionist-Israeli historical consciousness, with its internal ambiguities and inconsistencies, in its Hebrew (pre-1948) and Israeli (post-1948) stages. With the passage of time, especially from the 1960s onwards, crucial transformations took place in the patterns of memory and forgetfulness. These transformations can be attributed to the changes in the complexion of Israeli society and to changes in its balance of power. In the pre-state era the Jewish community was quite small (around 600,000 in the 1948 War of Independence) and fairly homogeneous, especially in terms of ethnic origins. Even though it was composed of several social sectors, all were united around a potent nation-building center. While the creation of the state even strengthened the hegemonic center, it was preceded and immediately followed by waves of mass immigration from both Europe and North Africa and the Middle East. Within three years the immigrants more then doubled the number of the Jewish population in Israel and transformed its ethnic and cultural complexion. The immigrants of the late 1940s and early 1950s were not educated or socialized as Hebrews or Israelis. In most cases they were not even Zionists. Rather they were Jews, forced to move from their diaspora locations to Israel.

Since the 1967 war (the Six Day War) another "forgotten" group re-emerged on the Israeli public agenda: the Palestinians. The occupation of the Gaza Strip and the West Bank, inhabited by Palestinians many of whom were refugees from the 1948 war, reminded Israelis of that part of the past they wished to put behind them. Later, the Palestinian rebellion beginning in 1987, the *Intifada*, brought the issue back to the headlines and television screens. Finally, since the 1980s, another factor began to challenge the Israeli national memory: a growing middle class of entrepreneurs and professionals, whose members tend to reject any form of collectivism and tradition in favor of a utilitarian and individualistic ethos.[24] While all these trends, traditional Jewish, Palestinian and individualistic, caused cracks in the solid façade of the national (that is to say Hebrew-Israeli) memory, a new group of faithful adherents and staunch defenders of it began to emerge, Gush Emunim (Bloc of the Faithful), which mixed old-Judaism with new-Hebrewism to forge a new model of religious nationalism.

Let us now consider the ethnic and civic paradigms of collective identity and memory in Israel, focusing, as above, upon selected emblematic manifestations of each.

Ethnic Nationalism

The neo-Zionist ethno-Jewish paradigm reinterprets Zionism and Judaism, fusing them in a new mold. From secular Zionism it adopts the territorial stipulation, the centrality of territory in the national project; from Orthodox Judaism it adopts the imperative of the Jewish codex, the *Halakhah*, and the expectation of messianic redemption. Fusing the two, territory and community become religiously sanctified. Thus Judaism, rather than being identified as a specific culture, is turned into a nationalist-territorial religion, that is, a political religion whose first principles are land and nation. This is not, as commonly assumed, a process in which Israeli nationalism is becoming more and more religious. On the contrary, it is a process in which Jewish religion is becoming more and more nationalistic. In fact, except for some closed ultra-Orthodox communities, Judaism in Israel has been totally transposed from the religion of a nation to a nationalistic religion.

This new creed of messianic Zionism was contrived in the pre-state Jewish community in Palestine by Rabbi Abraham Isaac Ha-Kohen Kook, at the time the Chief Rabbi of the Ashkenazi Jewish community. Kook differed from most Orthodox rabbinical authorities of his time in his support of secular Zionism. The three major religious approaches towards Zionism that prevailed then have continued to shape religious attitudes to Zionism ever since:[25]

(1) The ultra-Orthodox approach, according to which Zionism is a blasphemy because it is not for flesh-and-blood to hasten the steps of the Messiah. This is the ideological source of Orthodoxy's rejection of Zionism.
(2) The pragmatic approach, according to which Zionism has neither a positive nor negative sacred value but which concedes that it may have practical utility in rescuing Jews, which of course deserves support. This approach was guiding the mainstream of religious politics in Israel until 1967.
(3) Messianic nationalism, which was formulated by Kook. According to this approach, Zionism — even secular Zionism — is not merely endorsed, but endorsed on religious grounds. The actual process of Zionist immigration, conquest and settlement is interpreted as the first stage in the forthcoming transcendental redemption. Secular Zionists are unconsciously engaged in a larger divine scheme.

This latter trend was dormant until the Six Day War, with the exception of several religious-national educational and youth centers. It burst into the public arena after the 1967 war, and especially after the 1973 October war. The former war stimulated the sense of Israeli omnipotence, while the latter revived the anxiety that Israel was on the verge of annihilation.

This emotional and cultural crucible led to the emergence of Gush Emunim, the avant-garde of the Jewish settlers in the West Bank and other occupied areas. During the 1970s and 1980s Gush Emunim turned out to be "the tip of an iceberg," a nationalistic-religious iceberg that included some of the large right-wing political parties and substantial sections of the Israeli establishment.[26] The political culture and practice of Gush Emunim has already received extensive scholarly attention.[27] In contrast, this article is mostly interested in the spatial-temporal consciousness of Gush Emunim. One of the most lucid expressions of this paradigm of collective memory is provided by Harold Fisch's *The Zionist Revolution: A New Perspective*, published in 1978. Fisch, a professor and former rector at Bar Ilan University, was after 1967 one of the founders of the Movement for Greater Israel and a member of the Israeli delegation to the United Nations in the era of Prime Minister Menachem Begin. His work is used here as an illustration of the larger politico-cultural trend it represents.

While artist Larry Abramson is agonized by the "double map" of Israel, by the fact that a Palestinian layer lies submerged under the surface of Israeli territory, Fisch is troubled by another duplicity: the "double calendar."[28] He is concerned about the fact that Israeli chronosophy consists of two layers: a Jewish layer and a universal layer. While Abramson's work implies that the inclusion of the forgotten "other" is essential for the healing of the Israeli collective consciousness, Fisch is interested in the exclusion of the "other," universal humanity, from Israeli collective consciousness in order to purify it.

The double chronosophy is expressed symbolically in such texts as Israel's Declaration of Independence, where both particular Jewish ancestry and the recognition of the family of nations are mustered as a vindication of Israel's right to exist. The document carries two dates, which attests to this duality: the Hebrew date, 5 Iyar 5708, and the civil date, 14 May 1948. This calendric ambiguity reveals the fundamental duality of Zionism, which from the ethnonationalistic point of view has to be curtailed. As Fisch maintains, there are two Zionist perspectives. On the one hand, "political Zionism" considers national sovereignty to be a solution to the persecution of the Jews and Zion as "the place where Jews would go to end their abnormal condition in the world." On the other hand, there is a "Zionism of Zion," for which Zionism is considered "to be the fulfillment of Judaism in acknowledgement of the mystery ... a return to transcendent tasks and origins."[29] Zionism then, should be purified from its pragmatic tendencies and elevated to a spiritual state.

The itinerary of Jewish history is seen as a process of release from the double chronosophy, until the foreign calendar is finally discarded and Zionism returns to an uncorrupted Jewish essence. This journey of Zionism from a contaminated to a cleansed state has evolved through three "moments of truth."

The first such moment was the Holocaust. It revealed the treachery of humanity and the impossibility of progress and enlightenment. The ultimate conclusion from the Holocaust is that Jews cannot live and endure among gentiles. There are no lives for Jews in the foreign calendar: "... in the cataclysm of the war years [World War II] the hope of the emancipation ... was largely burned away. It may be that Israel was not ready for the Jewish Messiah, but there would be no non-Jewish Messiah either. The sting had, so to speak, been taken out of the non-Jewish calendar."

The second "moment of truth" was the Six Day War of 1967. Here, according to Fisch, a contrary truth was revealed: not the poverty of the foreign calendar, but rather the full glory and meaning of the Jewish calendar, "which binds us to a past echoing with ancestral obligations and a future of promise and redemption."[30] The conquest of vast areas of the biblical land had suddenly turned the remote past implicit in Jewish tradition into a vivid reality. The Six Day War, like other historical events, is not considered by

Fisch as an ordinary historical event but rather as a miraculous occurrence through which the past becomes the key to the future:

> It was a truly religious moment, the experience of a miracle, of sudden illumination. And what was illuminated was the significance of Jewish existence. We were suddenly living in the fullness of our own covenant history. It is here that we should locate the special metaphysical character of the Six Day War. The outcome of the war did not only call into question the armistice lines set up in 1949 between the divided halves of Palestine; it also challenged the lines which divided the Israeli people from within, the lines which divided their Jewish past from their contemporary existence in the twentieth century. The Six Day War revealed a new dynamic in the Jewish calendar. It was as though archaeology had come alive, or rather as though the past had become a key to the future.[31]

The symbolic meaning of the Hebrew appellation of that war is obvious: just as the universe was created in six days, so was the Land of Israel emancipated in six days. And so, in this way, a history of flesh and blood, in this case of war in a tragic literary sense, is extracted from mundane actuality and turned into metaphysics, and, indeed, eschatology.

The third "moment of truth" was the 1973 October War. Once more the Hebrew appellation of that war is particularly loaded: The War of the Day of Atonement. Hence, Fish claims, "it is no good talking about the October War":

> [E]very Jew, every Israeli knows in his bones that this was the War of the Day of Atonement. It was the war that "made us one": it made us not only one people, but a people subject to a special destiny, to special stresses, to special existential perils, a people with one calendar which stretches back from Creation through the agonies and storms of the present, through a wilderness where only the pillar of fire and the column of smoke mark the path to the future. ... Launched on Yom Kippur, at the most sacred hour of the Jewish year, it was a challenge to the Jewish calendar and all that it stood for, namely, the whole historical pilgrimage of the Jewish people, its covenant destiny. A metaphysical shudder, as it were, passed through the body of Israel. ..."[32]

The historical lesson from these three moments is evident: only one calendar remains, the Jewish calendar. In this neo-Zionist calendar the present does not have a validity of its own; it is a mere temporary link between the ancient past and the messianic future. Equally, individual lives have no validity of their own, they are mere temporary fillers of the eternal collective. Hence, Zionism is not a political option for its own sake, but rather a passing moment in a continuous and predetermined destiny. Pragmatic secular Zionism is ignorant of the role it plays in providential history. It misleads the youth to consider Israel as a regular state, one among many, as if being Israeli is similar to being French or Dutch. But fortunately the unfolding "moments of truth" expose the falsehood of this supposed "normalcy." In the calendar espoused by Jewish ethno-nationalism the Palestinians receive the status of a "non-nation," which "represents the inverted image of Israel. It thus hardly exists in its own right." "The Palestinian national identity was invented as a kind of antithesis, a parody of Jewish nationhood."[33] Speaking about Palestinian nationality, Fisch writes:

> There is an element of fantasy in all this. Of course refugees had local patriotism. Those who had fled from Acre had a feeling for Acre; those who fled from Jaffa a feeling for Jaffa, and so forth.... But does this add up to a corporate nationality? And does this constitute a claim for sovereignty? ... to construct a nationality and a claim to sovereignty on such basis would be a work of fiction.[34]

The historical debate of the 1990s was ignited by the radical critique of the "new historians," starting with Benny Morris's archival scrutiny of the origins of the Palestinian refugee problem and Avi Shlaim's interpretation of the Israeli–Jordanian collusion in 1948 at the expense of the Palestinians, and ending with Ilan Pappé's program for a new narrative of Israeli and Palestinian histories.[35] The debate moved from academia to the mass media (the controversy over the 1998 TV series *Tkumah* [Revival] on the birth of Israel) and to new history textbooks for schools (*Olam shel tmurot* [A World of Transformations] for the ninth grade was a matter of contention). Throughout, the Zionist and mainstream historians were busy defending their much-attacked left flank. Ethnic nationalism was in the main a nonacademic affair, except for isolated islands such as Bar Ilan University, where Harold Fisch taught. Yet since the late 1990s mainstream history has also come under attack from its right flank. In Jerusalem the right-wing Shalem Center became a hothouse of ethno-nationalist thought, and the book, *The Jewish State: The Struggle for Israel's Soul*, authored by its academic director, Yoram Hazony, became popular — though, interestingly, much more among Jews in the United States then in Israel (at the time this article was written the book was still not published in Hebrew).[36]

The neo-nationalist paradigm draws from the fountain of the older national historical paradigm. Zionism had imagined from the start an integral "people" united spiritually over periods and over continents, and a teleological history leading from ancient birth through dispersion in diaspora to national revival.[37] Yet historical Zionism was constrained by universal visions, be it liberalism or socialism, while neo-Zionism represents an unconstrained accentuation of the exclusionary perception of Israeli collective identity. This one-sided adoption of Zionism is offset by an opposite one-sidedness, that of post-Zionism.

Civic Nationalism

In 1988, a few months after the eruption of the first *Intifada*, Professor Yehuda Elkana published in the *Ha'aretz* daily a short article entitled "In Praise of Forgetting."[38] Elkana, a leading Israeli intellectual who established the Institute for the History and Philosophy of Science and Ideas at Tel Aviv University and has led a group of critical thinkers at the Van Leer Institute in Jerusalem, is known as a sympathizer of the Israeli peace movement. In this article Elkana portrayed some of the fundamental principles of the civic paradigm of Israeli historical consciousness, the opposite of the ethnic paradigm reviewed above. I shall use it here to illustrate the emergent civic paradigm in Israeli historical consciousness.

The opening sentence is forceful: "As a ten-year-old boy I was transferred to Auschwitz and passed through the Holocaust." The forgetfulness of Elkana is not born of oblivion or negligence; it is a deliberate forgetfulness, a forgetfulness with an aim. He then dryly states the lessons he has drawn from that dreadful experience: Nazi brutality was not exclusively German, there were others; such behavior may happen again, in any nation, and Jews are not exempt; such brutalities may be prevented by proper education and political context.

The direct trigger to Elkana's piece was a number of so-called "deviations" in the behavior of Israeli soldiers towards the rebelling Palestinians, or, in other words, repeated acts of brutal repression of Palestinian Arabs by Israeli Jews. A particularly horrifying instance was the burial alive under piles of earth of four Palestinians from the village of Salem. The Israeli press reported on "the covering of Arabs by gravel" and on a certain sergeant-major, Sharli Danino, who had smiled "when the idea was raised to pour gravel on a few people ... and during the whole event continued to watch the action and smile." "What could reduce Israelis to such baseness and cruelty?", asked Elkana. His response: "A profound existential anxiety which is fed by a particular interpretation of the lessons of the Holocaust."

The intensive and extensive inculcation of the Holocaust in Israeli consciousness paralyzes the positive creative potential in the country and in fact presents the greatest threat to the future of Israel. Prime Minister Menachem Begin (the historical leader of Israel's nationalist right wing) had led the attack on the Palestinians in Lebanon in the early 1980s comparing Yassir Arafat to Adolf Hitler. He thus avenged in the Middle East the murder of his parents and their community in Poland by the Nazis. The Jewish Holocaust and the Palestinian disaster (the 1948 expulsion) are lumped together in one indissoluble knot. Elkana wrote:

> It is for the first time now that I understand the severe consequences of our conduct, when for decades we have sent each and every child in Israel on repeated visits to Yad Vashem [the Holocaust memorial museum in Jerusalem]. How did we expect children to process this experience? We have proclaimed thoughtlessly and relentlessly, without explaining — REMEMBER! What for? What are children supposed to do with the memories? For very many of them the horrific images may be internalized as a call to hate. "Remember" may be interpreted as a call for blind prolonged hatred.[39]

Two lessons were extracted from the Holocaust, explains Elkana: one that "it should never happen again," and the other that "it should never happen again to us." The latter lesson has been fiercely disseminated in the Israeli educational system.[40] Elkana does not reject the former lesson on behalf of the latter, or the other way round. He rejects the very notion of living by a "historical lesson" and especially of such a terrible calamity as the Holocaust: "any life lesson or life perception whose source is the Holocaust is a disaster ... a disaster for a society that wishes to live in relative calm and relative security like all societies." He does not entirely rule out the function of collective or national history as such, not even the constructive role of myth. He draws a radical distinction, however, between two kinds of collective approaches to the past: one democratic, the other fascist. This most significant observation goes to the heart of our distinction between the post-Zionist and the neo-Zionist formations of historical consciousness and their contrasting cultural horizons:

> The very existence of democracy is endangered when the memory of past victims plays an active part in the democratic process. The ideologues of fascist regimes understood this very well. It is not by chance that research on Nazi Germany focuses upon political myths. Relying on lessons from the past in order to construct the future, the mobilization of past sufferings as an argument in current politics, is equivalent to the participation of the dead in the living democratic process. Thomas Jefferson, a founding father of American democracy, explicitly indicated in his writings that democracy and consecration of the past cannot endure together. Democracy is the cultivation of the present and the future; the cultivation of memory and the immersion in the past undermine the foundations of democracy.[41]

If we wish to lead normal peaceful lives, Elkana tells his fellow Israelis, we must forget; we must "stand by life, and devote ourselves to the construction of our future; we must stop dealing day and night with symbols, ceremonies and lessons of the Holocaust. We must uproot the dominance of the 'remember' imperative in our lives."

Elkana's position, although idiosyncratic, nonetheless exposes the historical orientation of post-Zionism, namely its preference and commitment to the present and future rather then to the past. A different post-Zionist option was raised by Moshe Zukermann, who has studied the use of Holocaust memory in Israeli political discourse.[42] Unlike Elkana, Zukermann considers forgetfulness to be a "curse" and draws a different line between past, present and future. While the common historical consciousness in Israel nourishes the dictum "this should never happen again to us," he insists that it is especially the "us," who had been the ultimate victims of racism and bigotry, who ought to live by the dictum "this should never happen again to anybody." Thus, in this post-Zionist version the past should shed light — or in this case a shadow — on the present and future, but the lessons of the past ought to be universalistic rather then particularistic.

The civic historical paradigm that emerged in Israel in the late 1980s broke out into the public arena in the 1990s. The controversy between two leading historical paradigms: the ethnic and the civic, the neo-nationalist and the post-nationalist, reflects the major schism in Israeli political culture in the 1990s, the schism between neo-Zionism and post-Zionism.[43] What space, what time, and what community are the issues being debated. I shall conclude with a recapitulation of these contested questions.

The Nation: What Space? What Time? What Community?

Nationalistic neo-Zionism emerged in the 1970s. Its constituency consists largely of the Jewish settlers in the territories and their many supporters in the so-called "national camp" throughout the country. It is represented by a variety of extreme right-wing parties, including core parts of the National-Religious Party (Mafdal) and the Likud Party,[44] as much as by splinter nationalist parties such as Tehiyah, Tzomet, Moledet, and the Israel be-Aliyah Party, established by immigrants from the former Soviet Union. This trend regards "the biblical Land of Israel" (identified with all areas under Israeli military control) as more fundamental to Israeli identity than the State of Israel (a smaller territory identified with the 1948 "green-line" borders). The motherland is conceived as a superior end, the state as a means for dominating it. The culture of neo-Zionism is an admixture of Zionist and Jewish ingredients, in which, instead of the discord between the two that characterized classical Zionism, secular nationalism is conceived as a stage in an immanent religious revival.[45] The political allegiance of neo-Zionism is to an ostensible "Jewish people," conceived as a unique spiritual-ethnic community, rather than to Israeli nationality in its down-to-earth sense of a political community defined by common citizenship. Legal (and practical) affiliation in the collectivity is considered secondary to the ostensible ascriptive national brotherhood. Neo-Zionism is thus an exclusionary, nationalist, even racist, and antidemocratic political-cultural trend, striving to heighten the fence encasing Israeli identity. It is fed by, and in turn feeds, a high level of regional conflict and a low level of global integration. Conflict vindicates its alarming messages, and global integration may erode its grip on the national mind.

Liberal post-Zionism started to emerge in the 1980s. Its constituency is composed mainly of the extensive "new" middle classes, typically concentrated in the country's coastal area, especially in the city of Tel Aviv and its vicinities (where a quarter of the population resides). This trend grants more esteem to individual rights than to collective glory. In blunt contrast to neo-Zionism, it considers the collectivity as a tool for the welfare of the individual. In its historical horizon the present ("quality of life") is much more important than the past ("history"), and the near future (the children) is more meaningful than the remote past (ancestors). One political avant-garde of liberal post-Zionism is the Yesh Gvul (literally: "there is a border/limit") movement, which surfaced in response to the 1982 war in Lebanon. It consists of reserve soldiers and officers who refuse to serve in the occupation forces in Lebanon and the Palestinian territories, arguing that the role of the military is defense, not repression. Though the movement is rather small, the principles of civil disobedience and, more broadly, of civic liberties that it represents have gained recognition by a larger sector of the population, which is committed to civil rights rather than to ethnic nationalism. Post-Zionism is, then, a trend of libertarianism and openness, which strives to lower the boundaries of Israeli identity, and to include in it all relevant "others." It is fed by, and in turn feeds, a lower level of regional conflict and a higher level of global integration. Conflict mobilizes nationalistic feelings, and thus disables post-Zionism; global integration draws people into a cosmopolitan culture, and is thus supportive of post-Zionism.

It should be emphasized that the traits of both neo-Zionism and post-Zionism are not entirely foreign to "classical" Zionism. In fact, their principles represent the two diametrical poles already implicit in Zionism. Their novelty consists precisely in their one-sided accentuation. Neo-Zionism accentuates the messianic and particularistic dimensions of Zionist nationalism, while post-Zionism accentuates its normalizing and universalistic dimensions. In their opposing ways both trends indicate a transition towards a post-nationalist Israeli collective identity. The nationalist stage was an imperative of the era of territorial colonization, nation-building and state formation. Decades later, a variety of internal and external pressures, some of which were reviewed above, are eroding the national cohesion and enhancing the emergence of post-national alternatives. Neo-Zionism and post-Zionism are "labels" for these emerging alternatives. Neo-Zionism elevates to an exclusive (and exclusionary) status, the ethnic dimension of Israeli nationalism; post-Zionism elevates to an exclusive (and in this case inclusivist) status, the civic dimension of Israeli statehood.

The demise of the dominant nationalist ethos of Zionism has generated a transformation in Israelis' collective identity, spatio-temporal perceptions and Israel's cultural scene. What we witness is the scrambling of the unilinear and teleological national meta-narrative by a variety of supra-narratives (post-Zionist cosmopolitanism), sub-narratives (empowered marginalized or excluded groups: women, Palestinians, *Mizrahi* Jews, Orthodox Jews), backlash narratives (neo-Zionist ethnicity); and subsidiary narratives (bourgeois-liberalism). Diverse social categories, whose voices had until recently been silenced, now emerge in the public arena, articulate their own versions of history, and retell it. Their "truths" diverge naturally, or rather historically, from the hegemonic "truth." Just as at the end of the nineteenth century and in the first half of the twentieth century Zionism was busy inventing a tradition and composing a historical narrative for itself, so today, in the globalist era of the end of the twentieth century and the beginning of the twenty-first century, a variety of groups in Israel are busy deconstructing that particular version of nationalist history and constructing their own histories, identities and cultural policies. The new politics of identity and memory are radically refurbishing the tissue of historical consciousness in Israel. The hegemony of the national paradigm is being undermined, and two diametrically conflicting alternatives are emerging: ethnic neo-nationalism and civic post-nationalism. Israeli historiography is one stage on which the collision of these two alternatives is being acted out.

NOTES

* The research for this study and its composition was made possible by a grant from the United States Institute of Peace, Washington DC, as part of a larger project on Israel in the 1990s. I am grateful to USIP for its generosity. My colleagues at the Ben-Gurion University of the Negev have provided a stimulating environment for the development of the ideas presented in this article (for which I am solely responsible). The contents of this article does not necessarily represent the positions of USIP.

1 Roger Brubaker, *Citizenship and Nationhood in France and Germany* (Cambridge, MA, 1992).
2 Haim Hazaz, "Ha-drashah," in idem, *Sipurim nivharim* (Selected Stories) (Tel Aviv, 1952), pp. 150–1.
3 Ibid., pp. 160–2.
4 See Uri Ram, "Post-Nationalist Pasts: The Case of Israel," *Social Science History*, Vol. 22, No. 4 (1998), pp. 513–45; and Anita Shapira, "Ha-motivim ha-datiim shel tnu'at ha-avodah" (The Religious Motifs of the Labor Movement), in Shmuel Almog, Yehuda Reinharz and Anita Shapira (eds.), *Tziyonut ve-dat* (Zionism and Religion) (Jerusalem, 1994), pp. 301–28.
5 Sasha Weitman, "Shemot pratiim ke-medadim tarbutiim: Megamot ha-zehut ha-le'umit shel

Yisre'elim" (First Names as Cultural Indicators: Trends in the National Identity of the Israelis), in Nurith Gertz (ed.), *Nekudat tatzpit* (Observation Point) (Tel Aviv, 1988).
6   Yael Zerubavel, *Recovered Roots: Collective Memory and the Making of the Israeli National Tradition* (Chicago, 1995).
7   See Idith Zertal, "Ha-me'unim veha-kedushim: Kinunah shel martirologiyah le'umit" (The Sacrifice and the Sanctified: The Construction of National Martyrology), *Zmanim*, No. 48 (1994), pp. 26–45; and Moshe Zukermann, *Shoah ba-heder ha-atum: Ha-'shoah' ba-itonut ha-yisraelit be-tkufat milhemet ha-mifratz* (Shoah in the Sealed Room: The "Holocaust" in the Israeli Press during the Gulf War) (Tel Aviv, 1993).
8   See Uri Ben-Eliezer, *Derekh ha-kavenet: Hivatzruto shel ha-militarizm ha-yisre'eli* (Through the Sight of the Gun: The Emergence of Israeli Militarism) (Tel Aviv, 1995); Amnon Raz-Krakotzkin, "Galut mitokh ribonut: Le-vikoret 'shlilat ha-galut' ba-tarbut ha-yisre'elit" (Exile within Sovereignty: Toward a Critique of the "Negation of Exile" in Israeli Culture), *Teoriyah u-Vikoret*, No. 4 (1994), pp. 6–23, and No. 5 (1994), pp. 113–32; and Oz Almog, *Ha-tzabar: Dyukan* (The Sabra: A Portrait) (Tel Aviv, 1997).
9   Yoram Kaniuk, "Tzomet akhzari" (Cruel Junction), *Politikah*, No. 17 (1987), pp. 2–8.
10 Yonathan Ratosh, "Ktav el ha-no'ar ha-ivri" (A Note to the Hebrew Youth), in idem, *Reshit ha-yamim: Ptihot ivriyot* (The First of Days: Hebrew Introductions) (Tel Aviv, 1982), p. 35.
11 For further elaboration, see Uri Ram, "Post-Nationalist Pasts: The Case of Israel."
12 Charles Liebman and Eliezer Don-Yehiya, *Civil Religion in Israel: Traditional Judaism and Political Culture in the Jewish State* (Berkeley, 1983).
13 See Tom Segev, *The Seventh Million: The Israelis and the Holocaust* (New York, 1993).
14 Benny Morris, *The Birth of the Palestinian Refugee Problem, 1947–1949* (Cambridge, 1987).
15 Baruch Kimmerling, "Dat, le'umiyut ve-demokratiyah be-Yisrael" (Religion, Nationalism and Democracy in Israel), *Zmanim*, No. 50–51 (1994), pp. 116–31.
16 Yair Oron, *Zehut yisre'elit-yehudit* (Israeli-Jewish Identity) (Tel Aviv, 1993).
17 S. Yizhar, "Hirbet Hizah" [1949], in idem, *Shivah sipurim* (Seven Stories) (Tel Aviv, 1971), pp. 35–88; A. B. Yehoshua, *Mul ha-ye'arot* (Facing the Forests) (Tel Aviv, 1968); David Grossman, *Sleeping on a Wire* (New York, 1992).
18 See Ben-Eliezer, *Derekh ha-kavenet*.
19 See Ruth Firer, *Sokhnim shel ha-hinukh ha-tziyoni* (The Agents of Zionist Education) (Tel Aviv, 1985); Oren Yiftachel, "Israeli Society and Jewish-Palestinian Reconciliation: Ethnocracy and Its Territorial Contradictions," *Middle East Journal*, Vol. 51, No. 1 (1997), pp. 1–16.
20 Tali Tamir, "Tsuba: Abstraction and Blindness," in idem (ed.), *Tsooba: Larry Abramson* (Tel Aviv, 1995), no page nos.
21 Ibid.
22 Ibid.
23 See Ella Shohat, *Israeli Cinema: East/West and the Politics of Representation* (Austin, TX, 1989); and Yehuda Shenhav, "Kesher ha-shtikah" (The Conspiracy of Silence), *Ha'aretz* weekend supplement, 27 December 1996.
24 See Uri Ram, "The Promised Land of Business Opportunities: Liberal Post-Zionism in the Global Age," in Gershon Shafir and Yoav Peled (eds.), *The New Israel* (Boulder, CO, 2000), pp. 217–40.
25 See Aviezer Ravitsky, *Messianism, Zionism and Jewish Religious Radicalism* (Chicago, 1996).
26 See Ehud Sprinzak, "Gush Emunim: Model ha-karhon shel kitzoniyut politit" (Gush Emunim: The Iceberg Model of Political Extremism), *Medinah, Mishtar ve-Yahasim Beinle'umiim*, No. 17, (1981), and *The Ascendance of Israel's Radical Right* (Oxford, 1991).
27 See Gideon Aran, "Jewish Zionist Fundamentalism: The Bloc of the Faithful in Israel (Gush Emunim)," in Martin E. Marty and R. Scott Appleby (eds.), *Fundamentalisms Observed* (Chicago, 1991); Michael Feige, "Tnu'ot hevratiyot, hegemoniyah ve-mitos politi: Behinah mashvah shel ha-ideologiyah shel Gush Emunim ve-Shalom Akhshav" (Social Movements, Hegemony and Political Myth: A Comparative Study of Gush Emunim and Peace Now Ideologies) (Ph.D. diss., Hebrew University of Jerusalem, 1995); and Ian Lustick, *For the Land and the Lord: Jewish Fundamentalism in Israel* (New York, 1988).
28 Harold Fisch, *The Zionist Revolution: A New Perspective* (London, 1978), pp. 79–96.
29 Ibid., pp. 78–9.

30 Ibid., p. 87.
31 Ibid.
32 Ibid., pp. 92, 94.
33 Ibid., pp. 153, 152.
34 Ibid., p. 151
35 Morris, *The Birth of the Palestinian Refugee Problem*; Avi Shlaim, *Collusion across the Jordan: King Abdullah, the Zionist Movement, and the Partition of Palestine* (New York, 1988); and Ilan Pappé, "Critique and Agenda: The Post-Zionist Scholars in Israel," *History & Memory*, Vol. 7, No. 1 (1995), pp. 66–90, and "Post-Zionist Critique on Israel and the Palestinians," *Journal of Palestinian Studies*, Vol. 26, No. 2 (1997), pp. 29–41, No. 3, pp. 37–43, No. 4, pp. 60–9.
36 Yoram Hazony, *The Jewish State: The Struggle for Israel's Soul* (New York, 2000). See also, Amnon Lord, *Ibadnu kol asher yakar hayah: Al shorshav shel ha-smol ha-post-yehudi* (We Lost All We Cherished: Roots of the Post-Jewish Left) (Tel Aviv, 2000).
37 See Uri Ram, "Zionist Historiography and the Invention of Modern Jewish Nationhood: The Case of Ben-Zion Dinur," *History & Memory*, Vol. 7, No. 1 (1995), pp. 91–124.
38 Yehuda Elkana, "Bi-zkhut ha-shikhehah," *Ha'aretz*, 2 March 1988.
39 Ibid.
40 Cf. Ruth Firer, *Sokhnim shel ha-lekah shel ha-shoah* (Agents of the Lesson of the Holocaust) (Tel Aviv, 1989).
41 Yehuda Elkana, "Bi-zkhut ha-shikhehah."
42 Zuckermann, *Shoah ba-heder ha-atum* (Note 7).
43 See Ram, "Post-Nationalist Pasts"; and Pappé, "Critique and Agenda."
44 See Sprinzak, *The Ascendance of Israel's Radical Right*; and Yoram Peri, "From Political Nationalism to Ethno-Nationalism: The Case of Israel," in Yehuda Lukacs and Abdala Battah (eds.), *The Arab–Israeli Conflict* (Boulder, CO, 1988).
45 Ravitsky, *Messianism, Zionism and Jewish Religious Radicalism*.

The Strategies of Historical Revisionism

Anita Shapira

Last year (2000), a minor scandal erupted in Israeli academe: a graduate research student at Haifa University whose M.A. thesis had been awarded the grade of "excellent" was charged with defamation in a libel suit brought by veterans of the Alexandroni Brigade (1948). His thesis, whose conclusions were given wide coverage in the Israeli press, deals with the conquest of Tantura, an Arab village on the road between Haifa and Tel Aviv, by IDF (Israel Defense Forces) soldiers in the Israeli War of Independence. The thesis described a massacre of villagers there allegedly perpetrated by members of the brigade after the inhabitants had surrendered.

On the face of it, one more incident was added to the so-called list of injustices committed by Jews against Arabs. Yet this time the scenario involved actors who are still alive, Alexandroni Brigade veterans who suddenly found themselves denounced as war criminals. They furiously denied the allegations and demanded that Haifa University reevaluate the thesis. When no response was forthcoming, the veterans turned to the courts. Subsequent to a court order, the plaintiffs obtained the protocols of testimony by Jews and Arabs on which the research is based. It then became clear that the author of the thesis had not always been very exact in quoting what the witnesses had stated, and, allegedly, in some instances had even written precisely the opposite of what had been said in testimony. The two sides came to an out-of-court compromise: the researcher would have to retract his allegations, concede there had indeed been no such slaughter in Tantura and express his remorse for having caused so much pain to the Alexandroni Brigade veterans and their families. It was agreed he should also publish a detailed statement on the affair in the Israeli press. But after the compromise settlement was officially approved by the court, one of the three lawyers for the research student requested that the court allow his client to cancel the agreement he had signed under "pressure from his family." The judge refused to grant this, arguing that a deal is a deal. This late appeal to the court provided a basis for the genesis of a kind of myth: that the researcher was some sort of martyr who was simply unable to cope with the social pressure — and so had decided to abandon his just struggle.[1]

This incident casts light on the close link that has developed in Israel in recent years between the writing of history and politics. The 1970s and 1980s saw the emergence of a historiography that sought to break free from the ideological ballast representative of the accepted notions regarding the pre-state period and the earlier decades of the state, and to describe historical events "in a nonpartisan way." In the late 1980s, that approach ruptured with the advent of the so-called "new historians." From that juncture on, historians have not been judged by the quality of their work but by the stripe of their politics: "post-Zionists" or their opponents. Recently a third current has surfaced. Its main intellectual organ is the journal *Azure* published by the conservative Jerusalem think-tank, the Shalem Center, headed by Yoram Hazony. One of its principal documents to date is Hazony's recent book, *The Jewish State: The Struggle for Israel's Soul*. As Hazony himself notes, the main thrust of his attack is directed against the professors, writers and culture makers in the Israeli mainstream who do not see themselves as "post-Zionists" but have been infected by their basic tenets.[2] So it is indeed possible to describe the current situation as a joint attack from the left *and* right on what today is considered the embattled "center." In this article I will attempt to sketch the shared features of this two-pronged attack from both ends of the spectrum.

The Creation of an Anti-Narrative

The historical narrative of the *Yishuv* and the State of Israel was based in large part on a description of developments seen through the prism of the Labor movement — the dominant current in Zionism and the Israeli state from the 1930s to the late 1970s. Its point of departure was the need of the Jewish people for a homeland, a need rooted in the rise of modern post-emancipatory nationalisms. The narrative was based on an assumption regarding the correlation between the Zionist enterprise on the one hand, manifested in the creation of concrete facts on the map of Palestine — through immigration, settlement, economic development and the creation of a defense force — and political headway on the other, progress determined in large measure by those material facts created on the ground.

That narrative was accompanied by an ideological-educational superstructure. It provided the explanation, the legitimization and stamp of moral value to the prosaic acts that wrought concrete changes in the landscape of Palestine. The conception that political change was the product of concrete settlement activity accompanied Zionist ideology from the time of the 1920 heroic stand at Tel Hai, on through the resolutions of the Peel Commission, whose 1937 partition proposal carved out of a part of Palestine a Jewish state, whose boundaries were based on actual Jewish settlement, and on to the Six Day War of 1967. The War of Independence was also presented as an amalgamation between a political achievement — the November 1947 UN

General Assembly resolution on the partition of Palestine and the recognition by the great powers — and action on the ground, namely the success of the Israel Defense Forces in standing up to the onslaught of five Arab armies and emerging victorious. In that narrative, the Arabs were relegated to secondary importance — they were strangers, marauders who came to attack Zionist settlers, bent on thwarting the hope of the Jewish people to return to their ancient land, motivated by xenophobia, a hatred of the Jews and locked in an insidious pact with British imperialism. Yet at times there was also a recognition of the fact that the Jews were coming into Palestine to alter the character of an Arab land and even gain dominance over it. One of the leaders of the settlement policy once noted that settlement is war, even if its ways are peaceful. Beginning with the War of Independence, the Arab–Israeli confrontation became a central element in the narrative of the state's history, along with the tale of the mass immigration and its problems.

The "new historians" changed the context of the narrative: their representation's axis has moved from the plight of the Jewish people in Europe and the need for a homeland to the history of Palestine and the pivotal issue of the Jewish–Palestinian (and later Jewish–Arab) confrontation. In that context, Zionism is not viewed as a national movement of liberation but as an enterprise of colonization, like analogous movements that were part of Western imperialism. The story is not one of socialists laboring to build a state, torn between their faith in socialist ideology and allegiance to their own nationalist vision and agenda, which usually proved decisive. Rather it is a tale of wicked invaders, who right from the outset aimed at dispossessing the indigenous Arabs and ousting them from their land, in Benny Morris's formulation, an enterprise "tainted by moral dubiousness" from its inception.[3] The development of the tale then centers on how those European invaders were able to realize their desired aims. In their narrative, the War of Independence becomes the pivotal axis, the founding event of statehood. The state's creation was tainted by handicaps: it uprooted and expelled the Arabs and prevented them from returning, and it also bears major blame for the fact that attempts to forge peace between Israel and the Arabs have borne so little fruit. That was not a war between David and Goliath. On the contrary: the Arabs were fewer in number and weaker, while the Jews, the aggressors, enjoyed the numerical and logistical edge in the field where it counted.

Yoram Hazony puts forward a totally different narrative. The question that interests him is: how did it come about that what he terms "political anti-Zionism" is today a pervasive influence, molding intellectual life in Israel and threatening to undermine the Jewish state? Analogous to the classic Zionist narrative, Hazony has no interest in recounting the tale of Jewish–Arab relations. Nor is he interested in describing the revolutionary changes in Palestine in the twentieth century brought by the Jewish settlement — an essential feature in the classic narrative. Rather, what intrigues him principally is the sphere of ideology. He draws a straight line from the controversy between Martin Buber and Theodor Herzl at the beginning of the twentieth century to the members of the Brit Shalom association, established in Jerusalem in the 1920s to promote an agreement between Jews and Arabs regarding Jewish settlement in the country, to Judah Magnes, Ihud and all the other short-lived organizations that arose in the period of the *Yishuv* and the early years of the state aspiring to the same goal. Hazony presents the history of Zionism as the chronicle of a clash between two ideological conceptions: the champions of the Jewish state and "Jewish empowerment" (whatever this means) and those who opposed this view. The history of Zionism and the *Yishuv* and the concrete political situations that arose are swallowed up by this overriding ideological description. A debate of some salience in its time, though it is doubtful that it had any real impact on the formation of the state, becomes in Hazony's book the narrative's central line. According to this line, it led on to the confrontation between David Ben-Gurion and the professors at the Hebrew University, and ultimately to the "deposing" of "the old man" and the victory of those who today wish to dismantle the Jewish national character of the state and to establish in Israel a binational state, the state of all its citizens, in which Jews will have no special standing. The struggle is not in the more material sphere of military might or nation-building but in the realm of ideas, of intellect and ideology. He argues that from the time Ben-Gurion was removed from the political arena, no successor has come to the helm of state to give the people a vision, an all-embracing explanation of the state's existence and survival. This is why all those wild weeds grew in the halls of academe at the Hebrew University. And today, they and their students have gained in stature throughout the entire structure of the Israeli cultural establishment.

Morality and Politics

In history, division between saints and sinners is never clear. With the exception of the Second World War, it seems there was no war where in retrospect it was not possible to discover elements both to the credit and liability of each side. The composite complexity of the historical picture stands in marked contrast with any reductionist attempt to point with absolute certainty to "villains" and "victims," which is why historical discourse has been wary of using concepts drawn from the domain of morals. From the time of Richelieu it has been customary in historiography to utilize the notion of *raisons d'état*, which makes a distinction between personal morality and the ethics of the state. While the individual is always obliged to adhere to accepted moral standards, the state, charged with preserving the well-being and peace of its citizens, sometimes finds itself constrained to deviate from the ethical path. There is no state free of the stain of arbitrary action towards its own citizenry or its neighbors, for reasons rooted in the general interest (as the state conceives it). The distinction between an ethical politics and *realpolitik* is characteristic of the shift in Europe from a political agenda grounded in religion to one based on nationhood. The "new historians" reinserted the discourse of ethics into the discussion: Israel was born in sin, wrote Benny Morris in his "charter essay" published in *Tikkun* in 1988, in which he coined the expression "new historians."[4] That began a wave of accusations that Zionism was from its very outset inherently flawed, a morally questionable enterprise both in its ends and means. These historians proclaimed that there existed ostensibly an a priori contradiction between the Jewish national liberation movement and the dictates of morality.

At first, the Israeli right subscribed to views quite close to those of the new historians: yes, Israel had always been the tough bad guy, had used force and acted in an arbitrary manner to achieve its ends. But the right's tone differed from the accusatory clamor of the post-Zionists: the latter moralized, the former extolled the same actions. The classic right believed it was necessary to expunge morality from politics and to act in keeping with egotistical national interests. That is why Vladimir Jabotinsky, the leader of the right-wing Revisionist Party, was able to assert so unflinchingly, already back in the 1920s, that the Jewish–Arab confrontation was unavoidable and that only an "iron wall," a military force, could provide security to the fledgling Jewish settlement.[5] It is no coincidence that Avi Shlaim, one of the "new historians", who is keen to lay the blame for the Israeli–Arab conflict at Israel's doorstep, embraced the model of Jabotinsky, entitling his 1999 book *The Iron Wall: Israel and the Arab World since 1948*. In contrast to Jabotinsky, Ben-Gurion and his left-of-center associates sought ways to realize Zionism without being pulled into the vortex of confrontation with the Arabs, since they were still reluctant to accept the notion that this conflict could only be solved by armed force. Against the absolutist notions of "moral" or "immoral," they staked out a middle ground that prescribed "reasons of state" only in small careful doses.[6]

Hazony's project is to criticize the center from the right, injecting issues of morality. In his view, the Jewish state is a moral value, infused with transcendental significance. Consequently, any criticism of the state is in effect an attack on morality. Buber and his confederates, who did not regard the idea of a Jewish state as something sacred, are presented as bent on undermining the state's foundations — not simply as exponents of a differing political view. Hazony does not explain what exactly he means by the concept of a "Jewish state," but he evidently does not have just a "state of the Jews" in mind. He aspires to ascribe special Jewish attributes to that state. Here is where things begin to become opaque. Does he think of Jewish religious attributes? Or special privileges for Jewish citizens? Or a messianic ideology of the brand he associates with Ben-Gurion? And is this messianism of a secular or a religious character? His references to Jewish state power and sovereignty are undoubtedly beyond the ambit of rational discourse on the state and its instruments. He explicitly opposes Rousseau's idea of the "social contract," according the conception of a Jewish state a weight and importance far beyond the "here and now." As a consequence, he endows its supporters with special moral values which he denies to its detractors.

Legitimization and Delegitimization — the Marking of the Boundaries of the Normative

The demarcation of the confines of consensus determines who is marginalized and who is left at the center. From the outset, the post-Zionists have defined themselves as outside the Zionist consensus and negated its legitimacy. Consequently, they are not offended if we present them as contrary to the consensus. By contrast, Hazony wishes to define the consensus in a different way, to exclude others from its perimeter, though he sees himself as squarely inside. Both sides subscribe to a politics that aggrandizes their own legitimacy while denying that of their opponents.

When Benny Morris proclaimed the advent of the new history and began to portray the "old historians" as not just outdated but guilty of willful concealment of the past and serving as intellectual lackeys to the powers that be, he staked out the right to define the boundaries of the normative in historiography. Hence, he defined a group of historians as the founders of the school of the "new history." The criterion entitling one to membership was a focus on Israel's wars, especially the War of Independence, and Israeli policies thereafter, coupled with a fiercely critical view of Israel and an interpretation that reinforces Jewish guilt while minimizing that of the Arabs. Whoever did not embrace these views, even if they were young in years, were labeled "new old historians." The concept "new" bestowed a special value, while "old" was a loaded term, with hints of scholarly laxity or even dishonesty. That categorization was catchy like a popular slogan and assisted the "new" historians in delegitimizing anyone who dared attack them or their findings.

Hazony employs a similar method: he asserts that the legitimate conception was that of Labor Zionism as formulated by Ben-Gurion in the early years of the state (as Hazony interprets that conception). He defines legitimate Zionism, the proper conception of the "Jewish state" — and whoever does not fit in with these definitions is labeled a "political anti-Zionist," a classification Hazony invented. Anyone who believes that fundamentally there is no contradiction between Judaism and universal values is presented as an opponent of the Jewish state, Jewish state power and sovereignty. Even a fundamental criticism of nationalism at large is viewed as something inimical to Jewish sovereignty. In his construction, anyone who ever said anything that might be construed as expressing a willingness to grant equal rights to Jews and Arabs in a Jewish state is unacceptable. He assumes that there is an inherent contradiction between a Jewish state and democracy. Consequently, those who champion a state that is Jewish *and* democratic have placed themselves beyond the pale of consensus.[7] Hazony introduces a new "negative" category: emancipationist German Judaism, which includes all the pupils and followers of Hermann Cohen and Martin Buber. In general, he seems deeply suspicious of all Jews, Zionists and non-Zionists alike, who hail from Central and Western Europe — except, of course, Herzl. By association and ideology, he splices a link between them and the Reform Judaism movement in the United States, a current he also roundly rejects. Hazony stretches this to the point that when he wants to criticize the professors from the Hebrew University, he notes their origin: they came from areas of German culture (Galicia) or were trained in German universities (Joshua Prawer, Jacob Talmon, Nathan Rotenstreich, Jacob Katz, Efraim Auerbach).[8] Hazony concedes that his definitions of Zionism and the Jewish state are not the accepted notions, which is why he speaks in his book about "the idea of the Jewish State as we have known it."[9] That is also why he invents concepts such as "political anti-nationalism" and "adulation of powerlessness," attributing to those Jews the purported "Jewish ideal" of "statelessness" and "disempowerment" (it is interesting to consider how one would translate this latter term into Hebrew, which is an additional proof of its superficiality).[10] After crafting the conceptual frame that defines the perimeters of the camp, he excludes anyone who in any incidental or even marginal remark ever said anything incompatible with the defined frameworks of legitimacy.[11]

Hazony presents himself as someone treading in the footsteps of the classic Labor Zionist movement. He is critical of some aspects of that movement, which he finds too "materialistic" and lacking in "spirituality."[12] To label Labor Zionism "materialistic" reflects a profound lack of understanding of the Labor movement and the texture of its value system. Nevertheless, this is Hazony's preferred model of statehood. He criticizes the individualistic tendencies that emerged in Israel after the end of the Ben-Gurion era, as a result of the treacherous influence of the intellectuals. Hazony admires the dedication of the individual to the community, the readiness to accept the authority of the great mentors of the generation and to refrain from critique, to postpone gratification on the personal and national level, traits characteristic of Israel's early years. He apparently does not realize that these characteristics were all integral to the collectivist world view whose sources and inspiration were socialist-revolutionary, the same "materialistic trends" of which he is critical.

Moreover, in those years Israel came close to being a kind of "guided democracy." Ben-Gurion sought to determine for the people what they should think and believe, what world view to espouse. It is doubtful that this all-embracing ideological order could exist in a Western democracy, which is why Menachem Begin did not try to implement it during his period in office, a fact Hazony criticizes.[13] It had been feasible in the 1950s and 1960s, when a large part of the world espoused similar concepts, Israel was isolated from the rest of the world, and the media were limited to a few channels, some of which were under state control. But even then these predilections on Ben-Gurion's part were viewed as idiosyncratic, unacceptable to either the right or center, and even the left was ambivalent about them. In other words: to long for the state of the 1950s and its intellectual climate is to pine for a world at odds with liberalism, individualism and Western democracy and imbued with unmistakably authoritarian features. There was a built-in contradiction between Ben-Gurion's placing of Israel squarely in the camp of Western democracy and his effort to engineer society. This contradiction was bound to cause a disruption of the "old values." Thus, one could say that Ben Gurion himself created the forces of change that Hazony is so critical of.

History as Conspiracy

One of the legacies of vulgar Marxism was the repeated attempts to depict history as the unfolding of a preplanned story, the making of history via prior conspiracy. As a rule, the tendency is to seek the present's roots in the past — that is, the present is not the result of unanticipated development, of trial and error, uncontrolled chance, contingency; rather, it is a virtually preprogrammed process, initiated by human actors, most commonly willful and malicious. Thus, Benny Morris attempts again and again to prove the Palestinian claim that the idea of expelling the Arabs from Palestine was integral to Zionist ideology right from the start. Although his description of the War of Independence is more complex, contradicting this simplistic thesis, it does not prevent him from repeatedly emphasizing every sliver of evidence that could indicate that this had been a part of the Zionist movement's agenda from its inception.[14] This is an example of an attempt to write history in reverse, moving from the present backwards. His point of departure is Israel's military might after the Six Day War and especially in the wake of the Lebanon War — not the actual situation as it was conceived in 1948.

Hazony uses a similar method: he looks for the roots of the anti-nationalist tendencies he sees in Israel today, anchoring them in a matrix dispute that began between Buber and Herzl one hundred years ago. And from this he unrolls the entire history of Zionism and the State of Israel. His description of the development of the Hebrew University into a kind of fortress of the anti-Zionists is an outstanding example of this process of writing history backwards: the story of the Elders of the Hebrew University who introduced the virus of anti-nationalist politics, infecting their pupils. For example, Professor Joshua Prawer, an authority on the Crusades and a staunch Zionist, is presented by Hazony as responsible for the unorthodox political views of his student Meron Benvenisti.[15]

In general, history for him is not what people *did* but what they *said*. He magnifies the importance of education, indoctrination, ideology. What is absent in his narration is history as a recounting of events, of shifts in ways of thinking and mentality, influences from the broader world, the welter of changing realities. This is a strategy designed to imbue a single segment of reality with decisive importance and to place it outside the flow of history: it was not the course of history that determined developments, but the machinations of a conspiracy. Thus, for example, Hazony makes no mention whatsoever of the harsh reality of Israeli occupation and the problematical situation of a democratic state as an occupier ruling over another people. That reality, which might provide an alternative explanation for certain pervasive tendencies among Israeli intellectuals today, is disregarded. In contrast, he sketches the process of passing on the microbe of German-Jewish defeatism from generation to generation.

Selectivity

On both the left and right, historical revisionists tend to disregard those aspects of reality that are incompatible with the main theses of historical revisionism . Thus, for example, one of the characteristic approaches of the "new historians'" project is to portray a uniform Zionist narrative: they seize on the narrative of the right in its simplistic form, styling it as the ultimate Zionist narrative, and then analyze its faults. Or in another tactic, they take an old-fashioned veteran military historian such as Netanel Lorch, who wrote under the auspices of the Ministry of Defense and in accordance with its directives on censorship, and then present him as an example representative of the "old" historians who preceded them. All the failed attempts at negotiation between Israel and her neighbors are given special emphasis. They present Israel's refusal to pay the price of peace demanded by her enemies as Israeli intractability, and tend to show much more sympathetic understanding for the other side. Violence perpetrated by Jews is underscored, violence by Arabs is downplayed or concealed.[16]

Hazony utilizes the same method in his presentation of the so-called opponents of the Zionist narrative: one tactic he employs is to cite incidental remarks out of context by those he classifies as "mainstream." Another ploy is to quote at length from post-Zionist thinkers and historians creating the impression that they represent the dominant current. Adi Ophir, Baruch Kimmerling, Tom Segev, Moshe Zimmermann, Zeev Sternhell and others are presented by him at length, and though he says that they belong to the new trends, he uses them to project an image of a widespread phenomenon of post-Zionism among mainstream scholars.[17] His criticism of the opponents of political nationalism concentrates only on secular Jews, avoiding the discomfiting fact that there is another category of opponents: ultra-Orthodox anti-Zionists. The ultra-Orthodox rebbes and rabbis were always opposed to political Zionism, but this fact is not mentioned in the book. In Hazony's construction, Yeshivat Merkaz ha-Rav, established by Rabbi Kook and his disciples, the spiritual authority for the religious settlers after 1973, emerges as the only conceptual alternative to the intellectual sabotage of the universities.[18] Yet in truth, the alternative to the universities is the ultra-Orthodox Rav Shach and Rav Ovadiyah Yosef and the Habad movement, who command the masses and whose attitude to the Jewish state is problematic, to say the least, not the religious-nationalist stronghold of Yeshivat Merkaz ha-Rav, which has a limited impact. All this complexity is absent in Hazony's book because it does not fit in smoothly with his central thesis. In this respect, his reductionist tack is reminiscent of the post-Zionists' tendency to present a monolithic Zionist narrative as they choose to define it, without nuances and depth.

Terminology

Whoever wishes to create an alternative narrative begins with the formulation of terminology that creates values and groups of affiliation. I have already mentioned the terms "new historians," "new old historians," "critical sociology" (a rejection of all previous approaches in sociology) and "emancipationist German," "adulation of powerlessness," "political anti-nationalism." I wish to expand now on the notion of terms of disparagement. In the past, we were accustomed to use the first person plural when relating to what Jews did or thought in Palestine, or simply used the concept "Jews." For the new historians, however, there was a "Zionist" versus an "Arab" side, ideology contra nation. This was the genesis of the discursive distinction between the Jewish people and the Zionist project: it was not the Jews who created the Jewish state but the Zionists. Jewish settlement in Palestine now became "Zionist colonization." The narrative of the War of Independence is not the narrative of the State of Israel but the "Zionist" narrative, the narrative of the ideological movement suspected of illegitimacy. There is no longer any talk of opposition to the State of Israel; it is supplanted by opposition to Zionism, an allegedly racist ideology that denies civil equality. The use of terminology referring to the War of Independence is indicative. Its combatants termed the conflict the "War of Liberation" because they thought they were fighting against Great Britain. Later it was renamed the "War of

Independence" in order to signify the quantum change that had occurred for the Jewish population with the birth of the state. Today people often use the neutral term "1948 War" so as not to offend the sensibilities of the Palestinians, for whom the war is etched in national memory as *al-nakba*, the catastrophe. When Avi Shlaim speaks of negotiations between Israel and King Abdullah of Jordan regarding the annexation of Arab parts of western Palestine, he does not talk about legitimate diplomatic dialogue but "collusion," as in the title of his 1988 book *Collusion across the Jordan*.[19]

Hazony also fashions a terminological/conceptual system: any mention by Hazony of someone connected with German culture is always derogatory. He translates the name of the organization *Brit Shalom* as "Peace Association" in order to avoid the more loaded biblical term "Covenant of Peace." He intensifies the concept of anti-Jewish excesses: thus, the Russian pogroms in the 1880s are termed "massacres," even though in actual fact they had relatively few victims. Hazony terms the economic legislation introduced by the Polish Interior Minister Wladyslaw Grabski in the 1920s, laws damaging to the Jewish middle class in Poland, "Grabski's persecution." Killings of Jews by Arabs in Palestine are "massacres."[20] The 1929 riots are called the "1929 slaughter." This appropriation of radical concepts recalls the traditional, ahistorical Jewish narrative of helplessness: all the world is always against us, and we are victims without salvation. The attribution of extra weight to the activities of the small pacifist group in the *Yishuv* is another feature in the presentation of the narrative. Thus, for example, he writes that when Judah Leib Magnes criticized the position of the Zionist Executive in 1930, he "was toppling the Zionist position like a house of cards."[21] Anyone who reads this cannot grasp how it was possible for the British government to abandon its anti-Zionist policy within the span of a few short months and to adopt a position that enabled the continued growth of the National Home.

Ben-Gurion as a Symbol

One thing Hazony has in common with the post-Zionists is the choice of Ben-Gurion as a peg on which to hang ideology. Ben-Gurion was at the helm of the *Yishuv*, the Zionist movement and the State of Israel for over 30 years. He is the founding father of the state of the Jews, so that anyone wishing to attack the state naturally tries to use Ben-Gurion as a historical punching bag. In Zeev Sternhell's attempt to demolish the image of Labor Zionism as a socialist movement and present it as a radical nationalist movement, he does his utmost to lower the stature of Ben-Gurion and to picture him as a poor leader, inferior to comparable socialist leaders in Europe. Tom Segev presents him as a mediocre helmsman at best, who did not succeed in rising to the requisite greatness of leadership during the Holocaust. Avi Shlaim portrays him as the neighborhood thug, opposed to all efforts at reconciliation with the Arab states and responsible for the exacerbation of the Israeli–Arab dispute. Benny Morris accuses him of responsibility for the expulsion of Palestinians and Israel's aggressive policy stance. There is a tendency among critical sociologists to blame him for the melting-pot policy of absorption which led to discrimination against Oriental Jews and Holocaust survivors, the dominance of statism in Israeli life and other ills.[22]

In contrast, Hazony presents a picture that is a mirror-image of the post-Zionist view. Ben-Gurion deserves praise not only for his role in the establishment of the Jewish state and Jewish "empowerment," but also because he gave the people a shining idea, thus on a par with the other great figure in Hazony's secular pantheon, Theodor Herzl.[23]

Just as the post-Zionists present a mythological image of Ben-Gurion, so does Hazony, though in an opposite way. Ben-Gurion would certainly have been astonished at the array of attributes he ascribes or denies him. Ben-Gurion saw Zionism as a revolt against everything he regarded as negative in Jewish life and East European Jewry: "In its beginnings, our movement was the fruit of the revolt of pioneering youth against the misery of the Jewish way of life, the wretchedness of existence in the Diaspora, the nullity of Jewish socialism and the sterility of declarative Zionism."[24] In one acerbic sentence he rejected traditional Judaism, non-Zionist socialism and a Zionism that sufficed in words not deeds, a criticism directed against the Revisionist right and the Jewish middle class. As late as 1939, Ben-Gurion stated that there was no link between the centuries-old longing of the Jewish people to return to their land and Zionism, a new, modern development: "The impetus driving Zionism is not the longing for *Eretz Yisrael*. That yearning was always there. But Zionism was something new, completely modern. The main stimulus behind Zionism is the plight of the Jewish people ... that Jews have finally ceased to acquiesce in."[25] It is true that *after* the state was established Ben-Gurion began to talk in another way. He sought to create a national narrative that would speak to the generation of "native sons" to whom the old Zionist ideology did not seem to appeal — and to the immigrants from Oriental lands, whose ties to Zion were anchored in messianic longings. Yet in so doing, Ben-Gurion deviated from the received notion that saw Zionism as a secular modern movement, tied to the pragmatic material world of action, not to ancient messianic Jewish yearnings for Zion that had always come to nought. The modern return to Zion was conceived as antithetical to messianic movements. Hazony attacks Gershom Scholem because he rejected the idea that the modern return to Zion had some kind of mystical, messianic meaning.[26] In truth, it is Scholem who represented the classic Zionist movement (including the religious Zionism à la Rabbi Isaac Jacob Reines) — not Ben-Gurion in his final years, when he spoke of the "messianic vision." Mainstream Zionists were on the whole apprehensive of the old Jewish messianic outbursts and saw them as a destructive force, detrimental to Jewish coping with the "here and now." In Hazony's portrayal, in the dispute between Nathan Rotenstreich and Ben-Gurion, it seems as if Rotenstreich, in opposing the inclusion of the messianic motif in Zionist ideology, is almost a traitor. The truth is that Rotenstreich defended an accepted view that Ben-Gurion in previous years had also championed. But the real contrast between the two was in respect to historical continuity: Ben-Gurion sought to skip over 2,000 years of Jewish creativity, while Rotenstreich stressed the wealth of Jewish creativity between the Bible and the Palmah, two millennia Ben-Gurion wished to discard onto the garbage heap of history.[27]

Hazony disposes of the entire matter of Ben-Gurion's rejection of Jewish tradition. He also disregards other aspects of the historical Ben-Gurion: at certain stages in his life Ben-Gurion was quite close to the idea of a "state of all its citizens" and to notions that Hazony today would regard as "post-Zionist": in the 1920s Ben-Gurion faithfully espoused the idea of "joint unionizing" of the Jewish and Arab worker.[28] In the 1930s, he spoke about a Palestine that was destined for the Jewish people *and* its Arab inhabitants.[29] In an interview he gave to the extreme right-wing activist Geula Cohen on 12 May 1967 — the eve of Israel's 19th independence day (and subsequently the eve of the Six Day War) — for the daily *Maariv*, he spoke in favor of the territorial status quo of 1949, refused to express any feelings of longing for a united Jerusalem and stated that the concept of "historical borders" was one appropriate for the coming of the Messiah, but not a practical one. In that same interview he seems to dispute what is Hazony's basic conception: "Words are not important. What counts are deeds. That was really Jabotinsky's big mistake: too much talk." In contrast with Hazony, for whom any reference to universalism is in total contradiction with the idea of Jewish power and sovereignty, Ben-Gurion stated back then: "In an independent Israel, we cannot make any distinction between Judaism and humanity. In the State of Israel, we have become citizens of the world, a free people with equal rights in the family of nations, and nothing human is alien to us."[30] The founders of Zionism, and Ben-Gurion among them, would not have endorsed the proposal that there is an irreconcilable contradiction between humanism and nationalism, universalism and the particularism of Zionism, democracy and the state of the Jews.

The image of Ben-Gurion that emerges from the descriptions of the post-Zionists and Hazony is monolithic, unfair to the reality of the historical figure. Ben-Gurion was not a philosopher or teacher, nor was he a spiritual leader. He was the leader of the people, and his views changed with the changing times. Since Ben-Gurion lived to a ripe old age and at times contradicted himself, anyone can select the Ben-Gurion of his or her choice. But the authentic historical picture must try to present a balanced figure, an image reflective of the changes the man experienced over time, what was a fixed and stable part of him and what was in flux, the positive with the negative.

Radical efforts from both sides to present a unified image of the father of the nation, for better or worse, reflect the process of politicization in historical inquiry: researchers are no longer at liberty to espouse their views on the basis of the historical materials at their disposal. Any position is ostensibly the product of a political outlook. Historical revisionism, from the left and the right, makes it harder for us to craft a more subtle and intricate view of history, with intermediate hues and shadings. All is perceived in stark black and white, in terms of what camp the scholar belongs to. In other areas marked by a sharp historiographical debate, a middle ground ultimately emerged, which embraced justified criticism from both sides. Will that also occur within the historical inquiry into the Zionist movement and the Israeli state, or will we see an ever-widening gap between the two extremes?

NOTES

1 *Ha'aretz*, 22 December 2000. See website www.ee.bgu.ac.il/~cesor/katz-directory for more details.
2 Yoram Hazony, *The Jewish State: The Struggle for Israel's Soul* (New York, 2000), p. 12.
3 Benny Morris, *Righteous Victims: A History of the Zionist–Arab Conflict, 1881–1999* (New York, 1999), p. 654.
4 Benny Morris, "The New Historiography: Israel Confronts Its Past," *Tikkun*, Vol. 3, No. 6 (November–December 1988), pp. 19–23, 99–102.
5 Ze'ev Jabotinsky, "Al kir ha-barzel" (On the Iron Wall), in *Ba-derekh la-medinah* (On the Way to Statehood) (Jerusalem, 1953), pp. 251–60.
6 For further discussion, see Anita Shapira, *Land and Power: The Zionist Resort to Force* (Stanford, 2000).
7 Hazony, *The Jewish State*, p. 50.
8 Ibid., p. 292, for example.
9 Ibid., p. 25. See also p. 309: "the Jewish state such as Herzl had advocated" (according to the author's interpretation of Herzl, of course).
10 Ibid., pp. 33, 193.
11 See, for example, how he treats Eliezer Schweid (ibid., p. 12) and Aharon Appelfeld (ibid., p. 26).
12 Ibid., pp. 332–4, 339.
13 Ibid., pp. 328–9, 331.
14 See Benny Morris, *The Birth of the Palestinian Refugee Problem, 1947–1949* (Cambridge, 1987), pp. 385–96, and *Righteous Victims*, pp. 252–4.
15 Hazony, *The Jewish State*, p. 294.
16 See my review article, "The Past Is Not a Foreign Country," *New Republic*, 29 November 1999, pp. 26–36, dealing with Avi Shlaim's book, *The Iron Wall*, and Morris's *Righteous Victims*.
17 See Hazony, *The Jewish State*, pp. 6–14. Most of the names mentioned are of scholars who indeed are conceived as post-Zionist. However, the reference to the scholars Menachem Brinker and Eliezer Schweid is a good example of taking words out of context.
18 Ibid., pp. 330–1.

19 Avi Shlaim, *Collusion Across the Jordan: King Abdullah, The Zionist Movement, and the Partition of Palestine* (Oxford, 1988).
20 See, for example, Hazony, *The Jewish State*, p. 192.
21 Ibid., p. 215.
22 See Eliezer Don-Yehiya, "Memory and Political Culture: Israeli Society and the Holocaust," in Ezra Mendelsohn (ed.), *Studies in Contemporary Jewry*, Vol. 9 (New York, 1993), pp. 139–62; Idith Zartal, *From Catastrophe to Power: Holocaust Survivors and the Emergence of Israel* (Berkeley, 1998).
23 Hazony, *The Jewish State*, p. 334.
24 David Ben-Gurion, *Mi-maamad le-am* (From Class to Peoplehood) (Tel Aviv, 1931), p. 306.
25 David Ben-Gurion, *Zikhronot* (Memoirs), Vol. 6 (Tel Aviv, 1987), p. 271.
26 Hazony, *The Jewish State*, p. 290.
27 For details see Anita Shapira, "Ben Gurion and the Bible: The Forging of an Historical Narrative," *Middle Eastern Studies*, Vol. 33, No. 4 (October 1997), pp. 645–74.
28 See, for example, David Ben-Gurion, *Anahnu u-shkhenenu* (We and Our Neighbors) (Tel Aviv, 1931), pp. 72–75.
29 Ibid., pp. 188–96.
30 Ben-Gurion's interview with Geula Cohen, *Maariv*, 12 May 1967.

Zionism and the Counter-Intellectuals

Mark Lilla

I feel I should preface my remarks with a truth-in-advertising disclaimer. I am not an Israeli, I am not a Zionist, or an anti-Zionist; I am not a Jew. My reasons for reading Yoram Hazony's book, *The Jewish State*, were therefore not the predictable ones.[1] I simply have an interest in religion and politics in modern life, and for anyone who takes such issues seriously the question of Zionism and the fate of Israel cannot but loom large. I have followed the debate over historiography in Israel from a distance for some time, and took up Hazony's book in the hope of hearing an alternative Israeli view of Zionism's past and future. Does his book offer an alternative to mainstream and post-Zionist orthodoxy? Absolutely. Is it an Israeli alternative? That is a more complicated question.

For this American at least, the experience of reading *The Jewish State* brought back distant memories, of books written and debated here decades ago in the heyday of American neoconservatism. Hazony's subject may be Israel and Zionism, but everything else about it — its tone, its quasi-militaristic rhetoric, its cavalier use of sources and quotations, its insinuations of intellectual bad faith and cowardice, even treason — mark it as American. Hazony's posture is that of the American counter-intellectual. He is not an anti-intellectual, any more than the American neoconservatives are. He and they present themselves as people who care deeply about ideas, or at least about the "battle of ideas," which they assume to be the same thing. Anti-intellectuals have contempt for intellectual life and see no reason to engage in it; counter-intellectuals think that ideas govern the world, which they may consider an unfortunate fact but a fact nonetheless. They are engaged in intellectual life, then, not out of curiosity or natural inclination but out of a purely political passion to challenge "*the* intellectuals," conceived as a class whose political tactics must be combated in kind. Whether he realizes it or not (and my guess is he does), Hazony has written a classic in American neoconservatism.

Does that matter? If all one cares about is the history of Zionism and getting that history right, does the intellectual and political background to the book contribute to our judgment of it? Can't Hazony's historical argument be considered in its own terms? Yes, it obviously can and should be. But neoconservative books like this frustrate attempts at straightforward engagement because they deny its very possibility. They therefore present the reader with a dilemma: either the reader must meet the author on his chosen terrain and argue over political motivations, conceding this to be the real issue; or he must renounce any hope of engaging the author, who has little interest in the historical record as such. Many Israeli readers, I presume, would like to meet Hazony's challenge, which means that they are prepared to discuss motivations. But to do so they will need to understand more than the political and intellectual landscape of contemporary Israel. They will also need to understand something about American neoconservatism and its peculiar conception of intellectual life.

To make my case, however, I need to make a second truth-in-advertising disclaimer. In the early 1980s I was an editor of *The Public Interest*, one of the flagship neoconservative journals in the United States and in my view still the best. I was a neoconservative but an unhappy one: satisfied with the neoconservative lines on domestic and foreign policy (these were Cold War years) but distressed by the blind hostility to intellectuals among my peers and embarrassed by their forays into cultural matters they did not understand. Many of my older friends had once been genuine intellectuals who made important contributions to history and criticism in the postwar decades, and their early works are still worth reading. But in their despair over the changes in American life since the 1960s, they had, by the 1980s, renounced any intellectual ambitions that did not serve the cause of restoring the cultural *status quo ante*. As for the young people they inspired and cultivated, they became counter-intellectuals without ever having been intellectuals — a unique American phenomenon.

Or perhaps not. To judge by his book, and by some of the articles his Shalem Center publishes in the magazine *Azure*, Hazony is intent on bringing counter-intellectualism to Israel. One only has to glance at some of his chapter titles to see this: Chapter 1, "The Culture Makers Renounce the Idea of a Jewish State"; Chapter 9, "The Intellectuals' Assault and Ben-Gurion's Response"; Chapter 13, "The Triumph of the Intellectuals." The attack on the intellectuals as a class is relentless. The Jewish state, he writes, is under "systematic attack from its own cultural and intellectual establishment," a "tight packed and intellectually monochromatic clique" whose attacks are "coordinated" by members of the Hebrew University.[2] These are people who understand that "the state need not be defeated militarily to be defeated utterly. The entire job may be done on the battleground of ideas."[3] Therefore "real resistance requires counter-ideas," which are in fact old ideas, belonging to "the old Labor-Zionist religion of physical labor [and] the power of gunpowder."[4]

Hazony can write: like Gramsci, in a *kippa*. But unlike Gramsci, Hazony displays no real interest in intellectual and cultural life apart from what he conceives to be its political uses. He is free to dislike the works of contemporary Israeli novelists and poets, and their politics, but to judge by his remarks on their works, which I too have read, he is incapable of engaging them as works of literature. He is probably right that the visual arts are in a bad way in Israel (as they are everywhere) but his praise of kitschy Zionist-Canaanite sculptures of the 1930s and 1940s will make any friend of art wince. His readings of the works of Martin Buber, Gershom Scholem and Jacob Talmon are so against the grain that one wonders how closely he has studied them. And even when he writes about Rousseau — who, I remind you, never taught at the Hebrew University — he gets him wrong, apparently unaware how much his own Zionist heroes owed to Rousseau's conviction that legitimate states must first be founded on an act of pure will — a notion of political guardianship for which Hazony shows great sympathy in his book (pp. 106–7).

Intellectually, then, the book displays a disconcerting confusion. But to judge by the American neoconservative experience, I doubt whether this will matter much to those whom Hazony hopes to reach in Israel and, crucially, in the United States. What will matter is that the book may help to create a network of writers, editors, academics and foundations who can act as a quasi-intellectual counterweight to those who he believes "control" or "dominate" Israeli culture. My prediction, again based on American experience, is that Hazony may succeed. And in succeeding, he will ultimately fail. Let me explain.

The history of American neoconservatism is a history of political success and intellectual failure. Neoconservatism was born in reaction to the political and cultural upheavals of the 1960s and reflected, at least originally, a disappointment with American liberalism among those whose sympathies were initially liberal, even socialist. Like all intellectual movements of this sort, neoconservatism eventually came to represent a whole complex of ideas, many of which bore only an indirect relation to the original animus: ideas about political principles, like equality, justice and the rule of law; economic ideas concerning taxation and regulation; social ideas having to do with modern bourgeois life, the family, morality; the list could be extended. But if there was one idea that permeated all these other ideas, and held them together, it was the idea of "the adversary culture": the notion that the important positions in American politics, the university, the professions and the press had fallen into the hands of a homogeneous class of persons who rejected the principles on which the liberal-capitalist order had originally been founded, and who were working, often without knowing it, towards a dissolution of that order.

The term "the adversary culture" was first used by the New York intellectual and critic, Lionel Trilling, in an introduction to one of his books in the 1950s. It was not a term of abuse, nor was Trilling's point a polemical one. He simply reminded his readers of something they already knew: that the modern intellectual, as a social type, defined himself in adversarial relationship to the bourgeois society that bore him. Trilling had no simple view of that adversarial relationship, nor should he have. He correctly saw it as simultaneously productive and stultifying, revealing and blinding. He also understood that it was not a uniquely American phenomenon, that it was a modern development to be found in all modern nations.

This idea of an "adversary culture" lay dormant until the neoconservatives, who genuinely admired Trilling, began to see it as a key for understanding all that was distasteful to them in the upheavals of the 1960s. In their minds, the student rebellions, drug use, the breakdown of authority, changing sexual mores, transformations in the family and distaste for the military could not be explained in terms of the affluence of the 1950s or the folly of Vietnam. The neoconservatives' reasoning was as follows: ideas have consequences; all social changes are therefore driven by changes in ideas; and ideas change due to the intellectuals' adversarial proclivities, out of irresponsible idealism, cowardice or self-interest. For all their frustration with the intellectual class, the neoconservatives display an intellectual megalomania one rarely finds among their adversaries, who generally feel put upon and ignored. Hence the focus on largely imaginary intellectual cabals in American neoconservative writing, and which we now see in Hazony's treatment of Israeli intellectual life.

As the American sixties began, those who would soon be called neoconservatives and who wrote for *The Public Interest* and *Commentary* adopted a mature and detached tone towards the chaos around them, following the lead of Lionel Trilling. They reminded their readers of the dangers of intellectual fanaticism and the *trahison des clercs*, they warned against the logic of political utopianism, and they offered a modest "two cheers" for capitalism and bourgeois life in the face of the alternatives. But then something happened. Whether out of frustration or ambition — or, more likely, both — neoconservatives took off their gloves in the late 1970s and decided that preaching moderation and common sense would get them, and their ideas, nowhere. As one neoconservative wag put it, "you can't beat a horse with no horse." Translation: you can't expect to win a cultural war without your own soldiers and arms. And so they armed themselves. Between 1975 and 1985 several important foundations were set up to support counter-intellectual writing and research, a number of magazines were founded (including college newspapers, which are still extremely important), and surprising alliances were made between the New York intellectuals (most of whom were Jewish) and fundamentalist groups, mainly within the Christian orbit but also, amazingly, with the Unification Church of Reverend Sun

Myung Moon. The slogan of the day was not moderation, it was "populism" — that is, an intellectual defense of populism in the hopes of turning the tide against the intellectual elites who neoconservatives thought controlled American culture. And when Ronald Reagan was elected in 1980 the neoconservatives harbored hopes that some sort of cultural counterrevolution was genuinely underway. Many of the younger ones joined the government as advisors and speechwriters, and the intellectual center of gravity of neoconservative life shifted from New York to Washington, DC.

The twelve years between the elections of Ronald Reagan and Bill Clinton marked the neoconservatives' political ascendancy and their intellectual decline. They rose to important positions in the Republican administrations, their writings could be found in most of the major American newspapers, their faces were seen on the talk shows, and their strictly political ideas — on everything from welfare reform to the college curriculum — had enormous influence. But at the same time their intellectual influence waned as they came to be seen as purely political creatures interested more in Washington beltway politics than in scholarship or criticism. They did little to erase that impression. To judge by the kinds of articles published in magazines like *Commentary* and even *Partisan Review* in this period, it was hard to imagine that writers like Lionel Trilling, Clement Greenberg and Delmore Schwartz had ever graced their pages.

The neoconservative dream of a cultural counterrevolution never came to pass. And for those who are wondering what fate awaits the program for Israel insinuated in Hazony's book, it is worth considering why. In many ways the Clinton years should have heartened the neoconservatives. After all, Bill Clinton announced himself to be a "new democrat" with a sound grip of economic principles, a president intent on reforming welfare, who preached individual responsibility, who was financially prudent, and who showed himself willing to use American military might around the world without shame. In matters of economic, domestic and foreign policy, the Clinton presidency represented the end of the sixties. But culturally, Clinton was very much a man of the sixties — and that is why he was popular. He had protested against the Vietnam war, he had smoked marijuana, he enjoyed rock and roll, and on the so-called social issues — race, abortion, sexuality, feminism — he accepted the sixties' dispensation. But how could that be, the neoconservatives wondered? How could one be a defender of bourgeois values by day and a member of the adversary culture by night? That was a contradiction — a contradiction that the whole country seemed to be living in the 1990s.

The neoconservatives never understood Clinton, and that is because they had ceased to understand Clinton's America. Their simple picture of the cultural landscape — in which the forces of cultural decency, led by ordinary working- and middle-class families, did battle against the adversary culture of professors and journalists – proved to be simply wrong. It may have captured something about American life in the 1950s, but by the 1990s it was nothing more than a counter-intellectual fantasy, a version of the noble-savage myth. Over the last five years there has been great confusion among those neoconservatives who do sense that the landscape has changed and wonder how to respond to it. Many have concluded that the cultural war was real, and that the adversary culture has simply won. Some of these then took the next step, declaring that modern philosophical liberalism was the enemy, or maybe American democracy itself. This happened in 1996 when a neoconservative religious magazine called *First Things* published a symposium on "the end of democracy" where contributors openly questioned the legitimacy of the American system today, now that, as the editors put it, law "has declared its independence from morality." Among the contributors was Robert Bork, once a distinguished jurist who nearly became a member of the Supreme Court.

It was during this period of neoconservative confusion and frustration with American life that Hazony's Shalem Center was founded, with American support. I, for one, find this very interesting, from a purely American angle. Someone with Hazony's polemical gifts and inclinations, which I don't possess, could probably write an article about all this. Such an article could pose interesting questions about just how well American neoconservatives understand Israeli life today, and whether they are as committed to "the old Labor-Zionist religion of physical labor [and] the power of gunpowder" as Hazony is. It could raise this question of the social contract and whether the neoconservatives now share Hazony's hostility to it — and whether one can, or should, have a liberal economic order without a liberal political one. Finally, it could ask whether American neoconservatives understand the dangers of flirting with populism in contemporary Israel, which is so divided over questions of religion and ethnicity. My guess, but it is only a guess, is that they do not. My guess is that the author of this article would discover that although the neoconservatives have always cared deeply about Israel, they remain astonishingly ignorant about it and that Hazony, paradoxically, has only reinforced their ignorance. But in the end, that may not matter, for the neoconservatives' primary interest in Hazony's enterprise is an American interest: it permits them to re-fight on foreign soil a counter-intellectual battle they feel they lost in America. Next year in Jerusalem.

I am not entirely satisfied with this conclusion, though. It smacks too much of the cabal-hunting that Hazony has himself engaged in throughout his book. But I do offer it as a hypothesis, one meant to help the Israeli readers understand why this book strikes them as so peculiar, so un-Israeli. It is not simply that Hazony has taken on some taboo subjects that left-wing Israeli intellectuals would rather not discuss, though he has done that, which is all to the good. What is foreign about this book is its aggressive counter-intellectualism, which is very American and which I have never encountered in Israeli intellectual life, or anywhere else for that matter. To judge by the experience of the neoconservative counter-intellectuals in the United States, it could be that Hazony's efforts will have a political effect in Israel. Books like his can have a short-term impact, either in changing particular public policies (like the content of school textbooks) or in giving coherence to the program of a political party. But as an *intellectual* exercise, counter-intellectual books like this one are always a dead end; they convince no one who takes ideas seriously. Hazony is not wrong to think that ideas matter and help to shape political life, in Israel as in America. But he is wrong to think that you can shape ideas in the long run by setting yourself against some imaginary conspiracy of the intellectual class and ignoring the rules of intellectual engagement. American neoconservatives have yet to learn that lesson. The bulky freighter of American culture life continues on its post-sixties course, and those on board are deaf to the apocalyptic shouts of the neoconservatives in their lifeboats. The ship sails on. And so, I imagine, will the Israeli one.

NOTES

1 Yoram Hazony, *The Jewish State: The Struggle for Israel's Soul* (New York, 2000).
2 Ibid., pp. xxvii, xxix, 4.
3 Ibid., p. 338.
4 Ibid., pp. xxx, 331.

Zionism, Colonialism and Postcolonialism

Derek J. Penslar

The relationship between Zionism and colonialism, long a highly controversial subject among scholars throughout the world, has in recent years become a primary source of friction between champions and opponents of revisionism within Israeli historiography and sociology. Until the 1980s, most scholars of Israel Studies teaching in Israeli universities denied or qualified linkages between Zionism and the high imperialism of the *fin de siècle*. This approach is still taken by a number of younger scholars in Israel, but in the past 15 years there has risen a cohort of Israeli academics who, following the lead of Arab and Western scholarship on the modern Middle East, have made linkages between Zionism and colonialism central to their scholarly endeavors.

Regardless of their political stance, historians of Israel have sought to reconstruct the sensibilities and mental universe of their subjects, just as sociologists of Israel have focused on broad sociocultural and economic structures. Traditional Zionist historiography emphasized that the founders of the State of Israel did not think of their enterprise as colonial in nature and, in fact, abhorred contemporary European colonialism for its parasitical profiting from the expropriation of native land and the exploitation of native labor. Classic Israeli sociology, in turn, has contended that the Zionist movement and *Yishuv* did not conform to any conventional model of a colonizing state and that the structural barriers between Jewish and Arab society before 1948 were so great as to render impossible any consideration of the Jewish–Arab relationship as one between colonizers and colonized.

Some of the more recent historical literature, on the other hand, claims that Zionist thinking, like that of *fin-de-siècle* Europeans as a whole, operated on multiple levels and that feelings of benevolence, humanitarianism and sympathy could easily blend with condescending, Orientalist and even racist views of the Palestinian Arabs. Israel's current crop of critical sociologists, claiming that Jews and Arabs in pre-1948 Palestine constituted a common socioeconomic and political matrix, argue that Zionism conformed closely with typical European settlement colonialism, in which, as Ronen Shamir has put it, "employers and employees belong to the same ethnic group ... and in which that ethnic group has effective control over the land in ways that enable it to extract and utilize its resources."[1]

One serious problem with the discussion on the relationship between Zionism and colonialism is the attempt to establish complete congruence or total separation between the two phenomena. Another, related problem is the failure to include additional categories of analysis such as anticolonialism (Zionism as an act of resistance by a colonized people) and postcolonialism (the Zionist project as akin to state-building projects throughout twentieth-century Asia and Africa). This article will contend that Zionism was historically and conceptually situated between colonial, anticolonial and postcolonial discourse and practice. I will do so by drawing upon some essential texts in postcolonial studies, especially the work of Partha Chatterjee.[2] Dialectically, my use of these texts to deconstruct current conceptions of Zionism's relationship with colonialism will deconstruct the texts themselves, for, I believe, scholars such as Chatterjee tend to essentialize anticolonial movements and do not sufficiently acknowledge their grounding in classic European nationalism. In other words, by claiming Zionism to be a form of postcolonialism, that is, placing Zionism in Asia, I will be re-placing Zionism in Europe, a continent distinguished by not only the great overseas empires of the West but also a sizable body of colonized, stateless peoples, including Jews.

***

Modern European colonialism frequently involved the expropriation of native lands and the exploitation of native labor for the economic benefit of the metropole. The two phenomena were, at times, causally linked, in that expropriation could stimulate the formation of a rural proletariat, which then provided cheap labor on plantations and in workshops and factories. On the other hand, the two could develop separately; settlement colonialism displaced the native from his land so that it might be worked by members of the colonizers' nationality. Settlement colonialism was usually sanctioned by a sovereign state, often via the licensing of one or more private companies to bear the risks of the colonizing venture.

Before 1948, the *Yishuv* and its Zionist sponsors abroad could not be considered a colonizing state, in that it exercised highly limited authority over small portions of Palestine. From 1918 to 1948, the role of the colonizing state was played by Britain. As has long been argued by economic historians of the *Yishuv*, and has recently been popularized by Tom Segev in his book *One Palestine: Complete*, the Mandatory British administration developed Palestine's physical infrastructure, sanctioned mass Jewish immigration and fostered the development of Jewish autonomous political and even military institutions. Moreover, the nation-building practices within the *Yishuv* itself conformed, in many ways, to both the exploitation and displacement models of colonial practice: the former through the heavy reliance upon Arab labor in the Zionist plantation colonies and in certain urban industries, and the latter through the assiduous purchase of Arab-owned land and its nationalization by allowing only Jewish ownership thereof and labor thereupon. There are a number of documented cases of such land purchases causing the displacement of Palestinian peasants, but the overall dimensions of the phenomenon are difficult to determine, as is the overall importance of displacement as opposed to other factors in the movement of Palestinian laborers from the countryside to the cities during the Mandate period.

More important than the consequences of Zionist settlement, however, were the means employed. The World Zionist Organization tried to assume the role of a colonizing state. It overtly emulated European practices by establishing a colonial bank, funding agricultural research and development and supporting capitalist joint-stock companies that were hoped to yield, eventually, a profit to their shareholders. That is, the instrumental rationality, bureaucratic procedure, and expectation of sustained profit that characterize modern colonialism (and distinguish it from mere conquest) were all present in the early Zionist project. The Zionist Organization's (ZO's) attempts to take on the mantle of the colonizing state failed, primarily due to a lack of means. Moreover, although the officers of the ZO had few qualms about linking their enterprise with European colonialism, they were not wont to conceive of the Arab as an enemy to be expelled or a body to be enslaved for profit. This was the case even when Zionists explicitly invoked European nationality conflicts as models for their own actions. Thus, for example, in 1908 the ZO planned to establish a publicly funded colonization company along the lines of the Prussian Colonization Commission, which sought to strengthen the German presence in Prussian Poland. Zionist bureaucrats blithely cited both the Prussian Commission and Polish countermeasures as models of the mobilization of public direction and expertise, on the one hand, and private capital, on the other, for the public good.[3]

Zionist discourse as well as practice conformed in many ways to the colonialist and Orientalist sensibilities of *fin-de-siècle* European society. Zionism contained a powerful *mission civilisatrice* to awaken the Middle East from its narcotized Levantine torpor, to shatter the fossilized soil of the Holy Land with European tools and technology. Zionists, like Europeans in general, romanticized the Bedouin as the true son of the desert, and some residents of the *Yishuv*, particularly students, laborers and guards, dressed in Arab fashion as an expression of their sense of return to reclaim their ancient Middle Eastern patrimony. This sentimental idealization of the noble savage, however, was overlaid by powerful feelings of moral and material superiority. The Palestinian peasant was more often perceived by Zionists as a rather ignoble savage, uncouth and backward. The most benign Zionist impulses to offer Arabs the fruits of Western technology and to present a model of bourgeois social relations were imbedded in a project to control, direct and regulate all affairs in the Land of Israel. These blended feelings of familial affinity and paternalist superiority were embodied in the Zionist claim that the Palestinian Arabs, or "Arabs of the Land of Israel," as they were called, were the descendants of ancient Hebrews who had been cut off from Jewish civilization and slowly devolved, preserving shards of the ancient Hebrew customs and language.

Zionism certainly contained Orientalist elements, yet it differed from colonial movements in its assertion of familial propinquity, however distant, with the Arabs. Moreover, whereas the topos of the Arab as sexual object figured prominently in Orientalist fantasy (the object was usually female but at times male, as in André Gide's novel *The Immoralist*), the sexualized Arab rarely figured as an object of Zionist desire. Thus we see in Zionism an apparently contradictory search for connection with and isolation from the Arab, a contradiction that can be resolved if we look beyond the obvious similarities between Zionism and colonialism and turn our gaze to the Jews' historic status as a colonized people and Zionism as an anticolonial movement.

***

In a well-known article on colonial practice in *fin-de-siècle* French Indochina and the Dutch East Indies, Ann Stoler writes of the profound anxiety caused to colonial administrators by the phenomenon of miscegenation between European males and native females. The offspring of such unions were said to create an economic problem by producing an underclass of paupers, yet the threat that these children posed to their colonial masters was clearly cultural in nature. A child neglected by his European father but dutifully raised by his native mother was said to have been abandoned, and thus subject to government action, whereas the abandoned children of native fathers were objects of neither concern nor tutelary policy. Children of mixed unions were considered potentially meliorable because of their European blood; in fact, if raised as wards of the state, they could form "the bulwark of a future white settler population, acclimatized to the tropics but loyal to the state."[4] In Indochina and the East Indies, argues Stoler, French and Dutch citizenship were granted to Creoles via an examination of the supplicants' racial fitness, mastery of the colonizer's language and culture and demonstrated commitment to leave behind the world into which they had been born.

Stoler's description of French and Dutch policies and attitudes towards their colonial subjects can be easily mapped on to attitudes and policies towards Jews in eighteenth- and nineteenth century Europe. Emancipation was granted on a quid pro quo basis. Cultural and economic regeneration, that is, mastery of the host society's language, the adoption of reigning cultural mores, and a movement from the traditional practice of peddling to livelihoods in crafts and agriculture, were considered either preconditions for citizenship (as in the German states) or immediate and necessary outcomes of the attainment of citizenship (as in France). For Jews in post-Napoleonic Prussian Poland, as for Creoles in colonial southeast Asia, citizenship was granted on a case-by-case basis, the result of a rigorous yet arbitrary examination procedure. Proposals made in the late nineteenth century by colonial officials to establish agricultural colonies for the regeneration of the Indo-European poor had their parallel in the era of enlightened absolutism, when reformist bureaucrats in Prussia, Austria and Russia championed, and at times established, colonies to train Jews in productive labor.[5]

Much of the recent literature on the colonial encounter probes the complex reaction of the colonized intelligentsia to the blandishments of the West, the inability to achieve full acceptance and the simultaneous desire to preserve and transform indigenous cultures. Throughout Asia and Africa, intellectuals compensated for their economic and military inferiority *vis-à-vis* the West by asserting the moral and spiritual superiority of the colonized nation versus the powerful, but allegedly spiritually bankrupt, European powers. For example, in India, Vivekananda's Ramakrishna mission, founded in 1897, refashioned Hinduism into a bulwark against the West, which allegedly inculcated spiritual discipline into its adherents through yoga and meditation and stimulated national solidarity by preaching the necessity of social action.[6] Here, as well as in such diverse lands as Thailand (Siam), Meiji Japan and late Ottoman Egypt, the locus of collective identity was presented by intellectuals as found in the realms of culture, religion and historical commemoration, which could lead to a purification of contemporary ways of thinking and a return to lost glory.

Moreover, colonized intellectuals in various lands claimed that the colonized peoples' material disadvantage was the result of their cultures' unjustified and tragic rejection of science and technology, which had been essential elements of the pristine sources of the indigenous culture (for example, Islam, Hinduism, Buddhism). For example, Siam's King Rama IV (1851–68) ascribed opposition to scientific inquiry within Buddhism to pollution from Hinduism, whereas in the predominantly Hindu Bengal, early Indian nationalists located the source of their technological decline in Islamic influences.[7]

King Rama's distinction between Buddhism's rich spiritual heritage and the cold truths of Western science, and his well-tempered statement that each is necessary to human well-being, find their Jewish-historical parallel in the *Haskalah*, the Jewish variant of the European Enlightenment. One of the *Haskalah*'s pioneering texts, Naphtali Hirsch Wessely's *Words of Peace and*

Truth (1782–85), distinguishes between the "torah of God" and the "torah of man" and calls for a new appreciation of the latter in Jewish education. Like Thai, Bengali and Egyptian intellectuals in the late nineteenth century, Wessely and his fellow adherents of the late-eighteenth-century German *Haskalah* claimed that their religious culture was inherently open to scientific inquiry but had been tainted by superstition. Moreover, as the Reform movement within Judaism developed in Germany in the first half of the nineteenth century, champions of Reform would attribute these superstitions to baleful Christian influences, just as Asian intellectuals besmirched neighboring or competing religions. And, like colonized intellectuals who used Western methods to study their civilizations' classic texts, nineteenth-century German Jewry pioneered the systematic study of Jewish texts following the norms of Western scholarship. The term given to this enterprise was *Wissenschaft des Judentums*, that is, the study of the Jewish lettered tradition outside the pietist parameters of that tradition. Practitioners of Jewish *Wissenschaft* adumbrated the colonized intelligentsia in their compensation for powerlessness by locating the essence of Jewish civilization, and its justification for continued existence, entirely in the realm of spiritual and literary creativity.

The division between body and spirit, between the physical and the metaphysical, that was central to post-Cartesian Christian civilization had worked its way into Jewish culture already in the seventeenth century, stimulating astronomical, medical and (al)chemical inquiry. The *Haskalah*, Reform Judaism and the *Wissenschaft des Judentums*, however, contained a revolutionary and totalizing agenda not found previously in the realms of Jewish thought. The modernizing movements within Judaism claimed the right to abrogate centuries of interpretive tradition and to base faith and practice entirely on a rationalistic reading of ancient authoritative texts. This transformation of Judaism was paralleled in early-nineteenth-century India by Rammohan Roy, who invented a laicized, rationalized Hinduism that drew solely on the ancient Hindu scriptures, the Upanishads and their philosophic commentaries, the Vedanta.[8]

The founder of German Liberal Judaism, Abraham Geiger, dismissed much of rabbinic Judaism as a lifeless husk encasing Judaism's biblical, monotheistic essence, and Leopold Zunz, the greatest of the early exponents of secular Judaic scholarship, excavated the literary riches of the Jewish past to demonstrate its superiority to contemporary arid talmudism. The Indian parallel to the work of these men, a *Wissenschaft des Hinduismus*, if you will, came into its own in the 1870s, with the founding by Dayananda Saravati of the Arya Samaj. The Arya Samaj saw in the Vedanta a fixed, textual base for a rationalized Hindu religion. The Arya Samaj presented ancient Vedic religion as monotheistic and egalitarian, far superior to its degenerate Hindu successor, which had allegedly been corrupted by polytheism and the introduction of the caste system.[9] Like the proponents of Jewish *Wissenschaft*, Hindu reformers accepted Western scholarly methods, for a rationalized religion depended upon standardized, critical editions of sacred texts.

Among both Jews and Hindus, religious reform and textual scholarship were part of a broad movement for cultural renewal, of which education was an essential part. Like the *maskilim* in Europe, the Arya Samaj founded schools to educate Indian children as an alternative to the schools of the colonizer, in this case, Western missionaries. Cultural renewal also sought to rearrange and stabilize gender relationships. According to Chatterjee, Bengali literature in the late nineteenth century contained a strong criticism of the politically emasculated and feminized babu, or middle-class male. Misogynistic discourse about women as seducers of and lords over men was a projection of the babu's fears of his own loss of traditional culture and emasculation at the hand of the colonial state. The babu, then, had much in common with the *balabat*, the Jewish householder, who was presented in classic Yiddish literature as talkative but impotent, and dominated by bossy females.

Comparing Chatterjee with recent work by the Jewish historians Marion Kaplan and Paula Hyman, we see both Jewish and Indian writers in the late nineteenth century accusing women of leaping to assimilate into the colonizers' culture, thereby neglecting their duties as mothers of the nation and preservers of religious ritual. These accusations were themselves yet another form of projection, for among both Jews and Indians, men comprised the bulk of the vanguard undergoing assimilation. Women, largely confined to the home, maintained religious traditions within the intimate sphere of the family while the observance of public ritual experienced decline.[10]

An essential component of early Indian and Jewish nationalism was a defensive, secular historiography that posited the continuous existence of a united people (what Benedict Anderson calls a bound seriality),[11] whose fall from ancient glory was the result of random chance and human action, not divine will. Traditional Hindu historiography, like the historical consciousness of biblical and rabbinic Judaism, interpreted the course of human events as the result of divine providence, which rewarded and punished the leaders of the faith and people according to their observance of the divine way, be it dharma or *Halakhah*. Although Jewish historical thinking began to secularize in the sixteenth century, in the wake of the expulsion of the Jews from Spain, Hindu scholars were accounting for the Muslim and British conquests of India within this sacred-historical framework as late as the mid-nineteenth century. But in the 1870s Hindu historiography adopted modern Western conceptual norms, with the result being a body of writing in many ways parallel to the great works of Jewish historical writing of the age. Heinrich Graetz's magisterial *Geschichte der Juden*, like Tarnicharan Chattopadhyay's *History of India*, blended staggering erudition with proto-nationalist apologetics. Both authors molded history by compartmentalizing it into distinct periods, separated by particular events that became synecdoches for the nation as a whole. History moved from the periphery to the center of consciousness; the nationalist project was presented as an act of restoration as much as one of revolutionary transformation.[12]

We have seen thus far that the secularizing Jewish intelligentsia in nineteenth-century Europe bore much in common with the Westernized intelligentsia in lands under European colonial rule. It is no surprise, then, that Zionist ideology bore many similarities to that of anticolonial national movements, although there were spectacular differences as well.

Chatterjee has traced the transition in nineteenth century Bengali thought between the rationalist and universalist trends of Hindu reform movements and the rejection of those trends late in the century by an antirational, mystical glorification of the Indian national spirit. The lower-caste mystic Ramakrishna, who became an object of a cult in the 1880s, glorified the "ancient Hindu national ideal" of ecstatic asceticism.[13] Ramakrishna's emphasis on myth rather than rationality, and on myth's power to fuel nationalistic sentiment, had its counterpart in a major stream of Zionist ideology, beginning with Micha Berdyczewski and finding its most scholarly exponent in Gershom Scholem, who rejected the rationalism of the *Wissenschaft des Judentums* and embraced kabbalah as the primary manifestation throughout the ages of Jewish vitalist spirit.

As the late Amos Funkenstein observed, the Zionist project was fueled by two contradictory conceptions of human nature, romantic and materialist. The former defined man as ineffable, spontaneous spirit, and the latter operated within grooves cut by economic laws, "stychic" social processes (to use the terminology of the Marxist-Zionist theoretician Ber Borochov), and a search for "human material" to be shaped by Zionist apparatchiks into a productive laboring nation.[14] The nationalization of the masses had to be rationally planned even when it involved stoking irrational collective feeling. Thus anticolonial movements, and the postcolonial states that succeeded them, featured aspects of hyperrational, utopian planning while pooling reservoirs of tribal solidarity and fury against the colonizer.

Consider the case of women's suffrage, which was the subject of almost two centuries of debate in the West and which came to France and Switzerland only after the Second World War. Yet as Sylvia Walby has noted, postcolonial states have granted women the franchise at the time of the states' establishment. Political citizenship is granted to all adults at the time of state creation as an expression of a populist sentiment and a legitimization of the overthrow of nonrepresentative colonial rule. As Chatterjee writes of India, nationalists asserted that the entire people had been nationalized, that is, vested with a distinct and unifying Indianness. The entire nation, having been feminized by the colonial power, was to be emancipated in one fell swoop.[15] This conceptual framework is of benefit for the study of Zionism, for it helps account for the World Zionist Organization's early granting of voting rights to women (for the second Zionist Congress of 1898, at a time when only New Zealand had national female suffrage) and the passion with which all but ultra-Orthodox members of the *Yishuv* advocated women's suffrage after the First World War.

State building in the postcolonial world demands direction, planning and regulation. Chatterjee's important essay on the role of planning and technical expertise in modern Indian nationalism helps us to pinpoint the point of departure between Zionism and anticolonial movements, and between Israel and postcolonial states.[16] For Chatterjee, economic planning, like the woman's suffrage mentioned above, is a form of state legitimization, through which the state appears to rise above individual interests and promotes a Gramscian "passive revolution" in which modest reforms are accomplished but precapitalist elites are not annihilated. Economic planning is outside of the politics of the state but deeply imbricated with it. For most third-world countries, India included, such planning has focused primarily on industrialization, with agriculture more likely to be left to the private sector.

The comparisons to the situation of the Jews in the twentieth century are striking. For the Jews, there has been, even after the creation of the State of Israel and certainly before it, no unifying state to orchestrate economic development. Yet world Jewry has formed a unit more cohesive than an ethnic group or stateless nationality. Thanks to their economic and philanthropic elite (often one and the same), Jews the world over have been joined up into a quasi-polity, whose members, unlike those of a state, cannot be confidently tallied up and located in a particular space. Rather, this entity resembles, to use another of Anderson's terms, an "unbound seriality," borderless but finite. Nor did twentieth century Jewry have to contend with precapitalist elites cluttering up the developmental landscape. Indeed, the Jews' elites have been among the West's princes of capitalism.

During the first half of the twentieth century, the Zionist movement created a proto-state, in which planning was indeed a form of legitimization, of imagining the nation by asserting the authority to set the course of the nation-building enterprise. Like postcolonial states, the Zionist movement and early State of Israel venerated technical expertise; the engineer, along with the farmer and warrior, was part of the pantheon of Zionist heroes. In Zionism, however, the position of the colonial state in third-world developmental nationalism was replaced by an opponent as amorphous and unbounded as the Jews themselves: the diaspora, which had allegedly distorted the healthy political, economic and spiritual structures of ancient Israel and had rendered the Jews dysfunctional.

Because Jews have constituted an unbounded nation, Zionists were not the only agents of Jewish social engineering in our century. During the formative decades of the *Yishuv*, a number of international Jewish philanthropic organizations, often better funded than the Zionists, attempted mass colonization of Jews in lands as far flung as Argentina and Ukraine. Zionism's developmental ethos and its program of massive Jewish social and economic change appealed to Jewish philanthropies of virtually every stripe. Thus in 1929 non-Zionists in the United States were mobilized to serve Zionist political goals through the expanded Jewish Agency for Palestine, while the *Yishuv*'s material needs were attended to during the interwar period by organizations such as the Palestine Economic Corporation, which received much of its funding from the New York-based Joint Distribution Committee. Both Zionists and the array of non-Zionist Jewish philanthropies shared an eccentric developmental agenda that focused, unlike the case in postcolonial states, on agricultural rather than industrial planning. The reason for this reversal was ostensibly because the Jews' particular concentration in urban occupations, particularly commerce, and the economic needs of the sites of Jewish social engineering (for the JCA [Jewish Colonization Association], the Argentinean pampas; for the Joint, the Ukrainian steppe; for the Zionists, Palestine) demanded the creation of a class of Jewish agriculturalists.[17]

Much of the motivation behind the agrarian orientation of the agents of Jewish social engineering, however, was ideological — apologetic, romantic or socialist. After all, contemporary Israel has become exactly what Revisionist Zionists, whose economic views differed sharply from not only Labor Zionism but also most Jewish philanthropies, called for: an industrialized city-state that imports raw goods and cheap labor and exports high technology products. Thus the motives behind the Zionist project had little in common with those of Western settlement colonialism but also did not fit well with the developmental world view of postcolonial state building.

Our discussion demonstrates that at a certain point, comparisons between Zionism, on the one hand, and colonialism or postcolonialism, on the other, are no longer valuable except as tools for highlighting the eccentric, distinctive qualities of the Zionist project on the world stage. Attempts to force the Zionist project into Chatterjee's theoretical framework of an anticolonial nationalism and postcolonial state fall short not only because of Zionism's unique features, but also because Chatterjee fails to distinguish satisfactorily anticolonial nationalism and postcolonial policy from their European predecessors, which are, in fact, Zionism's true parents.

Chatterjee's desire to essentialize the colonized nation leads him to juxtapose Western, liberal politics, allegedly based on the mechanistic principals of majority rule and legitimized by atomized, individual voters, and what he claims is the consensus-based politics of postcolonial states.[18] In fact, a politics of consensus characterized many modern European states, including Imperial Germany, in which the chancellor and cabinet were not responsible to parliament, and the Italian kingdom, which was managed through a constant process of give and take between members of a minuscule political and economic elite. The failure of the international Zionist movement or the *Yishuv*'s representative bodies during the interwar period to function as paragons of representative democracy, therefore, does not in any way remove the Zionist project from mainstream *fin-de-siècle* European statecraft, let alone the rough-and-tumble world of politics among socialists and national minorities in Eastern Europe.

Chatterjee attempts to refute Anderson's claim that the modern nation-state is a Western conceptual category that predetermined the form and content of anticolonial collective identities. Chatterjee posits a distinction between Western and postcolonial states, claiming that the former, having long performed their national identities through the free exercise of power, have been sufficiently secure in their identities as to leave the realms of education, religion and familial affairs to the private realm. Postcolonial states, on the other hand, have been forced to make such matters central to state policy, for these had formed the core of the colonized people's identity during the period of struggle with the West.[19] This distinction, of course, has not historically existed; the modern state has been an increasingly invasive entity from the days of absolutism through the era of social-welfare states in the mid-twentieth century. Moreover, virtually all forms of European nationalism have stressed the cultural uniqueness of the people and the obligation of the state, or, in the case of stateless peoples, the intelligentsia, to preserve and promote the national culture.

Zionism's *mission civilisatrice* was directed primarily at Jews, not the indigenous Arabs of Palestine. It was not primarily a manifestation of a colonial will to power, nor was it merely a response to centuries of Gentile criticisms of Jewish social and economic behavior. As a European nationalist movement, Zionism could not help but have a powerful pedagogic and developmental dynamic. In the late eighteenth century, German states expected Jews to undergo, as the bureaucrat Christian Friedrich Wilhelm von Dohm put it, "civil improvement," but the same expectations were held for other social groups considered to be unproductive. Hence the appearance in Germany in the 1780s of books with titles such as "On the Civil Improvement of Women" and "On the Civil Improvement of Monks." Similarly, the demand upon the Jews in revolutionary France to undergo "regeneration" had at first been applied to the people of France as a whole, as part of the revolutionary project to forge a homogenous French nation, language and culture.[20] A century later, French Jewry's ongoing efforts to fully acculturate were paralleled by the Third Republic's gradual transformation of, to cite Eugen

Weber's memorable phrase, "peasants into Frenchmen."[21] The Zionist aim of transforming "Jews into Israelis" was unique not so much in the project of nationalization as in its overwhelming difficulty, in that the nationalization of the Jews demanded the rapid and laborious creation of its own preconditions, for example, the presence of a population *in situ*, a rudimentary national economy and a body of indigenous folk culture.

Chatterjee depicts the historian as the craftsman of the modern Indian nation, but of course the same can be said of any land in nineteenth century Europe. Augustin Thierry and François Guizot in France, Johann Gustav Droysen and Heinrich von Treitschke in Germany, Pasquale Villari and Gioacchino Volpe in Italy, all claimed to engage in a scholarly enterprise, based on a careful accumulation of evidence and free of prejudgments, yet still compelled, in Villari's words, by not "merely a scientific need, but a moral duty" to demonstrate the historical roots of national unification.[22] (How rare was Benedetto Croce's tart statement of 1916 that "the history of Italy is not ancient or centuries old but *recent*, not outstanding but *modest*, not radiant but *labored*.")[23] Zionist ideology was well served by the Jews' unusually high level of textual production and by the long history of Jewish communal autonomy, which provided Zionist historians such as Ben-Zion Dinur ample evidence, reproduced in his multi-volume anthology *Yisrael ba-golah* (Israel in exile) that the Jewish collectivity had, throughout the historic depth and geographic breadth of the diaspora, comprised a coherent national body, which, through Zionism, was merely fulfilling its longstanding and inevitable destiny. Although Villari's object of study was a predominantly peasant culture, he, too, combed through the past to locate manifestations of the united *Volksgeist*, although in his case the evidence came largely from the realm of folk customs and lore.

The origins of modern European nationalism are steeped in controversy, as classic views emphasizing the centrality of nationalist ideology, created and disseminated by narrow intellectual elites, have been steadily replaced by a focus on socioeconomic transformation, uneven economic development and the reshaping of preexisting collective identities as the prime sources of popular nationalist sentiment. Nationalism may well have had eighteenth century manifestations outside of Europe, as Anderson has argued of the socially frustrated and independent-minded "Creole pioneers" of Latin America. Even within Europe nationalist sensibility could emerge from what was essentially a political conflict between metropole and Creoles, as in Ireland at the time of the Act of Union, when Anglo-Irish landowners claimed to be true Irishmen, the natural-born stewards of the indigenous thralls. But it was precisely this sort of political conflict that stimulated the European intelligentsia to formulate nationalist ideology as early as the sixteenth century, and to frame the cult of national essence within issues of cultural production. Thus in Elizabethan England the unparalleled beauty of the English language and the unassailable virtue of English liberty were totally intertwined.[24] French nationalism, in turn, equated collective identity, morality and culture and featured a defensive ethos in which England was perceived as the dominant enemy. German nationalism emerged as a response to French cultural and political hegemony during the Napoleonic era, and so the chemical equation for a defensive nationalist ideology spread eastward and southward throughout the European continent.

Nationalist ideologues associate primacy with legitimacy and nervously equate a reactive nationalism with a lack of authenticity. Similarly, Chatterjee's defensive posture *vis-à-vis* Western nationalism is not warranted. The fact that nationalism was a European cultural invention does not delegitimize or subordinate extra-European nationalist movements any more than modern mathematics in the West has been tainted by its dependence on the medieval Islamic invention of algebra. As in math and science, so too in the realms of philosophy and sensibility certain concepts take on universal value and appeal, enter global circulation and become permanent fixtures in human consciousness. Nationalism is the algebra of modernity: it isolates and brings to light the factors of ethnic solidarity and then initiates *al-jabr*, a reunion of broken parts.

In this essay, I have set Zionism against colonial, anticolonial and postcolonial equations, only to argue that although Zionism shares certain variables with all three phenomena, Zionism is not equivalent with the first and can, like the latter two, be simplified and rendered largely congruent with European nationalism. Zionism was a product of the age of imperialism; its adherents shared a number of common sensibilities with European advocates of colonial expansion in the Middle East. Yet the movement was not, in and of itself, a form of colonial practice. Due to myriad historical and ideological factors, Zionism sought to realize itself in the Middle East, in an area chosen not for its strategic value, natural resources or productive capabilities, but solely because of the Jews' historic, religious and cultural ties to the area known to them as the Land of Israel. Because Zionism's *mission civilisatrice* was directed almost entirely inward, to the Jews themselves, Zionism lacked the evangelical qualities of European colonialism in North America, Asia and Africa, where conversion of the heathen to Christianity served as a justification, consequence and at times a partial cause of colonial expansion.

Anticolonialism's emphasis on cultural renewal, akin to cultural nationalism in nineteenth century Poland, Bohemia, Ireland and many other European lands, had its Jewish equivalent in the *Haskalah* and *Wissenschaft des Judentums*. These movements, which often denied Jewish national distinctiveness, were not Zionist despite themselves, playing the role of unwitting soldiers in a teleological march to full-blown nationalism. The

Haskalah and Wissenschaft des Judentums were necessary but hardly sufficient preconditions for Zionism. Without challenges to emancipation in the West and brutal, state-sanctioned anti-Semitism in the East, Zionism would have been stillborn, just as modern Thai nationalism would not have developed from its mid-nineteenth century Bhuddist reformist roots had France not seized lands traditionally under Siamese jurisdiction in the Mekong river valley.

As a result of the 1948 war, Israel became an independent state, which, like a great many postcolonial states, oppressed an indigenous national minority thought to present a political and cultural threat to the fragile polity. One can certainly be critical of the new Israeli state's policies of expropriating Arab land and subjecting the Galilee's Arabs to a harsh military rule, but such policies were not necessarily a form of Western colonialism. Only after the 1967 war did Israel's relationship with the Arab minority change to a genuine form of colonialism: the demographic balance between occupier and occupied tilted increasingly towards the latter, Israel gained substantial economic profit from the occupation, and its military and security forces brutally combated Palestinian nationalism in a fashion similar to French rule in preindependence Algeria. True, Israelis justified the conquest of eastern Jerusalem and the West Bank via arguments, often sincere, about the religious and historical right of Jews to sovereignty over their alleged ancient biblical patrimony. Moreover, the seizure of the Sinai Peninsula, Gaza Strip and the Golan Heights was attributed to bona fide security concerns. The act of conquest was arguably not motivated by a desire to subjugate a people and expropriate its land, but the speed with which the Palestinian labor force and market became tools for Israeli economic exploitation, the harshness of the Israeli military occupation and the sheer numbers of Arabs brought under Israeli control quickly created a colonial regime in the occupied territories.

Classic Zionism and its ideological underpinnings grew out of, yet departed significantly from, European high imperialism and the Orientalist sensibilities that justified it. After 1967, however, Israel underwent a rapid evolution into a colonial state. Scholars would be well served, therefore, to consider the importance of ruptures as well as continuities within the fabric of Israeli history when evaluating the relationship between Zionism and colonialism.

NOTES

1 Ronen Shamir, *The Colonies of Law: Colonialism, Zionism, and Law in Early Mandate Palestine* (Cambridge, 2000), p. 17.
2 Partha Chatterjee, *The Nation and Its Fragments: Colonial and Postcolonial Histories* (Princeton, 1993).
3 Derek Penslar, *Zionism and Technocracy: The Engineering of Jewish Settlement in Palestine, 1870–1918* (Bloomington and Indianapolis, 1991), pp. 94–6.
4 Ann Stoler, "Sexual Affronts and Racial Frontiers: European Identities and the Cultural Politics of Exclusion in Colonial Southeast Asia," reproduced in Geoff Eley and Ronald

Grigor Suny (eds.), *Becoming National* (New York and Oxford, 1996), p. 295.
5 I discuss this subject in detail in my book *Shylock's Children: Economics and Jewish Identity in Modern Europe* (Berkeley and Los Angeles, 2001), Ch. 1.
6 Peter van der Veer, "The Moral State: Religion, Nation, and Empire in Victorian Britain and British India," in Peter van der Veer and Hartmut Lehmann (eds.), *Nation and Religion: Perspectives on Europe and Asia* (Princeton, 1999), pp. 32–4.
7 Compare Thongchai Winichakul, *Siam Mapped: A History of the Geo-Body of a Nation* (Honolulu, 1994), pp. 39–40, with Chatterjee's essay, "Histories and Nations," in *The Nation and Its Fragments*, pp. 95–115.
8 Van der Veer, "The Moral State," pp. 30–1.
9 Ibid.
10 Compare Chatterjee's, "The Nation and Its Women," in *The Nation and Its Fragments*, pp. 116–34, with Paula Hyman, *Gender and Assimilation in Modern Jewish History* (Seattle and London, 1995), and Marion Kaplan, *The Making of the Jewish Middle Class: Women, Family, and Identity in Imperial Germany* (New York and Oxford, 1991).
11 Benedict Anderson, *The Spectre of Comparisons: Nationalism, Southeast Asia, and the World* (London, 1998), pp. 30–45.
12 See Chatterjee's essays, "The Nation and Its Pasts" and "Histories and Nations" in *The Nation and Its Fragments*.
13 Discussed in Chatterjee's essay "The Nationalist Elite," in ibid., pp. 45–51.
14 Amos Funkenstein, "Zionism, Science, and History," in idem, *Perceptions of Jewish History* (Berkeley and Los Angeles, 1993), pp. 347–50.
15 Compare Sylvia Walby, "Woman and Nation," reproduced in Gopal Balakrishnan and Benedict Anderson (eds.), *Mapping the Nation* (London, 1996), pp. 235–54, with Chatterjee's essay, "The Nation and Its Women."
16 "The National State," in Partha Chatterjee, *The Nation and Its Fragments*, pp. 200–19.
17 These themes are further developed in my book *Shylock's Children*, Ch. 6.
18 Chatterjee, "Whose Imagined Community?" in *The Nation and Its Fragments*, pp. 3–13.
19 Ibid.
20 Penslar, *Shylock's Children*, pp. 29–32.
21 Eugen Weber, *Peasants into Frenchmen: The Modernization of Rural France, 1870–1914* (Stanford, 1976).
22 Cited in Mauro Moretti, "The Search for a 'National' History: Italian Historiographical Trends Following Unification," in Stefan Berger, Mark Donovan and Kevin Passmore (eds.), *Writing National Histories* (London and New York, 1999), p. 114.
23 Ibid, p. 118.
24 Despite its many problems, Liah Greenfeld's *Nationalism: Five Roads to Modernity* (Cambridge, MA, 1992) argues this point convincingly.

Forgetting Europe: Perspectives on the Debate about Zionism and Colonialism

Avi Bareli

The debate about the earliest attempts to form an alternative post-Zionist approach to the study of Zionism and the State of Israel has in part revolved around the issue of Zionism and colonialism. It was one of the prominent manifestations of the fact that this contemporary debate was also a somewhat recidivistic return to the stormy arguments about Zionism and its program that raged among the Jews of Eastern Europe at the start of the twentieth century.[1]

Starting in the 1980s, Gershon Shafir, Ilan Pappé, Baruch Kimmerling, Ronen Shamir and other scholars suggested that the history of Zionism and the State of Israel should be understood according to concepts typical of the Jewish Communists in Eastern Europe and the diasporas of East European Jewry some decades earlier.[2] They proposed that Jewish immigration to and settlement in the Land of Israel (*Eretz Yisrael*) should be seen as a European colonialist invasion, which began in the 1880s under the auspices of the declining Ottoman Empire and continued as an alliance of interests with the British Empire. According to these scholars, who constitute what can be called the Colonialist School in the study of Zionism and Israel,[3] the "colonialist reality" should be preferred to the Zionist narrative. Accordingly, they highlighted what they saw as the colonialist reality of exploitation or dispossession that underlay the construction of the new society and economy in Palestine/*Eretz Yisrael* and the conflict between the Jewish settlers and the Palestinian Arabs.[4]

The Colonialist School offered this alternative interpretation to replace the account of the return of the Jewish people to its land; the account of the development by the Jewish people, in its demographic center in Europe, of a modern and revolutionary national movement;[5] and the account of the success of the Zionist wing of that movement in inspiring emigration, investment, and settlement in Palestine, bringing Holocaust refugees there, and creating a bond between the immigrants from Europe and those from Middle Eastern and North African countries in order to create a sovereign, territorial and modern Jewish polity.[6]

Corroborating the thesis about the colonialist nature of Zionism was a central element in the alternative research program advanced by the post-Zionists. In the following I will argue that, from a research perspective, this is not a rewarding thesis, and I will try to uncover the source of its barrenness. I will demonstrate the severe methodological limitations of the Colonialist School in the study of Zionism and Israel and argue that it severs the object of its analysis from its causes and accordingly fails to fulfill the essential task of historical or sociological interpretation. The core of the article is a methodological assessment of the basic interpretive ploys of the Colonialist School, aimed at buttressing my contention that the Colonialist School detaches Zionism and its *Eretz Yisrael* project from their causes and thereby "forgets Europe";[7] that is, the Colonialist School ignores the economic, social and cultural processes that spurred the Jews in Eastern Europe to emigrate to Palestine over decades in the twentieth century, to settle there and invest their capital in the country. A methodological analysis of the Colonialist School exposes its failure to explain the sources of Zionism's intensity and staying power. It fails to explain how Zionism and the state it founded came to be an active and vital historical force at the start of the twenty-first century.

Obliterating the causes of any object of study distorts it to the extent of replacing it with an imaginary one. This it what happens to authors like Shafir and Pappé; their writing has no roots in the essential causal context of their subject and they consequently mislead their readers. It is impossible to understand the Zionist settlement and construction in Palestine in isolation from the productivization of East European Jewry, for example, just as it is impossible to understand the revival of the Hebrew language in Palestine without locating it in the modern cultural activity of European Jews. The Bilu and, later on, Ha-Po'el Ha-Tza'ir and Po'alei Zion were manifestations of a much broader sociological phenomenon involving the young intelligentsia of Eastern Europe; Po'alei Zion in Palestine was part of a worldwide Jewish labor movement that had branches in Europe and America; immigration to Palestine was a small fraction (though its magnitude increased steadily) of a very large Jewish migratory movement that went on for a number of decades. These are random examples of the mischief done by severing the activities of the Jewish immigrants to Palestine from their European roots. I cannot address this scholarly damage in depth, but my argument is not limited to pointing it out. The crux of my thesis is that "forgetting Europe" when trying to explain Zionism and its enterprise in *Eretz Yisrael* involves an overall methodological failure that drives its proponents to a fundamentally irrational position where effects are amputated from their causes.

The fact that in recent years the debate about Zionism and colonialism has focused on taxonomy also steers the discussion onto the methodological track, because in this track we can examine whether the question of the affinity between Zionism and colonialism, or lack thereof, is to be decided chiefly on the basis of some classification or typology of the colonialist phenomenon. This is, at base, a methodological investigation. Here it is conducted via a discussion of the meaning of such a classification within the overall analysis of Zionism. The discussion seeks to corroborate the assertion that there is indeed a methodological rationale for classifying Zionism alongside undoubted colonialist phenomena, but that this classification is merely a first step; that is, it is only one of several classifications that must be made as part of the preparatory stage of the historical analysis. But remaining immersed in taxonomy after that initial stage divests historical analysis of one of its most important goals — coming up with a causal explanation for its object — and reduces it to an inventory of characteristics. From a broad perspective, the Colonialist School remains stuck in the preparatory stage of orientation, in the preliminary stage of collection and sorting, and never takes off to conduct a full analysis of its object, since it is unable to weave a valid causal network for explaining the rise of Zionism and the State of Israel.

There is another reason for focusing on the methodological aspect of the debate. In recent years, the bulk of the Israeli debate about Zionism and colonialism has been conducted by academics.[8] This fact creates a common denominator, at least in principle, among the various participants in the debate: they are supposed to be dedicated to the quality of their research, to its being an inter-subjective activity; in other words, an activity that is possible only through the application of shared norms, which are crystallized in the discussions of research methodology. It is clear that while there can never be a final verdict in historical studies, they take place in a shared methodological context that is not anarchical. Of course the lack of consensus about scholarly interpretation extends to research and analytical methods as well; nevertheless, a discussion of methodology can be of use in debates like this one, for two reasons. First of all, the range of disagreement on the question of methodology is not that broad and there are boundaries that almost all agree must not be crossed; second, there is no overlap between the disagreements about various methodological approaches on the one hand and the debates about interpretations of historical processes on the other.

Another reason that a methodological perspective can benefit the debate about Zionism and colonialism is that the debate is loaded with political and ethical meanings. Few participants in the discussion can remain indifferent to these meanings — myself included. For me, Zionism is a vital historical and political element of the people to which I belong. But the need to understand historical phenomena is shared by all participants in the debate, whatever their political leanings. There is both a scholarly interest and a public interest in a preliminary historical clarification that is isolated, as far as possible, from its political and ethical implications. Attention to methodology is central to this preliminary clarification, because the methodology's criteria relate to the quality of the historical analysis and the solidity of its conclusions and are not decided on the basis of any particular position on specific questions of historical interpretation.

***

Today there is a fashionable, though regrettable, tendency to analyze colonialism through an analysis of discourse and text obsessed with the structure of consciousness and forms of expression. Colonialism was an aggregate of material phenomena — geographical, economic, political and social — and its focus was chiefly economic. Of course it had manifestations on the level of consciousness. We can certainly speak about colonialist ideologies and assume that their evolution was an essential aspect of colonialism itself. But these mental manifestations were not the constitutive center of that aggregate of phenomena, neither were they what defined it. If these mental manifestations of colonialism are set aside, the entire set of historical phenomena known as colonialism does not vanish with them. In any case, they cannot be the starting point or core of any discussion of the subject. The analysis must start from its unmistakable material manifestations.

This is precisely the problem with what are commonly called "postmodern" approaches, which are in fact a quasi-Hegelian subjectivism or idealism: idealism, because of their exclusive focus on consciousness and discourse; but only quasi-Hegelian, because of their inherent irrationalism. Hegel re-enters by the back door, stripped of the rationalism that is essential to his thought, except for the identification between being and mind, and returns thus transformed in the spiritual descendants of Nietzsche. They make an idealist identification between being and mind, even though Nietzsche's own philosophy was one of the milestones in the rejection of idealism (among the other objects of his criticism); that is, rejection of the view that history is the process of the emergence of mind (rational, according to Hegel; chaotic and idiosyncratic, according to the postmodernists). There is also no little difficulty in the fact that left-wing radicals, at least in their own eyes, concentrate the bulk of their theoretical attention on discourse and consciousness while ignoring society and economics. In any case, for our present purposes I will argue that such an approach is inappropriate, especially when the focus of the discussion is an essentially material phenomenon like colonialism.

These remarks are particularly relevant to the tendency to approach any discussion of the relationship between Zionism and colonialism with the analytical methods of Edward Said and Homi Bhabha, who discuss the colonialist mentality that prevailed in the West.[9] Although there is good reason to study collective mentalities, even of an object as broad as "the West"

— broad almost to the point of uselessness — there is no justification for limiting the discussion of colonialism to a subjective analysis or even beginning it that way. Such an analysis can be merely peripheral and supplementary, precisely because of the material nature of the object under discussion. There is no need to adopt Marxist materialism or Marxian critical thought in order to see that an analysis of mentalities and discourse is not the high road to understanding colonialism.

The demand that culture, politics and consciousness be analyzed in terms of their links to their contemporaneous socioeconomic structures is perhaps Marx's most obvious and enduring philosophical legacy and the one that has been least impacted by historical developments. When practiced by overzealous Marxists, however, Marxian criticism is fated to deteriorate into what is known as "vulgar materialism," a reduction of everything to economic power relations. But postmodern thought has gone to the opposite, absurd extreme, and in the humanities and social sciences has become merely a vulgar idealism that can bear no scholarly fruit. The most public manifestation of this sterile academic trend is to be found in the delusion of "political correctness," namely, that social injustices can be righted by changing the way we speak about them. In any case, vulgar idealism is a particularly damaging approach to the study of an essentially material phenomenon. A treatment of colonialism that deals exclusively with texts and mentalities simply is not appropriate to its object; it is employing the wrong tools for the task.

Said's and Bhabha's analytical methods took root in intellectual discourse not only because they suited the postmodern fashion but also because they suited the advocates of a widespread moralizing approach, whose main objective was to "catch the crook" and condemn him categorically. They go to the historical texts, uncover colonialist mentalities in several written and oral utterances, and proudly wave the smoking gun. Their goal is not an understanding of the historical processes but a puritanical judgment that frustrates such understanding. This does not mean that historical events cannot be subject to moral judgment, but such judgment must come after we have more or less clarified what we think happened. Otherwise it has no foundation. This can partly be seen as a manifestation of impatience, of a desire to jump straight to the bottom line. But the debate about the historical classification of Zionism requires neither moral judgmentalism nor apologetics on behalf of Israeli interests; what is needed is a focused and patient attempt to locate Zionism in its various contexts.

Having established the need to demarcate the debate within largely economic and political issues, we can now consider another methodological question: what is the scholarly purpose of examining the relationship between Zionism and colonialism?

When the starting point is the desire to understand, before judging or propagandizing, one of the first methodological questions is indeed that of classification. We must consider the justification of assigning the aggregate of phenomena known as "Zionism" to the aggregate of phenomena that we call "colonialism" and the scholarly benefit of such a classification. It is certainly needed before we have established precise definitions of "Zionism" and "colonialism." In other words, it is useful in the initial stage of amassing our research materials, when we are trying to orient ourselves and define the list of phenomena to be examined. However, classifying Zionism is only a methodological tool used to clarify its sources en route to a historical explanation. Classification in itself cannot be considered to be such an explanation. Like every historical phenomenon, you have not explained Zionism simply by attaching some label to it, whether it be "colonialism" or "nationalism."

When taxonomic questions are being asked, a certain vagueness in the definitions of the historical objects and their interrelations is normal because beginning with precise definitions is tantamount to begging the question. Since classification is based on conceptual boundaries, if we posit unambiguous boundaries, what is the point of discussing them when the outcome has been predetermined without proof? So vagueness is a necessary part of the first stage of the analysis, when we know, in a general and preliminary fashion, which phenomena fall under the conceptual rubric "Zionism" and which under "colonialism," and want to inquire into the affinities between these two aggregates.

Such an analytical classification is a methodological requirement because it is a preliminary tool for making comparisons, and comparisons can be of some help in illuminating the causes of Zionism, including a precise identification of those that have no parallel in otherwise comparable historical phenomena. The taxonomy tells us which groups of phenomena have plausible grounds for being compared to Zionism. Thus, if we wish to investigate the usefulness of comparing the Zionist settlement, for example, with the European settlement in America or Africa, we obviously need a very broad definition of colonialism, one that embraces almost everything conventionally included in this category. Since the object of the classification is to perform an exhaustive search for whatever may be usefully compared to Zionism, we ought not to exclude from our survey anything that may be *prima facie* relevant before performing a closer examination.

Some scholars have taken the opposite path and tried to define colonialism as narrowly as possible, to hedge in colonialism with so many conditions that it cannot include Zionism.[10] As we have seen, however, this approach is methodologically unsuitable and incompatible with the goal of the initial stage of the analysis because it limits the scope of the comparative study. What is more, it sidesteps clarification by means of largely formal arguments and leaves lingering doubts about the relations between Zionism and colonialism.

The concept of "colonialism" is by nature multifaceted, precisely because its prime function is to bring together phenomena that deserve to be compared. For this reason it is a sort of "bag" into which phenomena are tossed not according to some taxonomic principle but rather by freer associative links. The concept of "colonialism" belongs to the genre of umbrella concepts like democracy, nationalism and religion. Such overarching concepts, whose purpose is to lay the basis for comparative analysis, are frequently the victims of attempts to force them into narrow, a priori, and sometimes even legalistic definitions. This is what happened, for example, in the study of nationalism, at least in the beginning.

To the extent that colonialism is a broad and associative umbrella concept of this sort, it can certainly benefit the study of Zionism, alongside other umbrella concepts — such as nationalism, religion or postcolonialism (which relates to the process of constructing states and nations after colonialism and is also relevant for a comparative analysis of Zionism).[11] The historical phenomenon known as "Zionism" was mainly a movement of people of European birth to a country that was sparsely populated and predominantly agricultural. In a decisive period in its history it was allied to British imperialism. The Jewish newcomers competed for land and labor with the Arab residents and Arab immigrants from neighboring countries. A conflict developed that deteriorated to the point of civil war between the two national groups; at its conclusion, most of the Arabs who lost their homes were not allowed to return. The Jewish immigrants arrived in the country with an ingrained sense of superiority and cultural arrogance and a romantic yearning for the "East" as imagined in Europe. This romantic image was reinforced to some extent during their years in the country (it is no accident that this mental element is the last in the present list). These are some of the basic facts, and no attempt was made to assess their weight within their historical context. But this list is enough to support assigning Zionism to the set of colonialist phenomena, as long as we are aware that this assignment is a first step in a comparative analysis and that its goal is to identify all the phenomena that may plausibly be compared to Zionism.

***

At this point in our discussion, against the background of the general consideration that favors methodological comparison between Zionism and colonialist settlement enterprises, I shall take a short break in the methodological argument in order to make three comments. One has to do with the European character of the Jews, that is, with one of the traits that supports filing Zionism under the rubric of colonialism. The second involves the economic profitability of the Zionist settlement enterprise. The third has to do with the social fissure that divided Palestine/*Eretz Yisrael* into two national sectors.

Although all three of these merit articles of their own, in the present context I can only give them cursory attention. They embody the nucleus of three of the weightiest arguments against the Colonialist School in the study of Zionism and Israel, alongside the methodological argument we are making against it. It is important to mention them because they prevent the methodological discussion from being abstracted from its historical context. Although the methodological discussion could be conducted according to pure research criteria, it should nonetheless be located in the context of research questions of the sort discussed in these three comments.

First of all, from the Jews' own perspective, to the extent that they adhered to their group and cultural distinctiveness and did not assimilate, and to no small extent from the perspective of other Europeans, it is quite bizarre to see the Jews as Europeans who transferred themselves to the Orient, since the Jews' foreignness in Europe involved an Oriental and Semitic element, which was one of the causes for the emergence of anti-Semitism. Some of the old communities of European Jewry had existed there for centuries, yet their members had never managed to shake off their alien status on that continent. The Zionists actually cultivated that alien status and non-European identity: what else could the revival of Hebrew, the most important focus of the Zionists' cultural enterprise, be? Hebrew is hardly a European language like the ones used by European colonists elsewhere in the world.[12] By reviving it, the Jewish immigrants adopted a cultural element native to the region in which they settled. This was a feasible, albeit an immensely difficult, project, not a vain fantasy, because a certain "Semitic" foreignness separated the Jews from their countries of residence in Europe and because Hebrew, which may have withered but had not died, remained one of the "Semitic" cultural traits of the Jews of Europe.

There is a certain sad irony in describing the Zionists and the migration movement that they created as a movement of Europeans to the East, since the Jews were in effect expelled from Europe in a long, painful and complex process that reached its horrible nadir in the mid-twentieth century. Hence there is a problem in the naive description of these Jews, the vast majority of them Ashkenazi Jews, as Europeans. Nevertheless, in a broad and somewhat crude definition, the Ashkenazi Jews may indeed be considered a European group, albeit distinct and unusual in many respects. Consequently, if we are drawing up a list of European migrations there is no doubt that we should include that of Jews to Palestine and especially the movement that began in the 1880s, despite its distinctive characteristics. Unique traits are not valid grounds for denying membership in a common group. Those who rule out comparisons because of certain differences between the entities compared frequently confound the act of comparison with that of identification; yet the entire point of comparison is that there are points of difference as well as similarities between the phenomena compared.

Second, one of the distinctive characteristics of the Jews' migration is evident in the economic context of Zionism. The Jewish settlement in Palestine transferred capital in an opposite direction to that of colonization projects: it invested Jewish capital in Palestine and did not withdraw natural resources and capital from it to benefit an empire or enrich investors (whether investors in the home country or among the colonists themselves); that is, it was not an effort to gain riches for some imperial state or an enterprise conducted by settlers in pursuit of wealth. For a long time — and perhaps still today — it was actually an unprofitable project. It certainly was not a promising arena for individuals or groups who aspired to get rich. It is hard to point to any economic logic that motivated the Jewish migration to and settlement in Palestine, which was a poor country and almost totally devoid of natural resources. This, incidentally, is why the Zionists did not encounter rival European immigrants in Palestine, other than a trickle of European Christians who came for religious reasons, but only competition from Arab migrants from elsewhere in the Middle East; and many of the latter came in the aftermath of the economic development brought about by Jewish capital and Jewish immigrants.[13] The movement of the Jews to Palestine cannot be explained in primarily economic terms. The picture here is indeed very different from what we imagine when we think of colonialism, which, as noted, is an aggregate of mainly material phenomena.[14]

Nevertheless, the unprofitable nature of the Zionist migration to Palestine is not sufficient grounds for denying its affiliation with the aggregate of colonialist phenomena, even though it is one of the possible conclusions that may be derived from a comparative analysis of Zionism and other European emigration projects. In any case, arguments that seek to block such comparative analysis should be rejected.

The third comment involves the social fissure in Palestine/*Eretz Yisrael*, that is, its division into two largely discrete national sectors.[15] This is a crucial question, which I shall consider here only to the extent that it is essential for the methodological argument.

Several leading Israeli academics have contributed to establishing the thesis that, under the British Mandate (1918–48), the society and economy of Palestine/*Eretz Israel* developed as two more or less separate national sectors.

This thesis is compelling and well grounded and no significant refutation has ever been offered.[16] Among those who developed it are the sociologists S. N. Eisenstadt, Dan Horowitz and Moshe Lissak and the economic and social historians Jacob Metzer, Nachum Gross, Yosef Gorny and Anita Shapira. On the basis of this thesis Lissak also argues that there was a latent potential for colonial exploitation in the relations between the Zionist settlers and the Palestinian Arabs at the end of the Ottoman era and the start of the British Mandate. However, it was never realized because the Zionist socialists, the main Zionist group in the country, were determined to prevent their society from developing along the lines of colonial exploitation, and to this end they used the development of Jewish autonomy under British patronage, the gradual separation of the economies of the two national groups, and the circumstances of the national conflict from the 1920s onwards. According to Lissak, all of these factors fostered separation and the creation of a sustainable Jewish working class and prevented the development of a society based on exploitation of the Palestinian Arabs.[17]

Here we can add that the Zionist socialists' repeated failure in the struggle to establish a viable class of agricultural laborers in the Jewish citrus plantation villages (*moshavot*) was one of the factors that pushed them to found independent cooperative settlements on land owned by the Zionist movement, that is, to consolidate the segregation of the Jewish economy, in order to keep their society from developing into one of colonialist exploitation as well as to defend the class interests of the Jewish proletariat.[18]

In his reply to Lissak, Gershon Shafir tried to sever the link between the thesis that the economy and society in Palestine/*Eretz Yisrael* were divided into separate national sectors and the argument that it was this separation that prevented the realization of the colonialist potential in the relations between the Jews and the Palestinian Arabs. Shafir acknowledged that the Zionist settlement enterprise may not have created a colonialism of exploitation, but he argued that it fostered something even worse — a colonialism of dispossession.[19] This argument is at odds with the fact that the Zionist development actually attracted Arab immigrants to Palestine during the Mandate years, because the sectoral division was not absolute and the Zionist development created employment for Arabs as well. In any case, according to the logic of Shafir's argument, the separation during the years of the Mandate laid the groundwork for the next stage — the dispossession of 1948;[20] or, more precisely, the closure of the border to the Palestinian refugees who sought to return to their homes in 1949 at the end of Israel's War of Independence — which was also a life-or-death civil war between the Jews and the Palestinian Arabs.

But this kind of argument turns everything on its head because the Jews, through their elected leadership, relied on the same sectoral-national division to extricate themselves from the conflict with the Palestinian Arabs through a political institutionalization of the sectoral-national division, that is, through a political partition into two states. Twice, in 1937 and in 1947, they agreed in principle to such proposals; in 1946–47 they even made substantial diplomatic efforts on behalf of partition — that is, on behalf of living side by side, not one on top of the other (exploitation), and not one in place of the other (dispossession). The war broke out because the Palestinian Arabs rejected the principle of living side by side, even though it had been endorsed by the United Nations General Assembly, and sought to expel the Jewish immigrants from the country. When the Arabs' attempts to expel them were frustrated, at the end of the war, the Jews were no longer willing to return to the demographic and geographic conditions that had exposed them to mortal peril in late 1947.

***

Here we have no more than touched on all these questions — the European character of the Jews, the non-profitability of the Zionist settlement enterprise, and the evolution of the split into two national sectors. Despite their importance, and that of related questions, these and similar issues do not determine whether there is an affinity between Zionism and colonialism because they do not clarify whether the fundamental causal explanation of Zionism is essentially similar to the causal explanations of colonialist phenomena.

This argument is based on the methodological criterion that, at a more advanced stage of the historical analysis, remaining immersed in questions of classification and comparison diverts the analysis from its goal and even sabotages it. This is because at that stage the appropriate focus of scrutiny is the historical forces or causes that generate the phenomenon, rather than an inventory of characteristics and an assessment of how they correspond to the characteristics of other phenomena. Without the main objective — offering a causal explanation for the historical phenomenon of Zionism — the inventory is merely a sort of "shopping list" in which all observers can find whatever they want and which they can rearrange as they see fit.

This can be seen in the aforementioned dispute between Lissak and Shafir. Against every assertion of the distinctiveness of the Zionist case, another, more diversified definition of colonialism can be offered that will encompass these unique characteristics. The assertion that Zionism is not a colonialist phenomenon, because this or that distinctive trait disqualifies it as such, is doomed to be refuted by an argument that presents that distinctive trait as characterizing a particular type of colonialism. This is the course taken by Shafir, for example, following Fieldhouse and Fredrickson[21] — developing a complex typology of varieties of colonialism and assigning Zionism to one of them or to a combination of several types, by virtue of its so-called "distinctive" characteristics, which Shafir has elevated to the rank of a "variety" of colonialism.[22]

If questions of taxonomy have a purpose at the initial stage of the analysis, at a later stage they are liable to reduce the entire debate to shallow rhetoric. There is very little point to the question of whether Zionism is or is not colonialist when ultimately the question is decided as a function of how we define "colonialism." At this stage of the analysis, the discussion must rise to a higher level and move beyond a preliminary inventory and classification to a much more important question: what weight do these or other colonialist characteristics have, at one time or another, in an overall evaluation of the complex historical phenomenon known as "Zionism"?

Thus, for example, there could be a national facet as well as a colonialist facet to Zionism; Gershon Shafir and Ilan Pappé propose that we make do simply with stating that fact: "in our eyes, Zionism is both a colonial phenomenon and a national phenomenon," wrote Pappé without elaboration.[23] But if our goal is chiefly cognitive, we must continue to explore what Zionism essentially is, what its historical significance is and, above all, what its fundamental causes were. Neither Zionists nor anti-Zionists, neither Israelis nor Palestinians, can evade these questions because their answer is essential for understanding a historical phenomenon that had fateful consequences. For example, for Palestinians who really want to understand what factors account for the defeat of their people in 1948 there is a vital as well as a practical interest in this question. The answer will be determined not by a Jewish perspective as opposed to an Arab perspective. The disputants can overcome, at least to some degree, their national identification if they are really interested in understanding. Those who hope to overthrow the State of Israel and replace it with a non-Jewish or *de facto* Arab state, as well as those who want to defend the Jews' sovereignty in their own nation-state, both have an interest in seeking to understand the core of the historical phenomenon they want to overcome or strengthen.

The scope of our perspective will largely determine the outcome of this discussion: whether it is restricted to *Eretz Yisrael*/Palestine only or extends to Europe and the other Jewish diasporas. Shafir, along with other Israeli scholars of the Colonialist School, most of them sociologists,[24] choose to limit their research perspective almost exclusively to Palestine/*Eretz Yisrael*. For Shafir, Europe is nothing more than the backdrop or a source of ideological and moral inspiration for the Zionist settlement enterprise.[25] But no phenomenon can be understood in isolation from its causes — in our case, the political and economic causes; and the causes of Zionism are to be found far from Palestine (mainly in Europe but also elsewhere).

Shafir does not deny the national character of the Zionist movement, but he gives it only minor weight. For him, the national motivation of the Zionist settlers is "ideology," that is, a false consciousness, and the underlying colonialist "reality" of Zionism should be exposed.[26] Shafir quotes what he describes as an anachronistic statement by the English historian Hugh Seton-Watson that the Jews developed "a national consciousness" in their diasporas. For Shafir, Zionist Jewish nationalism developed only in the course of the settlement enterprise and not before it. Hence it is colonialist by nature, because it was born in settlement activity. The flaw in this approach is, of course, its inability to explain what motivated this migration and settlement enterprise. Evidently Shafir is aware of this flaw and tries to invoke Hitler to fill it: "Territorial nationalism — so different from and alien to the ethnic Jewish way of life — was, as it were, imposed on Jews as a last resort, in response to Nazi persecutions and genocide, and forced migration from Eastern Europe, North Africa, and the Middle East."[27] But if territorial nationalism — meaning Zionism — was "imposed" on the Jews by the crisis of the 1930s and if it was the Nazis who forced them to go to Palestine, what motivated the development of the Jewish *Yishuv* before the Nazi atrocities? Can the earlier historical development, without which the Jewish refugees would have had nowhere to go, be explained as a colonial enterprise in terms of its fundamental causes? Should we base an answer to this question on certain colonialist characteristics or should we rely on causal analysis that explains what motivated Jewish migrants and capital to move from Europe to the Middle East? This is the Achilles' heel of Shafir's analysis, which purports to provide a complete analysis — a Colonialist School of explaining Zionism — because it makes do with an inventory of characteristics and avoids causal explanation.

Both traits — the tendency to condense the entire discussion into an exclusive focus on taxonomy or affinities, based on particular definitions, and the subjectivist assumption that exposing the existence of a colonialist discourse suffices to determine the relationship between Zionism and colonialism — are particularly conspicuous in the work of Ilan Pappé, another member of the Colonialist School. When Pappé describes what he refers to in derogatory terms as "Zionist historiography," he writes that it follows the empirical-positivist approach which judges the nature of an ideological movement only as a function of its intentions. He goes on to explain that Zionist historians, as he defines them, have rejected characterizing Zionism as colonialism on the pretext that the national discourse had no colonialist intentions.[28]

However, the facts are rather different. "Students of Zionism" — to adopt, if only for the purposes of the debate, Pappé's sweeping generalization — describe the Zionist movement as a Jewish national movement that emerged against the background of certain very concrete needs of the Jews in Europe, chiefly in Eastern Europe. To the extent that one can generalize about "their" approach, it ascribes the origins of the Zionist movement and, for our present purpose, its project to settle in Palestine, to severe political distress on the one hand and demographic and economic growth on the other. More precisely, some have attributed the emergence and consolidation of Zionism to the aspiration to reconcile the painful contradiction between the increasing economic and demographic power of East European Jews and their lack of individual and political rights; others have elaborated a different analysis of the material situation of East European Jews and attributed Zionism to their desire to escape their political and economic distress. But both groups have analyzed Zionism in undoubtedly material, economic and political terms and assigned great weight to the push factor — the fact that Europe pushed the Jews out in a vast wave of emigration, of which *aliyah* to *Eretz Yisrael* was only one part. Some invoked cultural and religious motives to explain the sources of Zionism, but even scholars with such tendencies gave great weight to a political and economic analysis of Zionism.

Pappé simply attributes to those "Zionist historians," as he calls them, his own subjectivist proclivity. The historians he criticizes certainly did not restrict themselves merely to defining Zionism as a national movement, that is, they did not make do with taxonomy, but provided a causal explanation for the development of this national movement. By contrast, Pappé suggests that we examine the issue of Zionism and colonialism by analyzing the symbols of Zionism, that is, by analyzing its consciousness. He compares the symbolic language of the Zionist immigrants with the symbolic language of "Christian colonizers" in Ottoman Palestine, on the one hand, and with the symbolic language of the Basel Evangelical Missionary Society (the "Basel Mission") in western Africa, on the other. Pappé makes no attempt to compare the concrete societies in which these immigrant groups were born — German Protestant society and East European Jewry — because such a comparison would have exposed the superficiality of his analysis of symbols.[29] Thus Pappé merely takes a sample of Zionist discourse and its symbols, finds some colonialist characteristics and proudly displays his conclusions. This approach, as we have seen, is inappropriate for the consideration of an essentially material phenomenon like colonialism. Now we can see that it is also deficient when we try to understand the sources of Zionism, because it is based on "forgetting Europe," on forgetting the European causes of Zionism. We could say that Pappé and Shafir offer us two ways of forgetting Europe, that is, two ways of ignoring the concrete causes of Zionism — political, economic and cultural — as they developed among East European Jews: one focuses on the symbolic discourse of Zionism and finds that it has colonialist traits; the other focuses on the Israeli–Palestinian conflict and finds that it has such traits. Neither attempts to go beyond the bare catalogue of characteristics to assess their weight or to offer even the start of a comprehensive causal explanation.

The Colonialist School's approach thus clearly fails as an explanation and is fundamentally irrational. It ostensibly manages to isolate the object from its causes, but an object is in fact constituted by its causes and cannot be isolated from them.[30] The causes of Zionism are to be found in Europe, in the lives of millions of Jews, most of them in Eastern Europe, even long before the Holocaust.

***

Thus the Colonialist School is marked by a "Palestinocentric" shortcoming. Among the members of this school this shortcoming is particularly severe because it undermines their main arguments. To be fair, however, we should note that many Israeli scholars, proponents of diverse and even contradictory approaches, suffer from this flaw to some degree or other.

An interesting example is Idith Zertal's *From Catastrophe to Power*. One of her key arguments is the allegation that the Zionist movement exploited Holocaust survivors for its own ends, treating them with a mixture of indifference, condescension and arrogance.[31] But despite this thesis, and despite the fact that the object of her research is the clandestine immigration of Holocaust survivors to Palestine, Zertal nonetheless concentrated almost all of her research efforts on the actions of the Zionist institutions and their emissaries from Palestine and made almost no attempt to study the survivors themselves, their actions or their attitudes. She complains about the lack of consideration for the survivors' wishes and feelings but fails to investigate them herself, although the subject of her research and her key theses would require her to do so. She ostensibly deals with the "European causes" of Zionism, at the low point in the Jews' relations with Europe, but elevates (or rather demotes) the clandestine-immigrant survivors to the rank of victims of Zionism, thus in effect silencing them. In her study, the only people with a voice are from Palestine, the "carriers" and not the "carried," in her terms. It is no accident that Zertal totally omits any analysis of the attitudes of the clandestine immigrants, because such an analysis would have refuted her claim that they were merely manipulated and would have revealed the active Zionist aspirations harbored by many of them and their leaders.

Zertal does not deal with the question of colonialism; the Palestinocentrism that characterizes her study has been cited here to demonstrate that the Palestinocentric shortcoming of the Colonialist School in the study of Zionism is associated with a broader academic and intellectual trend that has diverse sources, which I can outline only briefly here. The disposition to "forget Europe" is rooted in part in the nature of an immigrant society. Israelis suffer from a lack of continuous group-identity, from a cultural rupture and a gulf between the places where they grew up and those which molded their parents or grandparents. They are disturbed by the awareness that they are the offspring of those who are strange and alien to them. This is an inevitable outcome of migration as well as of the Zionist revolution, that is, of modernization, of adaptation to sovereignty, of secularization and of radical changes in lifestyle. One response to this distress is to deny those origins or, more moderately, to ignore them and relegate them to the margins. This is typical of many Israelis (and Israeli society may have this in common with other immigrant societies). Here we have seen some of the theoretical manifestations of this tendency to "forget Europe," but it also has other symptoms that are not theoretical, because its source is structural or existential, that is, it grows out of the roots of Israeli society and the basic conditions that created it.

The "Hebrew ideology" or "Canaanism" was one of the manifestations of this tendency in the 1950s, the years of the great wave of immigration to the State of Israel. Its sources can be traced, however, back to the late 1930s and especially the first half of the 1940s, precisely when the Jews of Europe were being exterminated. The "new Hebrews" or Canaanites aspired to consolidate a local nationalism for the Jews — or former Jews, in their view — who had settled in *Eretz Yisrael*. The Canaanite program was to cut the link with the Jews outside *Eretz Yisrael*, to sweep the local Arabs into the Hebrew culture, to establish a large Hebrew nation-state in the Middle East, and to crystallize a national consciousness tracing its lineage to the ancient Hebrew culture and the states in what they called "Eretz Kedem" (the "Land of Old": *Eretz Yisrael*, Transjordan, Lebanon, Syria and northwestern Iraq). This cultural and political trend eventually split into those with more aggressive tendencies towards the Arabs and those who were more conciliatory towards them. For our present purposes, however, what is important is what both groups shared: the idea of a complete divorce from the Jews outside *Eretz Yisrael* and from Jewish culture.[32]

The Israelis' desire to overcome this cultural fissure and not see themselves as the descendants of those for whom they feel no affinity, but who are nevertheless intimately connected with them, may explain in part the particular attraction that the Canaanites had for the members of the first generation born and brought up in *Eretz Yisrael*. The tension between the sense of alienation from their origins and their intimate bond to them created a certain cognitive dissonance, which was "resolved" by means of various forms and various degrees of denying their origins and even attempts to forge a national consciousness that would be autochthonous-Hebrew and non-Jewish. The discarding of particular Jewish identities (Ashkenazi, Sephardi, and so on) was a relatively moderate form of resolving this dissonance and therefore remained within the pale of Zionist nationalism and for a certain period even characterized it to some extent. By contrast, the various hues of

Canaanism were characterized by a total rejection of Jewish identity as an ethnic, rather than a national, identity to be cast aside. The proponents of this idea also tended to deny the existence of a modern Jewish nation that had developed in Eastern Europe and whose creations included the Zionist movement. They saw the Zionist idea and its historical sources as an incidental and not particularly important backdrop for the migration to *Eretz Yisrael*. For them, the main thing was the crystallization of a territorial nationalism around the Hebrew language.

This position is not far from the constricting perspective adopted by the members of the Colonialist School. Forgetting Europe, or suppressing the memory of it, is common to the Canaanites and the Colonialist School. It is certainly possible that they have similar motivations for doing so. In any case, it is clear that these are two manifestations of a Palestinocentric bent that is very common among Israelis. But the Canaanite context is striking from another angle as well. While, as I have said, Shafir's and Pappé's description of Zionism is basically inadequate because it says nothing about its causes, it is much more appropriate for describing the right-wing or anti-Arab Canaanism of Uriel Shelah (the poet Yonatan Ratosh) and Adaya Gur Horon (a researcher in the Ancient East), characterized by an extremely aggressive attitude towards the Arabs, an aspiration to dominate them brutally, to subjugate them and to Hebraicize them — in short, to dispossess them or despoil them of their culture and language. It was based on a radically artificial ideology, much more artificial than any national ideology (for there is a measure of invention in all nationalisms); more important still, Canaanism was totally out of touch with the concrete material and cultural needs of precisely those Arabs and Jews whose political, religious, and cultural lives it sought to mold.

The Colonialist School creates, then, a historical fiction which it calls "Zionism," but which is not really Zionism. The description would have been somewhat more valid had the Canaanites been the political spearhead of the Jews (or rather the Hebrews) in *Eretz Yisrael* (or rather, *Eretz Kedem*). In any case, although Canaanism was an offshoot of Zionism and evolved in the Zionist world, it developed into a radical and outright rejection of Zionism. The description offered by the Colonialist School misses the core of Zionism because of the same Canaanite tendency to "forget Europe." This school is also a product of Israeli society, of the mental world created in the political society founded by the Zionist movement. What is more, the Colonialist School developed in part as a manifestation of distress with the outcome of the historical reality created by Zionism. It is a manifestation of the unease this new society feels with regard to its historical roots and of its temptation to deny them. In any case, whatever the sources of the Palestinocentric shortcoming of the members of the Colonialist School, it has deprived them of the ability to produce an adequate explanation of Zionism's historical enterprise and of the sources of its strengths, as well as its weaknesses.

NOTES

I would like to thank Yosef Gorny, Gilat Gofer, Gadi Taub, Gideon Katz, Orna Miller, Tuvia Friling, Nir Kedar, Nahum Karlinsky and Orit Rosin, who read earlier drafts of this article and made helpful comments

1 Throughout the years these debates have been political, ideological, propagandistic and sometimes diplomatic, as well as scholarly, insofar as the scholarly facet of so loaded a subject can be isolated. The charge that Zionism is no more than an act of European aggression and an invasion of the Arabs' land has been hurled against it from its earliest days. It was voiced chiefly by the Left and was very much influenced by the inclination of some European leftists to deny the validity of the national category in modern politics. Among Jewish leftists this tendency frequently supplemented the view that their collective Jewish identity was a negative and unnecessary relic of the Middle Ages.

2 For an illuminating analysis of communism's shift from negating Jewish nationalism to the need to acknowledge its sociological basis, see Matityahu Mintz, "Ha-umah ha-yehudit — amtza'ah tziyonit? Be-shulei pulmus ha-historiyonim" (The Jewish Nation — a Zionist Invention? In the Margins of the Historians' Debate), in Pinhas Ginossar and Avi Bareli (eds.), *Tziyonut: Pulmus ben zmanenu, gishot mehkariyot ve-idiologiyot* (Zionism: Contemporary Debate, Research and Ideological Approaches) (Sede Boker, 1996), pp. 31–51.

3 The formal designation "school" may not be appropriate, since it denotes a general explanatory structure, and the thrust of my argument here is that these scholars sidestep the obligation to provide a causal explanation of Zionism. In a more restricted sense, however, where "school" designates no more than a group of persons who share a particular position on a key theme discussed in the academic literature, the expression "colonialist school" in the study of Zionism and the State of Israel seems appropriate and I shall use it here. Among its members, Shafir is most central to our discussion, because he published the work that has the most comprehensive explanatory intention (see below).

4 Gershon Shafir, *Land, Labor and the Origins of the Israeli–Palestinian Conflict 1882–1914* (Cambridge, 1989), pp. 8–21; idem, "Karka, avodah ve-okhlosiyah ba-kolonizatziyah ha-tziyonit: Hebetim klaliim ve-yihudiim" (Land, Labor and Population in the Zionist Colonization: General and Specific Aspects), in Uri Ram (ed.), *Ha-hevrah ha-yisre'elit: Hebetim bikortiim* (Israeli Society: Critical Aspects) (Tel Aviv, 1993); Gershon Shafir, "Israeli Society: A Counterview," *Israel Studies*, Vol. 1, No. 2 (Fall 1996), pp. 189–213; Ilan Pappé, "Ha-tziyonut ke-kolonializm: Mabat hashva'ati al kolonializm mahul be-Asiyah uve-Afrikah" (Zionism as Colonialism: A Comparative View of Mixed Colonialism in Asia and Africa), in Yehiam Weitz (ed.), *Bein hazon le-reviziyah: Me'ah shnot historiografiyah tziyonit* (Between Vision and Revision: A Hundred Years of Zionist Historiography) (Jerusalem, 1998); Baruch Kimmerling, *Zionism and Territory: The Socio-Territorial Dimensions of Zionist Politics* (Berkeley, 1983); Ronen Shamir, *The Colonies of Law: Colonialism, Zionism, and Law in Early Mandatory Palestine* (Cambridge, 2000); Ronen Shamir, "Burganut yehudit be-Palastinah ha-kolonialit: Kavei mitar le-seder yom mehkari" (Jewish Bourgeoisie in Colonial Palestine: Guidelines for a Research Agenda), *Sotziologiyah Yisre'elit*, Vol. 3, No. 1 (2000), pp. 133–48; Amir Ben-Porat, "Lo shakhvu al ha-gader: Hizdamnut, tshukah, veha-pritzah le-Palastinah" (They Didn't Lie on the Fence: Opportunity, Desire and the Breaching of Palestine), *Iyunim Bitkumat Israel*, Vol. 4 (1994), pp. 278–98.

5 Given that in modern times the Jews of Eastern Europe constituted an overwhelming majority of all those who could be considered Jewish by any definition whatsoever, it follows that Europe was the center of the political, religious and cultural developments in Judaism of that era. The Jews of Europe produced political movements that ignored non-European Jews (such as the Bund) and movements that included non-European Jews in

their programs (notably Zionism); but all of them were movements or historical phenomena whose emergence was fueled by European processes. Thus Europe was the site of the causes of the multifaceted process of emigration and settlement and the construction of a Jewish polity in Palestine; processes that took place in the countries of origin of the Jews of the Middle East and North Africa are an important part of the explanation for the consolidation of that construction after the murder of the Jews in Europe and the establishment of Israel.

6 The Colonialist School is also marked by other forms of forgetting or suppression in addition to those considered here, including ignoring the processes that motivated the Jews of the Middle East and North Africa to immigrate to the State of Israel, which had been founded in Palestine by the Zionist movement, thus expressing their preference for Zionism over "Arabism" (to use a shorthand term). Instead of studying the internal life of the Jewish communities and their relations with their Arab milieu in order to identify the reasons for that fateful historical decision, they prefer to hint at the "machinations" of the Zionist movement and the State of Israel and to attribute the large and rapid transfer of population to this slender explanation. Of course this important issue merits attention in its own right.

7 From other perspectives, of course, the Colonialist School certainly does "remember Europe" — colonialist Europe — since the European character of the Ashkenazi Jewish immigrants plays an important part in establishing the argument that the Zionist enterprise is a colonialist project. See below on the problematic nature of describing the Jewish immigrants as European. My expression, "forgetting Europe," has to do chiefly with ignoring or willfully omitting the European causes of Zionism. Incidentally, this school's very use of the European character of the Jewish immigrants to Palestine is rather misleading; for even if the Ashkenazi Jews are considered to have been a European nation (which I regard as a simplistic description), there is no question that they were a subjugated European nation, fleeing and emigrating from Europe, and settlement in Palestine was the national manifestation of this emigration/flight. It is misleading, for example, to lump together Irish and Jewish immigrants to the United States or Palestine, who were refugees from hunger or repression, with English settlers in the colonies of the British Empire.

8 It is true that much of it took place in the press, but the main participants were academics and the "quest for the truth" was a central motif in the journalistic reflection of the debate as well. In any case, the public debate is based chiefly on that among scholars.

9 Edward W. Said, *Orientalism: Western Concepts of the Orient* (New York, 1979); idem, *Culture and Imperialism* (New York, 1993); Homi Bhabha, *The Location of Culture* (London, 1994).

10 For example, Ron Aharonson, "Ha-hityashvut be-Eretz Yisrael mifal kolonialisti? 'Ha-historiyonim ha-hadashim' mul ha-geografiyah ha-historit" (Was settlement in *Eretz Yisrael* a Colonialist Enterprise? The "New Historians" vs. Historical Geography), in Ginossar and Bareli (eds.), *Tziyonut*, pp. 340–54.

11 Given the era when the State of Israel was established (the late 1940s and early 1950s) and the circumstances of its birth (the withdrawal of a colonial power from the country), it is certainly essential to compare the process with its parallels — the building of nations and postcolonialist states around anti-colonialist movements in Asia and Africa, sometimes accompanied by ethnic conflicts. Hence postcolonialism, too, is an umbrella concept that should be applied in preparation for a comparative analysis of Zionism and the State of Israel. I believe that this is a fruitful research approach — limited, of course, like any classification, but not vitiated by "forgetting Europe." See Derek Penslar's article, "Zionism, Colonialism and Postcolonialism," published in this issue of *The Journal of Israeli History*, pp. 84–98. Penslar notes: "by claiming Zionism to be a form of postcolonialism, that is, placing Zionism in Asia, I will be re-placing Zionism in Europe, a continent distinguished by not only the great overseas empires of the West but also a sizable body of colonized, stateless peoples, including the Jews." (p.85) See also Partha Chatterjee, *The Nation and Its Fragments: Colonial and Postcolonial Histories* (Cambridge, 2000).

12 See the short discussion of this point in Yoav Gelber, "The Status of Zionist and Israeli History in Israeli Universities," in this issue of *The Journal of Israeli History*, p.142. Gelber points out that the Jewish immigrants behaved totally differently from European settlers in that they renounced their countries of origin and their native languages.

13 The Arab immigration to Palestine in the wake of the Zionist development can be seen as a counterweight to the displacement of Arab peasants from the land that Jewish institutions purchased for Jewish settlement. I am not aware of a statistical study that weighs the significant phenomenon of Arab immigration to Palestine against their dispossession as a result of Jewish land purchases. In any case, it is well known that Arabs immigrated to Palestine during the British Mandate and anyone who argues that Zionism was a dispossessing force must deal with this fact.

14 There is another significant economic difference: in countries colonized by Europeans it is hard to find a parallel to the competition that developed in Palestine between Jewish and Arab laborers in agriculture and industry. See also the next few notes.

15 This thesis about the social fissure in Palestine/Eretz Yisrael and the existence of two separate national sectors has been developed most strongly in Jacob Metzer, *The Divided Economy of Palestine* (Cambridge, 1998); and Dan Horowitz and Moshe Lissak, *Mi-yishuv li-medinah: Yehudei Eretz Yisrael bi-tkufat ha-mandat ha-briti ke-kehilah politit* (From *Yishuv* to State: The Jews of Palestine in the British Mandate Period as a Political Community) (Tel Aviv, 1977), especially pp. 19–46. See also Moshe Lissak, "Sotziologim 'bikortiim' ve-sotziologim 'mimsadiim' ba-kehilah ha-akademit ha-yisre'elit: Ma'avakim idiologiim o si'ah akademi inyani?" ("Critical" Sociologists and "Establishment" Sociologists in the Israeli Academic Community: Ideological Struggles or Pertinent Academic Discourse?), in Ginossar and Bareli (eds.), *Tziyonut*, especially pp. 72–89.

16 In a study published in 1996, Zachary Lockman tried to offer a relational paradigm, an alternative research paradigm to that of Eisenstadt and of Lissak and Horowitz and its parallel among Palestinian and other Arab academics and among academics looking in from outside the conflict (if there are any). In brief, I believe that Lockman does not refute the macroeconomic proofs later advanced by Metzer to support his "division paradigm" (in *Divided Economy*). Metzer made it clear that the division paradigm does not necessarily assume total disengagement between the two national sectors (aside from their involvement in the political and military conflict) and that it can be corroborated if one can show, as Metzer does, that there was a large degree of socioeconomic isolation between the sectors. This was also the main thrust of Lissak and Horowitz's work, and Metzer offered a macroeconomic basis for this view. See Zachary Lockman, *Comrades and Enemies: Arab and Jewish Workers in Palestine, 1906–1948* (Berkeley, Los Angeles, London, 1996).

17 Lissak, "Sotziologim," pp. 80–5. The validity of Lissak's argument stems from the political power of the Zionist socialists. To counter it, several members of the Colonialist School have attempted to point to the economic power of the Jewish bourgeoisie. See Amir Ben-Porat, *Heikhan hem ha-burganim ha-hem?* (Where Have All the Bourgeois Gone?) (Jerusalem, 1999); Shamir, "Burganut"; Ilan Pappé, "Ha-mano'a, ha'meni'ah veha-korbanot: Mekomah shel ha-burganut ha-yehudit ba-historiyah ha-mandatorit" (The Motor, the Motive, and the Victims: The role of the Jewish Bourgeoisie in Mandatory History), *Sotziologiyah Yisre'elit*, Vol. 3, No. 1 (2000), pp. 149–54. Disagreement is possible as to the political influence of the Zionist socialists on the economy of Palestine, including its split into two national sectors; I think that Lissak's evaluation is correct. In any case, though, the colonialist version of the history of Palestine society is not sustained by the contradiction between the influence of the Zionist Labor movement and of the Jewish bourgeoisie; for, as Nahum Karlinsky argued in his rebuttal to the aforementioned articles by Shamir and Pappé, the farmers and bourgeois did express reservations about the hegemonic collectivism of the Labor movement, but they also saw themselves as an integral part of the Jewish national project in Palestine and as living "in a context in which, under one colonial roof, there existed two national societies that were fighting against each other, while both of them were at the same time also fighting against the same colonialist regime." Nahum Karlinsky, "Orkhei-din ke-vinyan av: Hirhurim induktiviim al 'Burganut yehudit be-Palastinah ha-kolonialit'" (Attorneys as an Archetype: Inductive Thoughts about "Jewish Bourgeoisie in Colonial Palestine"), *Sotziologiyah Yisre'elit*, Vol. 3, No. 1 (2000), p. 160. The Zionist socialists did have an anti-colonial commitment that influenced them and their political leadership, as Lissak holds; and they were the ones who led the Jewish national society in both struggles, against the Palestinian Arabs and against the British. Nevertheless, the Jewish bourgeoisie and the right wing were full partners in these

THE DEBATE ABOUT ZIONISM AND COLONIALISM 119

struggles and accordingly were engaged in the processes that led to the separation of the two national societies.

18 The Jewish workers' relative failure in the contest with Arab laborers for jobs in the citrus groves was evident in the first years of the twentieth century. In 1909–13, this failure gradually led one of their first political parties, the Marxist Po'alei Zion, to support development based on non-private Zionist capital and to think about autonomous workers' settlements. The second workers' party, too, Ha-Po'el Ha-Tza'ir, adopted this approach around the same time. See Yosef Gorny, "Be-hevlei tmurah (le-hitpathut ra'ayon ha-hityashvut ha-ovedet)" (The Travails of Change [on the Development of the Idea of Cooperative Rural Settlement]), *Baderekh*, Vol. 2 (April 1968), pp. 71–85. Cooperative Jewish agricultural settlement was implemented through an organization founded by the two parties, the General Federation of Hebrew Workers in *Eretz Yisrael* (the Histadrut); this settlement sector played a role in the separation of the Jewish and Arab economic sectors from the 1920s on. On the private farmers' concept of settlement, see Nahum Karlinsky, *Prihat he-hadar: Yezamut pratit ba-yishuv, 1890–1939* (Citrus Blossoms: Private Initiative in the Yishuv, 1890–1939) (Jerusalem, 1991), pp. 27–57. Anita Shapira described the later and decisive stage of the same struggle, which took place in the 1930s, when the cooperative rural settlement campaign was going strong. She noted the failure of that struggle as well. See Anita Shapira, *Ha-maavak na-nikhzav: Avodah ivrit, 1929–1939* (The Struggle that Failed: Hebrew Labor, 1929–1939) (Tel Aviv, 1977). At the same time, the citrus groves were only one branch, however important, of the economy, and the struggle was more successful in other sectors.
19 Shafir, "Israeli Society," pp. 192–3. In fact, Shafir had already adopted this position in his book, and the debate between Lissak ("Sotziologim") and Shafir in his above reply is only one round in the debate. See Shafir, *Land, Labor*, pp. 8–21.
20 Shafir, "Israeli Society," p. 192.
21 D. K. Fieldhouse, *The Colonial Empires: A Comparative Survey from the Eighteenth Century* (New York, 1966); idem, *Colonialism 1870–1945: An Introduction* (London, 1981); George M. Fredrickson, *The Arrogance of Race: Historical Perspectives on Slavery, Racism and Social Inequality* (Middletown, CT, 1988).
22 Shafir, *Land, Labor*, pp. 8–21.
23 Pappé, "Ha-tziyonut ke-kolonializm," p. 350; Shafir, "Israeli Society," p. 192.
24 See also Kimmerling, *Zionism and Territory*; Ben-Porat, "Lo shakhvu al ha-gader."
25 See, for example, Shafir, "Karka, avodah ve-okhlosiyah," (note 4), p. 104.
26 Shafir, *Land, Labor*, p. 3.
27 Ibid., p. 8.
28 Pappé, "Ha-tziyonut ke-kolonializm," pp. 345–6 and 353–4.
29 Ibid., pp. 348–63.
30 The logical structure of the Colonialist School's failure, detaching the object of the discussion from its causes, is the same as that of the failure discussed at the start of this article, because the tendency to view colonialism in isolation from its largely material context also involves detaching it from its causes. It is interesting to see the same logical pattern in Edward Said, who would limit the treatment of colonialism to a cultural analysis, and in the tendency to detach the analysis of Zionism from Europe and embed it exclusively in *Eretz Yisrael*/Palestine. It is true that Shafir opts for a distinctly materialist approach and is not tempted by Said's path. Nevertheless, he does not ascribe Zionism to its main material causes, which are European.
31 Idith Zertal, *From Catastrophe to Power: Holocaust Survivors and the Emergence of Israel* (Berkeley, 1998).
32 For the main tenets of the "Hebrew ideology," see Yonatan Ratosh, *1967 u-mah halah? Shalom ivri* (1967 and What Then? A Hebrew Peace) (Tel Aviv, 1967); idem. (ed.), *Mi-nitzahon le-mapolet: Me'asef Alef* (From Victory to Collapse: The Aleph Anthology) (Tel Aviv, 1976); idem., *Reshit ha-yamim: Ptihot ivriyot* (The First of Days: Hebrew Introductions) (Tel Aviv, 1982); A. G. Horon, *Kedem ve-Erev, Kenaan — eretz ha-ivrim* (Kedem and Erev, Canaan: The Land of the Hebrews) (Tel Aviv, 2000). Horon's book (edited after his death but with no indication of what is his own and what was contributed by the editors) does not directly

express the Canaanite ideology, but one can learn about it from the book. For conciliatory attitudes towards the Arabs among the Canaanites, see Uri Avneri, *Milhemet ha-yom ha-shvi'i* (The Seventh Day War) (Tel Aviv, 1969); idem., *Milhamah o shalom ba-merhav ha-shemi* (War or Peace in the Semitic Zone) (Tel Aviv, 1947). See also Boas Evron, *Jewish State or Israeli Nation?* (Bloomington, 1995); Joseph Agassi, *Liberal Nationalism for Israel: Towards an Israeli National Identity* (Jerusalem, 1999). For research on this phenomenon, see Yehoshua Porath, *Shelah ve-et be-yado: Sipur hayav shel Uriel Shelah (Yonatan Ratosh)* (With Spear and Pen in Hand: The Biography of Uriel Shelah [Yonatan Ratosh]) (Tel Aviv, 1989); Yaacov Shavit, *The New Hebrew Nation: A Study in Israeli Heresy and Fantasy* (London, 1987).

The Status of Zionist and Israeli History in Israeli Universities

Yoav Gelber

The Pandora's Box: Ramifications of the Tantura Thesis Scandal

Far beyond its mediocre academic significance, a single MA thesis submitted four years ago to the Department of Middle Eastern History at the University of Haifa opened, as it were, a Pandora's box of issues that for a long time had been swept under the carpet. Consequently, the ramifications of this thesis agitated the Israeli academe. The writer claimed to describe the fate of two Arab villages during Israel's War of Independence in 1948. Relying almost exclusively on oral testimonies of Arabs and Jews, he argued that in one of these villages, Tantura on the Mediterranean coast, soldiers of the IDF's (Israel Defense Forces') Alexandroni brigade had committed war crimes that had caused the death of 200–250 villagers. The outstanding grade of 97, which the supervisors and readers granted the student, eliminates the possibility that they might have failed to read his work.

This MA thesis would have probably remained anonymous and harmless had it not been discovered by an astute journalist who published its principal arguments and conclusions. He also interviewed some of the Arab witnesses and collected a few supporting and objecting responses of academics. Sensing an opportunity for anti-Israeli propaganda, Arab members of the Knesset promptly demanded a judicial investigation of the alleged war crimes, and the charges were widely discussed on Israeli radio and TV.[1]

Veterans of the Alexandroni brigade sued the author of the thesis for libel. An association of Arab lawyers and Jewish groups of the radical left launched a fund-raising campaign to finance the author's defense. They aimed to turn the legal proceedings into the *Nakbah* ("disaster," the Palestinian term for the 1948 war) trial – besmirching Israel as covering up war crimes and blaming it for the Palestinian sufferings in 1948 and after. However, from the beginning of the court's sessions, serious doubts emerged about the scholarly weight of this thesis and about the integrity and competence of those faculty members who had been involved in the process of writing, supervising and reading it. Far from sponsoring a historical debate on Israel's responsibility for the *Nakbah*, the trial dealt with falsifications and distortions. Under these circumstances, the University of Haifa appointed a commission of experts in

Arabic language and Middle Eastern History that found in the thesis several cases of negligence, fabrication, falsification, ignorance and disregard. The fact that they all reflected the same tendency eliminates the chance that these instances were only a matter of incompetence.[2]

Having lost its anonymity, this MA thesis had implications that by far exceeded its merit and extended to an unexpected variety of fields, generating three groups of issues. The first group concerns what really happened in Tantura on the night of 22–23 May 1948, implying by extrapolation the general course of events in that war and their ramifications for the lasting Arab–Israeli conflict until the current *Intifada*. Basically, such questions have long been a historical problem, at least for Israeli scholars. It is impossible, however, to ignore the actual ideological and political atmosphere that often affects historical judgment.[3]

The libel suit has added legal aspects to the historical, ideological and political arguments. The limits of the questionable catchphrase "academic freedom" have been put to test: What does "academic freedom" really mean? Does it include the liberty to libel, defame, fabricate, falsify, neglect, ignore and disregard? A negative answer should have been self-evident. However, reactions to the judicial rulings and to the findings of the university's committee proved that this has not been the case: what some academics regard as libel, falsification and defamation, others consider erudite research at its best.

The legal proceedings have irritated many academics who deny in principle the court's right to interfere in an apparently academic case. On the one hand, the competence of a judge to resolve historical controversy is indeed doubtful. Previous historical libel cases have displayed the incompetence of courts in handling such cases within the framework of the law's procedural limits.[4] On the other hand, it is inconceivable that the law should stop at the gates of the university in matters of libel and defamation precisely as it is unthinkable that universities should enjoy immunity in conducting illegal experiments on animals or human beings even if these tests are carried out for the sake of promoting research and knowledge.

In the second group of issues, this affair has cast a shadow over the standards of teaching and supervision in the academe: the selection and competence of supervisors and lectors; the criteria for evaluating papers and theses; the responsibility of the university for what is taking place under its banner versus the academic freedom of students and teachers; the accountability of professors and the limits imposed on academics by the constitution of the university. Furthermore, the *post factum* conduct of certain faculty members who were involved in this thesis raises the suspicion that they used the principle of academic freedom for promoting other ends.

The third — and most significant — group of issues concerns the situation of historiography in face of the postmodernist attack on its qualification and competence. Is historiography still a scholarly discipline with principles, research methods, rules of the allowed and the forbidden, as well as conventions of accepted and unaccepted interpretations? Or has postmodernism succeeded in bringing historiography back to the eighteenth century, when the writing of history was a literary genre dealing with the past, and in turning history into a conglomerate of narratives? Other questions in this group concern the authenticity and value of historical sources and the validity of the historian's methods of analyzing and interpreting them. Followers of the new trends have criticized the historicist tradition of relying on authentic documents as the primary historical source material and preach their preference for new methods of research that have been developed in the social sciences such as anthropology, psychology or political sociology. Semiotic and hermeneutic facilities that have been developed in other fields of cultural and social research also stand at the focus of disputes over their aptness for historical research and the proper ways to adopt and use them.

Furthermore, the application of comprehensive theories and relativist historiography to the historical and present realities of the Middle East and the history of Zionism and Israel reveals very little innocence and integrity. Eloquent and complicated theoretical arguments, often formulated in unintelligible language, conceal ulterior motives as well as ideological bias and political manipulations. Past experience has shown that Jewish history contradicts global theories. Jewish historical existence has already challenged Arnold Toynbee's theory of civilizations, Marxist-Leninist theories of nationalism and class solidarity, Edward Said's theory of Orientalism and current theories of colonialism as well.

Zionist Historiography in the Israeli Academe

Questions of academic legitimacy overshadowed Zionist historiography (that is, the writing of history by Zionist historians and the writing of the history of Zionism, not necessarily by Zionists) from its inception. For almost two generations, Zionist historiography developed and flourished outside the Zionist and Israeli academe. Throughout the 1930s, the Hebrew University of Jerusalem treated with suspicion Zionist historians and wished to avoid the ideological and academic implications connected with studying Zionism on campus.[5] Only in the early 1960s did the study of the Zionist movement and the *Yishuv* penetrate into the Hebrew University and, subsequently, into its younger sister-universities.

Academic research, and eventually the teaching of the history of the *Yishuv*, confronted the researchers with those who had made that history. Many heroes of this saga were still alive and held senior leadership posts in various fields of the state's life. Naturally, the younger scholars who embarked on studying this history disputed axioms that had struck roots in the public's consciousness. Furthermore, they had to examine critically a consensus created by official and factional histories that had been written in the previous years outside the universities. These young scholars, and certainly their supervisors, had been educated in the light of this consensus and these axioms. The process of liberation from these traditions — or challenging their myths — has been slow and is yet incomplete.

Gradually, academization has transformed the features of Zionist historiography. Prevailing trends in Western historiography concerning the goals, subject matters and methods of historical research influenced the study of Zionism as well. The contents of Zionist history, previously written in a national-epic and romanticist style in the manner of Ranke or Michelet, were apparently incompatible with the universal and absolute concepts and values that Western historiography increasingly drew from the social sciences. This gap illustrated the precarious status of Zionist historiography in the academic world and emphasized the quandaries of its penetration, consolidation and acceptance.

The Six Day War in 1967 marked a turning point in the development of Zionist historiography. Especially prominent was the embarking on the study of topics that had been almost taboo in the 1950s and the earlier 1960s: Zionism's attitude to the plight of European Jewry before, during and after the Holocaust, and the Jews' relations with the Arab world. These two issues, together with the transition from the melting pot concept to a multicultural society, still play a principal role in Zionist and Israeli historiography.

Ben-Zion Dinur — among many other accomplishments, the sponsor of Yad Vashem — and Yehuda Bauer — one of the leading pioneers of Holocaust research in Israel — separated the history of Zionism and the *Yishuv* from the Holocaust. In his first book, dealing with Zionist diplomacy during the Second World War, Bauer wrote only one sentence on the *Yishuv*'s attitude to the Holocaust:

> The response of the *Yishuv* (and world Jewry in general) to the news on the extermination of the European Jews is one of the most crucial and awful issues that confront modern Jewish historiography. Certain aspects of this issue have not been clarified yet, to say nothing of being settled.[6]

Several comprehensive histories of the *Yishuv* that were written during the 1960s and even in the 1970s also evaded the issue of Zionism's attitude to the Holocaust. Noxious weeds soon grew up in this historiographic void, reviving the prewar Orthodox-religious, Bundist, communist and assimilationist anti-Zionist polemics and the domestic arguments between Labor and Revisionist Zionism.[7] Initially, the Israeli academe remained mute in face of these arguments. It was only in the early 1970s that scholarly research of this topic began in earnest, bearing fruit in the mid-1980s. By that time, what had originally been critical and revisionist conclusions appeared almost orthodox and apologetic.[8]

The Arabs of Palestine interested Zionist scholars mainly as an independent neighboring society, not in the context of their relations with the *Yishuv*. Comprehensive historical projects as well as monographs on Zionist policies did discuss Jewish–Arab relations, but as a subsidiary subject to the principal topic — the political and military struggle for the implementation of the Zionist enterprise. In this respect, historiography reflected policy. Zionist leaders believed the fate of Zionism would be decided in London, New York and Washington, not in Baghdad, Cairo, Damascus or Nablus. Similarly, the historiographic effort concentrated on Zionist–British relations, and in this framework the Arabs had a minor place. A certain exception to this rule was the historiography sponsored or inspired by Ha-Shomer ha-Tza'ir. Due to their ideological background and belief in the fraternity of nations, historians who belonged to this movement ascribed greater importance to Zionism's relations with the Arab world and their studies deviated earlier from the common presentation of the subject.[9]

Western and Israeli Historiography

Israel Kolatt — a pioneering scholar in the study of the history of the *Yishuv* — summarized this chapter of the developing Zionist historiography in his meticulous essay "On the Research and Researcher of the History of the *Yishuv* and the Zionist Movement," which was written in the early 1970s and republished in 1976.[10] Kolatt linked the penetration of Zionist historiography into the universities with a broader change of generations in the Israeli academe and indicated the difficulties that academic research should anticipate in this minefield, which was still a fallow field:

> This project of uncovering the past below the heaps of stereotypes, images, memoirs, polemics and phraseology is a huge enterprise. ... Even harder is the scholar's intellectual need to overcome inherited concepts, criticize his prejudices, experiences, memories, feelings and preferences and regard the research object as a historical phenomenon. The burden of Zionist ideology and apologetics has turned the reassessment of Zionist history into a complex and delicate process.[11]

A generation before the "post-Zionist" controversy, Kolatt forecast the condemnation of Zionism by revisionist historians. He linked their emergence to the Arabs' anti-Zionist propaganda and to the ideas of the contemporary New Left in Europe and in the United States. Kolatt also identified the widening gap between the concepts prevailing in Western universities and the roots of the Israeli phenomenon. Enlightenment (*Ne'orut*), progress and liberalism notwithstanding, "the complex linkage between [Jewish] religion and nationality, the historical yearning for the Land of Israel and the international features of Jewish existence have been and remain a mystery exposed to libel."

Besides the lasting ideological confrontation between Zionism and its adversaries, Kolatt pointed out the difficulty in reconciling the needs of Zionist historiography with the trends of Western historiography:

> As far as the respect for the facts, the unbiased appreciation of the truth and the rejection of utilitarian myths are concerned — we are part of the Western world. However, the character and level of development of the *Yishuv*'s historiography make it difficult to adapt the new methods that have developed in the West to the subjects that stand at the center of Zionist and *Yishuv* history. ... Western historiography now gives preference to the critical and cognitive role over the constituent role. The needs of Zionist historiography are different.[12]

A generation later, Kolatt's observations and the accuracy of his predictions on the development of Zionist historiography in face of the pressures exerted by the social sciences, the media and press, the impact of Western historiography and the influence of postmodernist trends appear amazing. At the same time, there is room for reexamination of these observations in the light of recent developments in Western historiography, the study and teaching of Zionist and Israeli history and the transformation of Israeli society.

History in a Polarized Society

Kolatt wrote his article at the peak of the Israelis' euphoria, between the Six Day War in 1967 and the Yom Kippur War in 1973. Those years also witnessed the first cracks in the cohesiveness of Israeli society, but the significance of these signs was yet unclear. By contrast, in the first decade of the twenty-first century Israeli society is in a state of spin. Divided by profound controversies over its identity, source of authority, composition, contents and symbols, this society has lost the balance between authority and accountability, reward and punishment, rights and obligations, success and failure, collective and individual, service and parasitism, goals and results, wealth and poverty, labor and capital, solidarity and competition, reality and virtuality, words and deeds, truth and falsity. Ramifications of this spin are noticeable in the academe as well, and under increasing pressures from the political system and the market forces the universities ponder upon their national mission, social role and academic direction.[13]

Historical debates have mirrored the variation and perplexity of Israeli society. Israeli historiography, too, has entered a state of spin and lost its orientation between professionalism and charlatanism; opposing or competing historical schools and traditions; integrity and opportunism; the self-belittling imitation of the social sciences and the preservation of professional and disciplinary distinctiveness; the apparent need to conform to academic fashions in the West and the adherence to traditional and rational principles; the depth and comprehensiveness of scholarly work and the ambition to take part in public debates on TV, radio and in the daily press. Submissiveness to the media has often lowered the standards of historical discussion to the framework, language and time or space limits of talk shows and opinion columns.

On the other hand, this unrest has taken place amidst growing scholarly activity and may well have contributed to its prosperity. In the last five years, the major universities (Jerusalem, Tel Aviv, Bar-Ilan, Ben-Gurion and Haifa) have held more than 300 undergraduate and postgraduate courses dealing with various aspects of Zionist, *Yishuv* and Israeli history. Taking into account courses delivered several times throughout this period, the total is 420 classes across the country studying introductory courses or various specific aspects of Zionist and Israeli history. These figures relate only to courses that were held in the framework of historical and interdisciplinary departments. Taking into consideration departments such as sociology, political science and international relations as well as special programs, the real number should be considerably higher.

Having special departments for Land of Israel Studies or State of Israel Studies, Haifa (136 courses) and Ben-Gurion University (130) lead the list, while Tel Aviv (69) and Jerusalem (64) follow and Bar-Ilan closes with only 21 courses. Probably, the gaps stem from the different structures of historical and Jewish studies in the universities. In 1997, the universities offered 68 courses in this area. In 1998, the number rose to 90 and fell to 80 in 1999. In 2000 and 2001, the annual number of courses was 91. 15 percent of all the courses (64) were MA seminars.[14]

The variety of topics has been impressive. Using this database, I have divided the 300 individual courses into categories and subjects. The distribution reveals that in the last five years social history has been the largest category with 71 courses (of which I have defined seven courses according to their titles as "sociocultural history," one as social-ideological, three as sociomilitary, eight as sociopolitical, two as socioeconomic history and three as social-colonizatory). Under the category of political history come 54 courses, of which four are political-cultural, 16 political-ideological, eight deal with politics and society, and seven deal with politics and the military.

Zionist and Israeli policies have been the subject matter of 57 courses. 20 were military-political, dealing mainly with the struggle for statehood and the Arab–Jewish conflict. 44 courses focused on the history of the *Yishuv*'s military organizations, the IDF and the Arab–Israeli wars. Zionist ideology has been taught in 44 courses from various aspects: political (ten courses), cultural (two), social (one) and colonizatory (one). In this category I have included also ten courses that concentrate on anti- or post-Zionism. Alongside social history, cultural history is also conspicuously on the ascent, and 42 courses on various cultural issues from identity through literature, films and music to historiography have been taught during the years under examination.

The most neglected field of Zionist and Israeli historiography is the economic history of the *Yishuv* and Israel (five courses only). The number of general or periodical introductory courses is also low (13), but in certain universities the introductions are part of the general surveys of modern Jewish history. Jewish colonization has been the subject of 18 courses and is apparently on the decline — particularly courses on the kibbutz movement (three only). Eleven courses deal with five Zionist and Israeli leaders: Herzl (one), Weizmann (one), Jabotinsky (one), Ben-Gurion (six) and Dayan (one).

The variety of topics within these categories is large, and many courses can be ascribed to more than a single category or field. Without a parallel database on a previous equal period, it is difficult to definitively indicate changes. Nonetheless, it is possible to discern several issues that have lost their popularity while others, which would not have appeared in this list several years ago, are attracting growing interest. A typical example of the first group is Zionism's relations with Britain (eight courses only). The unsettled and relatively new *historical* issue of Israeli identity, or identities, has been the topic of 15 courses. Gender (six courses), memory and commemoration (five) and Zionist versus anti-Zionist historiography (eight courses) are other trendy topics occupying a growing part of the courses' list.

Social and cultural problems emanating from the influx of immigrants in the 1950s have been the topic of 13 courses — a figure that testifies to the revived interest in the ethnic aspect of Israeli society. However, it is noteworthy that none of the professors who teach courses of this sample emerged from the social circle of the early 1950s mass immigration. Scholars of this backdrop who specialized in the problems of Israeli society gained prominence in sociology or political science, but historians have remained basically a cast of WASPs (White, Ashkenazi, Sabra, Protectionist). The few exceptions to this rule focus on historical issues other than Zionism or Israel, and only one teaches ethnic relations in Israeli society.[15]

Actual relations between secular and religious Israelis are probably the reason for a growing number (twenty) of courses that focus on the history of relations between Zionism and Jewish statehood on the one hand and Jewish religion on the other hand. This variety includes courses on state and religion, religious Zionism, the Orthodox opposition to Zionism and the Orthodox community in the *Yishuv* society and during the early years of statehood.

This impressive activity notwithstanding, the status of Zionist and Israeli history in the universities has suffered from the general decline of the humanities. This decay has been quantitative — reflected by numbers of students — as well as qualitative. Many students come from a social backdrop that was not part of the Zionist experience in the pre- or early statehood years. In the peripheral universities and colleges, the percentage of non-Jewish students (Arab, Druze, Bedouin) studying in the history departments is growing. Some of these students consider the Zionist experience hostile, discriminating or oppressing. Furthermore, many students do not turn to the humanities because of curiosity or interest, but because admittance is easier. Students who take courses in Zionist and Israeli history, Jews and non-Jews alike, are deeply involved in the subject matter, yet at the beginning of their studies they lack basic information. This combination of involvement and insufficient knowledge presents special difficulty in classrooms. The history of the *Yishuv* and the early years of Israeli history are the story of an ideological, committed and mobilized society. Most present students — and some of their younger teachers as well — are the products of a highly competitive and individualistic culture. Their ability to comprehend the past in its own terms is doubtful as well as their capacity to grasp the *Zeitgeist* of the twentieth century's first two thirds.

Historiography as a Discipline

An even more significant threat to the status of historiography in general, and Jewish, Zionist and Israeli historiography in particular, stems from the postmodernist and relativist trends that to a large extent dominate current Western historiography. 25 years ago, Kolatt indicated some of these fashions in his above-mentioned essay and pointed to their menacing potential. Yet, he did not appreciate the destructive effects of these developments on traditional historiography to their full extent. Kolatt devoted a considerable part of his essay to the precarious situation of historiography between the humanities and the social sciences, and to the proper training of the historian. While concurring with most of his observations, I would like to elaborate on some and add a few of my own.

Historiography has acquired a special niche between the humanities and the social sciences. Its uniqueness derives from the simultaneous and balanced handling of both the text and its various contexts. The linguistic, artistic and literary disciplines concentrate on particular texts. Philosophers and social scientists embark on the wider context by speculating, generalizing, modeling and theorizing. At the same time, historiography aspires to maintain a proper dynamic equilibrium between the context and the text. Historical interpretation cannot be detached from the relevant source material (or "texts"), and at the same time a purely philological and textual interpretation of sources would be historically meaningless if offered out of the proper chronological, geographic, political, ideological, social, genealogical, psychological as well as many other contexts.

Asking students what are the historian's primary tools, I usually get the prompt and wrong answer: "source materials!" However, among the various intellectual faculties that serve the scholarly work of the historian, the sources — despite their importance — are not the first and foremost. The fundamental precondition is broad education and vast historical knowledge. If the unique essence of historiography is preserving equilibrium between text and context, the extensive infrastructure of general learning, and particularly historical erudition, is essential to comprehending the source material. Moreover, this education and knowledge prevent the historian from being misled by his sources — written as well as oral — and enable him to treat them critically. Broad education affects the historian's associative thinking and thereby his ability to establish relevant links between thoughts, events, people, organizations and institutions, and to place them in their true contextual frameworks.

Linguistic skills are the next essential prerequisite, serving the textual aspects of the historian's role. Mastery of languages and an understanding of their semantics and etymology — enabling thereby the textual and philological analysis of documents — are among the historian's most significant professional tools. This is particularly true in the case of a revived and rapidly developing language such as modern Hebrew. Another must of writing history requires familiarity with the geographic arena of the research. Lack of such acquaintance may lead to funny pitfalls and even to misunderstanding and misinterpretation of documents. It reminds me of a certain Ph.D. thesis written in England about the Palestinian Arab revolt in 1936–39. The author referred several times to "the rivers." Since in Palestine there is only one river worthy of this definition, the Jordan, I wondered what the author had in mind. Finally it came to me that he meant Rutenberg's electricity plant in a place called in Hebrew *Naharayim*, literally — two rivers. Certainly, this person had little knowledge of Hebrew and none of the Holy Land's geography.[16]

To be meaningful, the historian also needs the proficiency of conceptualizing his findings and showing his ability to see the wood, not only the trees. Furthermore, he must be a fluent writer if he wants to reach any substantial audience. In the wake of all these properties come the self-evident tools — the source materials: documents, newspapers, journals, books, memoirs, oral testimonies, statistical data, pictures, films, posters, advertisements, etc. Yet, the historian's use of these facilities is subject to a set of agreed though unwritten rules, on which I shall dwell below.

Until recently, most scholars in the history departments of the Israeli universities were educated in the historicist tradition that had emerged in the late nineteenth century in Europe and Britain. Those who studied in Israel are the third and fourth generations of the "Jerusalem School" that the teachers (Ben-Zion Dinur, Itzhak [Fritz] Baer, Israel Halperin, etc.) of our own teachers (Shmuel Ettinger, Hayim Hilel Ben-Sasson, Yehuda Bauer, etc.) had founded. This school was a variant of historicism, shaped for the study and teaching of Jewish history. Similar equivalents developed in the departments of world and Middle Eastern histories.

From the beginning, historicism has exacerbated criticism and opposition from various sides. It has been attacked by Marxists, by the New Historians who emerged in America in the 1930s and by the school of the *Annales* in France. The meaning of the concept has been blurred by different and varying usages. Nevertheless, it has remained a central historiographic trend.[17] For some unknown [to me, at least] reason, present opponents of historicism erroneously call it "positivism" and historicists have become "positivist" historians. Originally, however, positivism was a short-lived historiographic school that emerged in the middle and second half of the nineteenth century and soon disappeared into oblivion. Its followers — such as Henry Thomas Buckle — strove to turn historiography into "human sciences" in a sense similar to "natural sciences." They attempted to discover "laws of history" similar or parallel to the laws of nature — in other words: to predict the future on the basis of the past — and soon had to admit their failure.[18] Increasing the confusion, a different usage of the concept *historicism* has been introduced by Karl Popper to denote determinist religious or philosophical overall interpretations of history — both cyclical and dialectical — from Herodotus and Plato to Hegel and Marx. Criticizing the total philosophies of history, Popper denies the existence of any "meaning of history" that divine laws or rational rules can define or interpret. However, this usage of the term *historicism* has nothing to do with the historiographic movement bearing this name that I discuss here.[19]

A significant contribution of this historicism was the postulation that studying the past requires special principles, rules and methods of research — albeit, a scholarly discipline — that were different from those of other sciences. This methodology is essential for the study of past phenomena in all fields, including those that apparently belong to other disciplines. Hence, to study economic history one should be primarily a historian and not necessarily an economist. The research and teaching of legal and constitutional history demands primarily historical, not legalistic, training and education, and the study of military history demands a historian, not a warlord. This statement does not mean that military historians do not need experience and understanding of military matters or that economic historians are exempt from knowing economics. It claims, however, that the primary tools of the researcher of any past phenomenon are historiographic.

By applying this postulation, historical research has expanded into a variety of new fields, and the innovative school of the *Annales* has extended its limits further. However, this basic historicist supposition also provoked plenty of disapproval because of its far-reaching ambition to explain all facets of human activity as well as their development and transformation throughout the ages. The critics of historicism have argued that this pretense to dynamic comprehensiveness is beyond human capacity.[20]

A second axiom — dating back to Leopold Ranke, the forerunner of historicism — assumes the existence of historical truth and maintains that the historian's duty is to look for this hidden truth and to describe history "as it really was." Even if the historian is unable to uncover the historical truth completely and definitively (as even historicists now admit), he should try to approach it as far as possible. Heaps of futile polemics based on abstract theories and argumentations have already accumulated around this controversial surmise. On the one hand, history — namely the events of which it consists — could and can take place in a single way only, otherwise it contradicts the laws of nature. A certain person could either be killed in a battle or slaughtered afterwards, but not both because he could not die twice. The number of Arab casualties in Tantura (or Deir Yassin) could be either 80 or 250 but not both numbers, and so forth. On the other hand, those who are involved in making history or witness it by doing, writing, filming, observing or listening — and later serve as sources for its reconstruction, interpretation and learning — perceive and interpret what they did, saw or heard in an endless variety of ways and versions. Scholars who study history on the basis of this source material later add their own subjective and contradictory input of analysis and interpretation to this diversity.[21]

The principal purpose of historiographic methodology is, therefore, to reduce to the utmost the gap between the objective occurrence of the historical event and the contexts in which it took place on the one hand, and its representation through the subjective perceptions of witnesses and scholars on the other hand. This reduction brings us closer to the historical truth, but the process of approaching it is probably infinitesimal in the mathematical sense of calculus and will never end.

Striving to verge on the historical truth is often confused with "objectivity." Truth, however, is not necessarily objective in the sense of being neutral, impartial or detached. Historians should not pretend to be "objective" in their handling of testimonies, evidence, claims or traditions if and when they conflict and contradict each other. The historian's goal is to uncover the source material, select, analyze and evaluate it professionally and eventually approach the truth that may well contradict the views of one side in a conflict or more, and sometimes even his own beliefs. Of course, at his point of departure the historian should be free of bias and prejudice. However, he may adopt a point of view and take a position when he has learnt the evidence and concluded the process. His final test is not how far he succeeded in avoiding taking sides, but how professional, methodical, meticulous and thorough were the gathering, analysis and presentation of the source material and the degree to which his conclusions stemmed from the evidence at his disposal.

Truly, this enterprise is an enormous intellectual effort, demanding longer time, painstaking work on details, careful analysis of ever more documents and other source materials, an open mind, and a sensitive heart capable of displaying empathy and using it for nearing the truth. I submit that despite the many requirements and obstacles in fulfilling them, this demand is a feasible endeavor that no true historian is free from undertaking.

Sometimes, the campaign that relativists wage against "objective" history and/or the existence of historical truth seems an excuse to dodge this exacting commitment and make life easier by repudiating the very necessity of approximating the historical truth. Arbitrarily denying its existence, they confuse such truth with nonexistent "objectivity." Asserting that everything — knowledge included — is a question of power relations, they imply that there is no use in seeking "objective" historical truth. In any case the winner, or the stronger, dictates his subjective "truth" and this truthfulness will change only if and when the power relations change. However, I maintain that the historiographic application of Michel Foucault's theory of knowledge and power essentially serves postmodernist historians to exonerate their unwillingness to invest the effort necessary for seeking the truth while simultaneously neutralizing the subjective impact of power on it. In applying his theory, Foucault's less sophisticated partisans have gone far beyond what he originally meant.[22]

Historiography differs from other scientific disciplines, as well as from journalism and the writing of fiction, which may also deal with the past. A historical study striving to move towards the truth and comprehend it demands that the researcher examines his topic in the framework of the terms, concepts, semantics and values of the researched era and society, and not of those of his own times and environment. Unlike the jurist, the anthropologist or the philosopher, the historian ought to abandon temporarily the terminology, values and ethics of his own age and plunge into the past and different world of his subject matter. He should learn and appreciate that world from the inside and then "return" to his time and surroundings and translate his findings, their essence and his conclusions into a "language" — terminology and semantics — intelligible to his audience.

This demand, to partially strip oneself of one's own individuality and enter into that of one's research object, is not an easy one. Prior to embarking on a research project, the scholar should be aware of this prerequisite and confident of his ability to fulfill it in that specific case. Thus, for example, a nonbeliever coming from a secular social, educational and family background may find it difficult, if not unfeasible, to detach himself from his established world view, a detachment essential for studying the history of any community of believers. Moreover, having successfully done so, the researcher should then penetrate into the spiritual world, symbols, concepts, terminology, power relations, internal codes and values of a religious society and comprehend them from the inside. Finally, he has to translate them as they are (and not as he would like them to be) into a modern language that will be both intelligible to his audience and preserve the original meanings. In other words, historians who choose to research topics at variance with their own personal views are obliged to greater sensitivity and efforts in distinguishing between findings and positions, and to greater effort in displaying empathy to their research objects. As a matter of course, the search for the truth binds the historian when he studies his own folks as well. He should be equally careful to avoid the pitfall of turning into a propagandist of his world view, gender, sexual identity, nation, ideological movement, political party or any other entity with which he identifies and, sometimes, even of his friends and family. The obligation of treating everything — including one's own favorites — skeptically and critically binds the historian in all directions, 360 degrees around.

The adoption of anthropological, sociological, sociopolitical or psychological concepts and research methods by historians has indeed extended the perspective of historical research and enriched its capacities. At the same time, however, indiscriminate imitation of these methods has increased and complicated the hurdles at the historian's doorstep. For example, the formulation of a preliminary basic hypothesis is a key point of the social sciences' methodology and is ever more adopted in historical research as well. The social scientist begins the procedure of research by formulating a central hypothesis. Then, he examines it throughout the process of studying and ultimately verifies or rejects his preliminary guesses. Applying this procedure, however, the historian is misled to speculate. History deals with what actually happened and not with the endless number of possible events that for various reasons did not take place. The question "what would have happened if...?" may be very attractive and challenging, but it should remain outside the historian's vocabulary. To a large extent, a hypothetical research question is of a speculative nature. As such, it may determine the outcomes and conclusions of the study by dictating in advance the scope, direction and trend of seeking and selecting the source material. The alternative to a preliminary and speculative hypothesis should be a broad but clear definition of the research topic, scope, parameters, possible contexts and relevant source material. The questions then would emerge during the process of examining the source material while the gathering of documents would not be the known-in-advance consequence of a predefined theory.

The duty to suspend judgment, all the more so hindsight or moral judgment, entails other restrictions on the historian's freedom of action that singles him out in comparison with other disciplines. The historian's roles are to describe, to interpret, to analyze and to conclude — but not to judge. His wider perspective, and *post factum* knowledge of what his heroes could not know because his past was their future, commands the historian to be extremely cautious while appraising his objects and drawing his conclusions. Retroactive activism is the prerogative of politicians, not historians.[23]

Numbers and statistics fascinate many historians, particularly those who specialize in economic, demographic and social history. In certain cases they are relevant also to political and military historians. Numerical figures seem to possess an absolute value and unequivocal nature that are so much absent in words.[24] Like any other text, however, numbers do have terminology and semantics, partly open and partly hidden between the columns and rows of the statistical tables and the numerical results of censuses, polls, balances, surveys, reports, summaries of data tables, etc. Moreover, the statistical tools that serve well the economist, the demographer, the political scientist or the sociologist, and are accepted by them without undue questions about the way they were produced, may often prove insufficient and sometimes even misleading to the historian. As any other text, numbers and tables require a skeptical and analytical approach. They are subject to the usual questions of who produced them, by which methods, for what purpose, what could be the open or ulterior motives behind their production, what was the author's access to the data, under what definitions the columns fell and why, and many others.

Giving in to the fashionable catchphrase "interdisciplinary research," historians may confuse "interdisciplinary" with "nondisciplinary." The first means combining research methods from different disciplines that supplement each other for attaining a common research goal, while adhering to the disciplinary principles of all involved disciplines. The second term refers to ignoring or blurring disciplinary principles in the name of some higher and nonexistent framework, "postmodernism," for example.

Imitation of social sciences' modern methods of teaching is also dubious from the standpoint of training historians. In the social and educational sciences the learning process partly functions through methods of self-experiencing, such as group dynamics, psychodrama, role-play, etc. At the beginning of my teaching career, I enthusiastically tried some of these methods on my students only to learn the lesson that previous knowledge and understanding — in the old manner of reading and rehearsing a topic as a preparation for discussing it — was an essential precondition and not an alternative obsolete way of learning. The use of modern technology for purposes of illustration — so popular in school-instruction and in American universities — is also hardly recommended. Where would the students acquire the faculty of abstract thinking if not in their academic studies? The audiovisual technology is important to the extent that it represents history, but not in illustrating it. By adhering to audiovisual illustrations, we may find ourselves teaching virtual history as we are driven by the TV and film industry into living virtual reality. On the other hand, the history departments of the universities in Israel make too little use, or no use at all, of more important illustrative facilities at their disposal. The history of the *Yishuv* and Israeli history took place mostly in the country, and all significant sites are within reach. Yet, excursions for learning purposes are few, and most students have not been trained in the use of old maps and air photographs as significant historical sources to political, military, urban, demographic, economic and even social histories.

The Onslaught of Postmodern Relativism

Since the 1970s, almost each of the above-mentioned principles has been subject to attacks that denied its validity. Some prominent critics had practiced research in intellectual (Foucault) or medieval (Hayden White) history before relinquishing their research in favor of theorizing. However, the criticism of historiography comes mainly from scholars outside the discipline. Partly, the disapproval of historiographic principles has emanated from political correctness, but principally it has represented interdisciplinary polemics. There are few postmodernist or relativist practicing historians who have been radical to the point of negating altogether the existence of historical truth and the historian's duty to approach it. Usually, the critics are theoreticians. Philosophers such as Karl Popper censure the pretensions of historians, and social scientists — particularly political scientists — are annoyed by the doubts that historical research, based on archival material, cast on their theories and findings. Often, the conclusions of the social scientists dealing with the near past are based on incomplete source material of dubious value such as newspapers, interviews and memoirs. Therefore, the opening of archives usually brings about a revision or rejection of their theories.

Contrary to the earlier and constructive historical relativism of Charles Beard or Raymond Aron in the 1930s and 1940s,[25] present relativist theories are quite harmful — and not to historiography alone. Stemming from postmodernism, these theories deny or ignore any rules, principles, codes and obligations. The escape from authority might be acceptable — and even productive — in art. However, this freedom is highly problematic in literary research, where it concerns the issue of the text's ownership: does it belong to the writer or to the reader? Such chaos is destructive in science and dangerous in the practical political, military and social life. Postmodern relativism brings historiography back to the eighteenth century and reduces it to the status of a literary genre — an endless collection of narratives that in the absence of an agreed basis to assess them all carry equal weight.[26] As stories, we appreciate narratives by literary, not historical standards. According to the relativist credo, there is no technique to measure the truthfulness, validity, accuracy and reliability of narratives in a way that makes it possible to determine their historical value in terms of accuracy or truthfulness. Hence, the dominant criteria are their eloquence, fluency, beauty, sensitivity, empathy, ability to create identification and arouse the reader's sympathy, political correctness, conformity with prevailing trends, and other historically irrelevant parameters.

In recent years, these postmodern theories — casting doubts on the very existence of facts and truths, and repudiating the validity of any rules or principles — have won over large segments of Western historiography. Concepts such as narrative, discourse and their derivatives have acquired a dominant position in Western historical writing. Consequently, these theories and concepts have gained considerable influence also in Israeli universities whose faculty members are influenced by and dependent on American academic institutions — and to a lesser degree on British, French and German universities and institutes as well — for postdoctoral scholarships, visiting positions on sabbaticals, invitations to conferences and publications in refereed journals which are essential for their promotion. This dependence encourages opportunism, and at least in the matter of promotion the universities can and, in my opinion, should change their policy. In the case of Zionist and Israeli history, scientific expertise, competence and authority have concentrated primarily in Israel, so dependence on foreign advice is less essential.

The Changing Historiography of the Arab-Jewish Conflict

In Israeli historiography, the new trends have focused on three major fields of Zionist ideological and political history: Its attitude to the Arabs, to the Holocaust and to the new immigrants who arrived in Israel after statehood. This combination assaults the justification of Zionism and Jewish statehood in three systems of relations: between Israel and its surroundings; Israel and its people, as well as Israel and its own allegedly discriminated citizens.[27]

So far, the first of these issues — the history of the Arab-Jewish conflict — has been the most popular and complex. I know too little about the historiography of conflicts in the Balkans and the Caucasus to make any comparison. However, historians writing about other wars and conflicts during the nineteenth and twentieth centuries can now detach themselves to the necessary degree from the objects of their studies because these encounters — such as the two World Wars, the Korea and Vietnam Wars and even the Cold War — are over. Historians studying these wars and their repercussions are free of the enmity between Nazis and Communists, Britons and "Huns" or Americans and Chinese. Hence, their writing and teaching are relatively relieved of the past's tensions and passions. By contrast, a historian writing on the Arab–Jewish conflict deals with a persisting confrontation. None of the problems involving Jews and Arabs that emerged before, during and after the War of Independence in 1948 have been solved. Every word on that war, or on the subsequent major military confrontations and endless skirmishing along and inside Israel's borders — written in a book or article and spoken in class or conference — may have actual ramifications and is often interpreted and discussed outside its historical context and in terms of the continuing struggle at the present time. In this sense, the historiography of the Arab–Jewish conflict is as unparalleled and unprecedented as the conflict itself.

Already during the 1970s, the academic circles in the West changed their attitude to Israel. The same Palestinian slogans that had made no impression between the World Wars and in the aftermath of 1948 gained popularity against the new backdrop of Europe's postcolonial guilt feelings. Arab donations and other forms of funding encouraged this process, which expanded also to American universities. Early signs that the transforming attitude in Western universities towards the Arab–Jewish conflict had penetrated Israeli historiography appeared in the late 1980s, with the emergence of the so-called "new historians." Their principal contribution to the study of the Arab–Israeli conflict has been the diversion of the focus of historical attention from Israel's accomplishments to the ordeal of the Palestinians. They portrayed the Palestinians as the hapless objects of violence and oppression (Israeli), collusion (Israeli–Transjordanian) and treacherous diplomacy (British and Arab).[28] Some of them have described the Israelis as intransigent, merciless and unnecessarily wicked usurpers who cynically used the Holocaust to gain the world's support for Jewish statehood at the expense of the Palestinians' rights to their country.[29]

The emergence of this group has not brought about a scholarly breakthrough, neither in revealing new horizons nor in methodological originality. Benny Morris can be defined as historicist, strictly adhering to archival sources belittling the significance of oral history and memoirs, and open to conviction by the evidence. Ilan Pappé poses as a radical relativist, and under cover of his academic position he is merely grinding several personal and political axes and does not let the facts confuse him. Avi Shlaim allows himself an immense freedom of interpretation that far exceeds his documentary basis. Characterizing the new historians, Anita Shapira has stressed the differences that have made any generalization difficult, if not impossible. She has suggested age (biological and scholarly) as a common denominator, but even this explanation is unsatisfactory: there are substantial age differences among them, while several "new historians" or sociologists are not much younger, if at all, than their colleagues who do not proclaim this title.[30]

This self-proclaimed title "new historians" — implying possession of objectivity and open-mindedness that was not the province of "old" historians, who are alleged to harbor partisanship and involvement — has been particularly irritating.[31] The revisionist historians have indeed generated a questionable revision of the accepted standards of presenting the war of 1948 and its aftermath, but their (different) methodological approaches, practical performance and analysis have been open to criticism no less than those of their predecessors.[32] Supposing the revisionists' posture to be impartial and free from ideological bias is equally unwarranted. Pappé and, to a lesser extent, Shlaim have rendered the Palestinians' charge that Israel was "conceived in sin" a valuable service by sketching the Palestinians of 1948 and after as innocent victims of others' conspiracies and atrocities. This simplicity appears unconvincing to anyone familiar with the sources — unless the reader is utterly prejudiced. In his recent writings Pappé has relinquished the academic mask, joining the Palestinian propagandists openly and wholeheartedly.[33]

When revisionist historians (and sociologists) appeared on the stage in the 1980s, they were outsiders attacking the historiographic and sociological "establishment" of the Israeli universities. At present, most of them belong to the academic "establishment" in Israel and abroad, and hold university positions and tenure. Thus, the polemics between "old" and "new" schools has expanded from research and writing to teaching and supervising. The scandal of Tantura may well be a forerunner of a wider trend in the forthcoming years.

Confronting Palestinian Historiography

After several decades of separate and independent development, the present fashion of positive discrimination in treating the "other" has confronted Israeli historiography with its Arab and Palestinian counterpart. During the 1950s and 1960s, Israeli early historiography and fiction exalted the War of Independence as a miracle, reminiscent of ancient models such as David and Goliath or the Maccabees. The writers described the war as the triumph of few over many, the weak successfully challenging the strong, the right cause winning against the wrong one. To amplify the heroic achievement, they blamed Britain for covertly directing the Palestinian onslaught on the *Yishuv* and the Arab states' invasion of Israel. Several Israeli scholars have devoted their careers to studying the Arab side of the conflict. However, very little parallel interest in the Jewish perspective has developed among their Arab colleagues.[34]

Arab narratives of the war and its consequences — usually polemic or apologetic memoirs and rarely scholarly research — have concentrated on assigning guilt rather than on analyzing events and processes. Since it was inconceivable that the tiny *Yishuv* could inflict this defeat on the Arabs single-handedly, it was essential to mitigate the disaster by suggesting accomplices. The Arabs accused Britain of betraying them; blamed the United States for supporting its Zionist protégé and finally vilified King Abdullah of Transjordan, who was the only Arab ruler that benefited from the general debacle.[35]

A typical obsession of Arab historiography has been the question of justice and unfairness. Arab scholars have scarcely endeavored to find out what really happened, when, how and why. In place of this, they have elaborated on whose case was right and whose arguments were illegitimate. Hence, Arab scholars ascribe excessive significance to official documents of judicial and declarative character, such as UN resolutions, and disregard the huge corpus of the archival source material on the war. A partial exception to this rule — despite its apologetic character — is Arif al-Arif's six volumes of the war's history that were written in the 1950s. Unfortunately, this work has not been translated and is inaccessible to a wider Israeli audience. Recent Arab works on the conflict are more sophisticated and use the fashionable jargon of Western universities, but none of them approximates al-Arif's thoroughness, self-critical method and accuracy. Nur Masalha, as well as Walid and Rashid Khalidi, sometimes refer to the works of Israeli scholars, but their choice is highly selective and tendentious and usually confined to works in English edition.[36] An interesting question is what would be the findings of Arab "new historians" should they ever emerge in the Arab countries and among the Palestinians.

Representing "the other," Palestinian historiography is now thought by certain Israeli historians to deserve treatment on an equal basis with Israeli historiography of the conflict. Having tried to organize common discussions, I am afraid, however, that there is no common ground yet for such a parley. Any serious discussion of the evidence (or lack of it) behind the Palestinian "narrative" without accepting it in advance is promptly rejected. Objections rely on the argument that the demand itself is arrogant and reflects an "Orientalist" attitude. Arab historiography, as well as some Israeli revisionist historians and sociologists, draw heavily on Edward Said's theory that denies the possibility for a person born into one culture to understand intimately and profoundly "the other" culture. Coming from Said — claiming to be a Palestinian refugee who teaches English literature at an American university and has built his career on a Polish sailor by the name of Joseph Conrad who became a British writer — this argument appears peculiar, to say the least.[37]

The Colonialist Paradigm of Zionism

Following in Said's footsteps, Palestinian scholars as well as some Israeli revisionist sociologists, jurists, geographers and historians, attempt to prove the colonialist nature of Zionism and all the more so of post-1967 Israel.[38] Deriving from current theories on colonialism, this claim relies on very little historical evidence, which usually shows the opposite, and mainly on a tendentious interpretation that confuses past and present and serves primarily as a propagandist and ideological weapon in the persisting Arab–Jewish conflict.

The association of Zionism with colonialism did not begin with "new" historians, sociologists or geographers. It is as old as the conflict, dating back to the first Palestinian congress in Jerusalem at the beginning of 1919, if not earlier — as Rashid Khalidi has recently shown.[39] Presented simply, the essence of Zionism is indeed immigration and colonization — pure colonialism in the manner of the Spanish Conquistadores, the pioneer settlers in North America and a long succession of Europeans who occupied, immigrated to and settled in America, Southeast Asia, Australia and Africa. Similarly, Zionism was temporarily assisted by an imperialist power, Britain, though for more complex reasons than plain imperialist interests. Here, however, the similarity ends and when the colonialist paradigm confronts reality it fails to explain adequately the Zionist phenomenon.[40]

Unlike the Conquistadors and their successors, the Jewish immigrants who came to *Eretz Yisrael* since the 1880s did not come armed to their teeth to take over the country by force from its natives. If we try a semiotic approach, until 1948 the Hebrew word *kibbush* (occupation, conquest) related to wilderness, manual labor, grazing and at most to guarding Jewish settlements. Military terms such as *gdud* (battalion) or *plugah* (company) also related to labor and not to military units. Economic theories of colonialism and sociological theories of migration movements are also invalid or insufficient when applied to the Zionist experience. Palestine differed from the typical countries of emigration primarily because it was underdeveloped and poor. Contrary to their European contemporaries and predecessors who had emigrated to countries rich in natural resources and poor in manpower to exploit them, the Jewish immigrants came to a country that was too poor even to support its indigenous population. Natives of Palestine — Jews and Arabs, Christians and Muslims — emigrated at the end of the Ottoman period to America and Australia. Zionist ideology and import of Jewish private and national capital compensated for the lack of natural resources and accelerated modernization. Ideology — excluding the missionary that did not exist in Zionism — and import of capital were two factors that were totally absent in any other colonial movement. The imperialist powers usually exploited the colonies for the benefit of the mother country and did not invest beyond the necessities of exploitation.

Until 1948 — with no parallel among colonial movements — the Zionists bought, and did not conquer, lands in Palestine. The list of sellers included all the prominent clans of the Palestinian elite — al-Husayni, Nashashibi, Abd al-Hadi, al-Alami, Tabari, al-Shawa, Shuqairi and many others — who despite their radical political postures could not stand the temptation of the rising land prices in Palestine. Palestinian and "new" Israeli historians usually blame foreign landowners, such as the Sursuq family of Beirut, for the eviction of the Palestinian tenants and conceal the role of the resident elite families who led the Palestinian national movement.[41] After statehood, state land was requisitioned and private lands were sometimes expropriated. Yet, the state compensated private owners and buying of tracts from individual Arabs continued.[42] By the same token, during the Mandate period and the early years of statehood Jewish immigrants competed with the (Arab) natives in the market of urban and rural manual labor — a competition inconceivable in any other colonial country.

Cultural examination also excludes Zionism from the colonialist paradigm. In contrast to the colonial stereotype, the Jews that immigrated to *Eretz Yisrael* severed their affiliation to their countries of origin and their cultures. Instead, they revived an ancient language and on the basis of Hebrew created a totally new culture that spread into all spheres. Furthermore, colonialist emigrants all over the world either escaped from a gloomy present or sought a lucrative future. Jews who immigrated to *Eretz Yisrael* shared these incentives, but were driven primarily by a unique motivation that distinguished them from all other colonial movements: reviving an ancient heritage.

This should be enough to refute the identification of Zionism with colonialism. However, this seemingly historical argument has significant ramifications for the present. Palestinian argumentation has always adopted the paradigm of a national-liberation movement (Palestinian) struggling against a colonial power (Zionism). After almost all other national-liberation movements have achieved their goals and ejected colonialism long ago, the Palestinians — who have enjoyed far greater international support — are still treading in the same place. This fact alone should have brought Palestinian intellectuals and their Western and Israeli allies to reexamine their traditional paradigm. However, by cultivating the Zionist-colonialist prototype, Israeli academics continuously provide the Palestinians with the excuse to dodge such reexamination and encourage them to proceed along a road that apparently leads to a dead end.[43]

The Holocaust and Jewish Identity

The second major field of Zionist historiography since the 1970s has been the Zionist movement's and the *Yishuv*'s actions during the Holocaust and their attitude to the plight of European Jewry before the Second World War and of the surviving remnant in its wake. An initially subsidiary field that gradually became a major issue has been the impact of the Holocaust on Israeli society, identity and even politics. In recent years, however, the issue of Zionism and the Holocaust has somewhat lost its central place in contemporary historical debates. Apparently, the issue has exhausted itself, or the critics of the Zionist movement's demeanor such as the psycholinguist Yosef Grodzinsky have failed to present a convincing and attractive case to sustain a serious public debate.[44]

While Zionist leaders or the *Yishuv* were minor players during the Second World War, and could hardly do more than they did, the question of their attitude to and treatment of the surviving remnant after the war has been a domestic Zionist issue and has left no room for excuses. Tom Segev and, particularly, Idith Zertal have accused the Zionist leadership of manipulating the survivors for advancing Zionist political goals and of ignoring the survivors' sufferings. Zertal's book is an example of the damage caused by the formerly mentioned fashionable trends: good and well-written research spoiled by superfluous meditations, inarticulate jargon and baseless interpretations.[45]

Having become a main pillar of Israeli distinctiveness, the Holocaust has been mobilized by critics of Israel to serve their campaign. In an anti-historical hindsight judgment that projects upon the past the concepts, values and realities of the present, they attribute to the leaders of the "state in the making" the values, powers and capabilities of the present Jewish state. Furthermore, they appraise the conduct and attitude of Ben-Gurion and his colleagues in the framework of our own rather contemporary terms.

While the issue of the *Yishuv* and the Holocaust has become less attractive to scholars and new research in this field has dwindled, the problem continues to play a significant role in public debates in Israel and abroad. As the Holocaust has become a basic component of postmodern Jewish identity, Israelis and Jews outside Israel argue about its essence and lessons. Are they primarily universal or uniquely Jewish, humanist or nationalist? Striving to participate in and expected to contribute to this public debate, Israeli historians were drawn into the polemics. 60 years after assimilated, emancipated, socialist and Orthodox religious Jews perished in the extermination camps, the axiom that the Holocaust was the ultimate proof justifying the Zionist solution to the modern Jewish Question could not be taken for granted as it had been hitherto. Zionism's prewar ideological adversaries, who had apparently disappeared into oblivion after the Holocaust, have reemerged under the fashionable mask of "post-Zionism" — religious, leftist-liberal or assimilationist. Both in Israel and elsewhere, they have severely disapproved of Zionist "monopolization" of the Holocaust and condemned the emphasis that Zionist leaders and historians have laid on its uniqueness.

Two elements have been prominent in this condemnation of the Zionist approach. One, dating back to Hannah Arendt in the 1950s, has portrayed the Holocaust as a crime against humanity rather than against the Jews. In terms of the Jews' relations with non-Jews, it was a German–Jewish — not European–Jewish or world–Jewish issue. The second refers to the Holocaust as one of several genocides that took place in the twentieth century, beginning with the persecution of the Armenians by the Turks in the First World War and ending with the wars in Cambodia, Bosnia or Chechnya. The first element is conspicuous to every visitor at the Holocaust Memorial Museum in Washington, where French, Dutch, Romanian, Hungarian, Croat, Slovak, Polish, Lithuanian and Ukrainian satellites, anti-Semites and collaborators hardly exist. This evasion, typical of a bestselling study such as Daniel Goldhagen's *Hitler's Willing Executioners*, is easy to understand.[46] Living in a country with large communities of East European ethnic origin, most American Jews and Jewish historians feel more confident within the limited concept of the Holocaust. Israeli historiography, however, cannot and should not be content with this narrow interpretation and should continue to emphasize the crisis of emancipation and integration as well as that of the traditional Jewish society.

The second element is even more crucial. Treating the Holocaust as genocide among others and denying its uniqueness continues the assimilationist approach of concealing or blurring any Jewish distinctiveness. The genocide concept contradicts the widely accepted periodization of the Holocaust, placing it between 1933 and 1945. How many Jews were massmurdered — or what genocide took place — in 1935, 1938 or even 1940? Indeed, the Holocaust was genocide, but it was much more than mass killing. It is precisely this increment that relativist historians in Israel and elsewhere strive to repudiate by comparing the Holocaust with other atrocities under the trendy slogans of "comparative" and "interdisciplinary" studies.

This comparative tactic has been particularly far-fetched when applied to Israel's attitude to the Palestinians since 1948, and particularly after 1967. The radical left in Israel and abroad introduced this link into its daily jargon as early as the 1970s, deriving from Yeshayahu Leibowicz's catchphrase "Judeo-Nazis" and similar pearls. Israeli historians joined this barrage for the first time in the summer of 1982, when Israel Gutman went on a sit-down strike at the entrance to Yad Vashem in protest against the war in Lebanon. Moshe Zimmerman's language while attacking Jewish settlers in Judea and Samaria, calling their youth *Hitler Jugend* and comparing the Bible to *Mein Kampf*, was another landmark in promoting an apparent analogy between Israel's policies towards the Palestinians and the Nazis' persecution of the Jews.[47]

Pappé has been most extreme in making the link between the fate of the Palestinians and the Holocaust. Ignoring the pre-1948 phase of the Arab–Jewish conflict in order to avoid dealing with Palestinian violent opposition to Zionism and massacres of non-Zionist Jews in Hebron and Safed, he argues that the Palestinians have been victims of the Holocaust as the Jews were. Although Pappé does not adopt completely Said's assertion that Palestinian suffering has priority over the Jews' ordeal during the Holocaust, his apparently evenhanded treatment, degrading the Holocaust by the very comparison to a few isolated atrocities in the midst of mutual fighting in 1948 and after, is very close to a denial of the Holocaust.[48] Similarly, Ilan Gur-Zeev defines the Zionist claim for uniqueness of the Holocaust as "immoral" because it denies others' (particularly the Palestinians') holocausts and genocides.[49] Despite their differences, Gur-Zeev joins Pappé in a highly tortuous attempt to show that the Jews have transferred to the Palestinians what the Nazis did to them. The ulterior motive behind these allegations has been to introduce the idea that the world, which under the impact of the Holocaust had deprived the Palestinians of their homeland to compensate the Jews, should now make up for its historical fault.[50]

From "Melting Pot" to Multicultural Society

Research of the third key issue of Israeli history — the absorption and integration of the mass immigration that arrived in the country during the 1950s and shaped the post-*Yishuv* Israeli society — is still at an early stage. Sociologists such as Shmuel Eisenstadt, Moshe Lissak, Rivka Bar-Yosef and Reuben Cahana wrote several works in the 1960s and 1970s describing and analyzing the absorption of new immigrants and their integration into the veteran mainstream society. In recent years, a school of "new" or "critical" sociologists assaulted the older generation, blaming their teachers for concealing the ulterior motives behind the processes of immigration and absorption, and ignoring the cultural repression of the new immigrants. Revolting against the older generation, the "new sociologists" have turned the focus of sociological research from the mainstream of Israeli society to its peripheral groups, and accused the veteran nucleus of the *Yishuv* society of all possible crimes, from deliberate discrimination towards Jews to militarism towards Arabs. They have even suggested extending the colonialist paradigm of Zionism (see above) to its handling of Jews coming from Islamic countries.[51]

Sociologists are not committed to historiographic methods of research and are entitled to their own professional views and conclusions. Their findings, however, are not "history," and the allegations about the absorption of the mass immigration are no exception. The outcomes of the few historical studies that have dealt with the same period and issues deny categorically any allegation of deliberate conspiracy against the new immigrants, whether survivors of the Holocaust or Jews from Islamic countries. These relatively new studies describe many mistakes that were made at the time, albeit innocently and under extremely dire conditions that those "critical" sociologists incline to ignore.[52]

In historical perspective, the "melting pot" concept may appear a fiasco at the present moment, when "multicultural" is the winning catchword. However, the present quandaries of Israeli society prove very little about the past and nothing about its future. The multicultural characteristics are not the outcome of any failure of absorption but stem from various other processes that Israeli society has undergone in the last two decades: decreasing external pressure, additional immigration, influx of foreign laborers, strengthening of minorities and widening economic gaps.

History in Schools

Against the backdrop of this extensive and transforming research activity, the school system too has changed its programs and updated the syllabus of Zionist and Israeli history. Several prominent historians have been involved in shaping the policies of the state's Ministry of Education on teaching history as permanent advisers or members of ad hoc committees. As could be anticipated, the penetration of revisionist polemics into the universities has been followed by the intrusion of revisionism into the school system, where the teachers and pupils are far less equipped for the encounter than university colleagues and students.

Public attention to the way Israeli history has been taught in schools has focused mainly on the approval and contents of new textbooks. The controversial books, however, are just the tip of the iceberg of more fundamental changes. The issue of teaching history in schools and the involvement of historians from the academe in monitoring the school syllabus deserve wider consideration, which is impossible in the framework of the present article.[53] Briefly, the academic advisers of the Ministry of Education strove to integrate Jewish and world history in a joint syllabus and in the same textbooks. Nonetheless, the utility and necessity of this merger are highly questionable. This amalgamation may indeed be appropriate in universities, whose task is to train their students in the disciplines that they choose to study. Precisely in Israel, however, each university maintains three or four history departments practicing the same discipline, while everywhere else History is a single department embracing all histories.

Unable to unite the history departments of the universities, some historians attempted to make the experiment in the lower educational system. They ignored, however, the profound difference between teaching history in school and in the university. Although the name "history" is identical, the purposes are almost opposite. While the school systems should bequeath the present generation's pictures of the past to the next generation, the role of academic research and teaching is to review, reexamine and reconstruct these pictures.

The fierce discussions on the various historical pictures and interpretations take place mainly within the secular state education, which is indeed approaching disintegration. Unlike the university, however, the school should educate its pupils and has nothing to do with their disciplinary training. Everywhere in the world, the emphasis in the school system is laid on the national history. World history is taught as essential background to American, British, French, Italian or Polish histories respectively. The dubious Israeli innovation of concealing the national history by wrapping it inside an envelope of world history should be rapidly revised.

History and Memory

One aspect, however, of the debate over history in schools does belong to the comprehensive discussion of historical revisionism in Israel. This aspect is usually referred to as the shaping of "collective memory." The school system fulfills a central role in forming this "collective memory" through various channels, from lessons in classes (not only history lessons) to excursions, ceremonies and celebrations.

Daniel Gutwein has defined the revisionist criticism of Zionist and Israeli historiography as "privatization of the collective memory" — a phenomenon that he rightly perceives in a broader framework of privatization processes that Israeli society has been undergoing.[54] However, the definitions of the collective and, consequently, what exactly its shared memory is, are obscure. Is the collective Israeli — including Arabs, Jews, Bedouins and other non-Jews? Is it Jewish — excluding minorities but consisting of non-Israeli Jews as well? What about those who joined the collective later, such as younger people and new immigrants? Is collective memory an aggregate of private recollections or is it detached from individual remembering and has an independent essence? Who decides what in this is independent essence, or which memory is "collective" and which is not — the government? The media? The academe?

I know of no convincing answers to any of these questions. Historiography has not yet solved satisfactorily the problems emanating from individual memory — the proper handling of oral testimonies.[55] Psychological research, too, has so far focused mainly on quantitative parameters of memory — how much people remember and for how long. Only recently, psychologists have resumed a systematic study of memory's qualitative properties such as accuracy, bias, foreign impacts, autosuggestion and many others. The outcomes of these studies are not encouraging as far as the links between memory and truth or accuracy are concerned.[56] The problem of oral testimonies aggravates as historical research expands into micro-history — the recording and study of undocumented objects such as small settlements or military units, or of societies, tribes, clans and families having mainly oral traditions, or sometimes, clandestine activities that because of secrecy or security considerations were not documented. In these novel fields, individual memories and oral traditions are the principal sources and there are very little — if at all — other types of sources for comparing and verifying the stories. The practitioners and theoreticians of oral history speak of it in literarynarrativist rather than historical terms. They regard their practice as an independent discipline and place it in the areas of anthropology, folklore and literature rather than historiography.[57]

Nonetheless, the phrase "collective memory" has become a common usage even when it is not clearly defined and should be treated accordingly. Apparently, its closest relative is the old and familiar "myth." Originally, myths were stories told by the ancestors to explain mystifying natural phenomena. Later, myths were concocted to support temporal or secular claims for status, power, jurisdiction, and so forth (that is to say, medieval myths such as the presents of Emperor Constantine and King Pépin to the Church). Modern myths are what the undefined collective believes — or is led to believe — happened in its past. Usually, modern myths are instructive — seeking to teach lessons — and polemic or apologetic — excusing or explicating. Zionist and Israeli myths are no exception. Like other nations' myths they, too, cover up failures or exonerate fiascoes. True success and triumph speak for themselves and do not require myths.

Various agents shape the myths and propagate them: persons involved in the making of history who try to affect the way they will be remembered; chroniclers, biographers, poets, dramatists, journalists; writers of fiction; filmmakers; school curricula and teachers; radio and TV producers, etc. Recently, the Internet has become a significant facility of creating and disseminating old and new myths and its role in the empire of information will probably continue to grow in the future. When historians are breaking long-established myths, the role of creating them has become unpopular. Hence, instead of cultivating myths these agents now "shape collective memory."

The question, however, is what myths, alias collective memories, have to do with history. Postmodernist historians and thinkers assert that historiography is just another one of the many agencies that produce collective memory, shape and change it, and historians are, therefore, agents of collective memories. This opinion is compatible with their general approach that reduces history to a collection of narratives. Regarding historiography as a scientific discipline I submit, however, that the historian is not — and should not be — a mediator echoing individual or collective memories. His task is precisely the opposite: to distrust, scrutinize and criticize the memories, not to endorse and repeat them.

History is not equivalent to memory — neither on the individual nor on the "collective" level. However, lack of access to official and personal archival material compels Israeli and other historians to rely on sources such as memoirs, oral testimonies, coverage by the media, fiction and arts. These categories of sources are valid for describing the manner in which events have been remembered, conceived or represented, but they hardly tell how they happened. In a secular and individualist age such as ours, they may also contribute to an understanding of the way identities have been shaped. Yet, the affiliation between history and identity has not been explained satisfactorily. As much as history can contribute to the shaping of identity, people also escape from their history in the course of shaping a different or new identity.

Consequently, the research and study of the history of memory have been rapidly expanding. A growing number of scholars study the roots and development of Israeli myths, images and stereotypes. They research the background from which the myths emerged, the reasons for their emergence, the motives behind and methods of their cultivation.[58] The study of myths belongs to cultural history. Significant as it is, this work should not be confused with researching the events — political, diplomatic, military or social. The virtual history, or history of the representation of history — through fiction, poetry, art, films or other popular methods — is not a substitute for the real history of people, nations, organizations, institutions, societies, ideas and other features of the human activity throughout the ages. Sharl De Koster's *Till Eulenspiegel*, or Henryk Sienkiewicz's *Pan Zagloba* are virtual fictions, yet the Netherlands' struggle for independence and the Poles' wars of the mid-seventeenth century were real — and different.

Concluding Remarks

In recent years, the means of disseminating information about and knowledge of the past have undergone profound changes. In the eyes of the public, books and articles, even popular, have ceased to be the principal channels of learning what happened, how and why. Watching audiovisual media such as films and TV documentary programs and surfing the Web are gradually replacing reading books and listening to lectures as the main avenues for gaining information and digesting it. In these respects, Israeli historiography lags far behind. We have no History Channel on TV as in America. The universities' Academic Channel is still poor and experimental, and the history of Zionism and Israel does not occupy a significant role in its programs. Even the flagship documentary series on the history of Zionism — Yigal Losin's *Amud ha-esh* (Pillar of Fire) — is far from being free of shortcomings. Its equivalent on the history of Israel — the series *Tkumah* (Revival) — has been a spectacular fiasco to which, unfortunately, I was a partner. The number of good and balanced documentary historical films on Zionist and Israeli history is abysmally small.[59] My experience in *Tkumah* taught me that producers and directors ignore historical advice, and their attitude towards the historical issues — almost without exception — causes revisionist historians to look nearly orthodox.

The situation of Israeli historiography on the Internet is even worse. Preparation of computerized courses accessible through the Web is still in its inception. A few research institutes and university departments have websites, but excluding the Ben-Gurion Institute and archives in Sde Boker they are poor and primitive. While the Public Record Office (PRO) in London enables users to read on its website the list of documents in a file throughout 1,000 years of British and Imperial history, the Ben-Gurion archives are the only archives in Israel accessible through the Web. Most painful is the total lack of reliable and authoritative websites that provide information on Zionist and Israeli history, and on the historical background of current events in particular.[60]

So far, the historical perspective of studying the history of Israel has been confined to the period ending more or less with the Sinai Campaign in 1956. Limitations and delays in opening significant archival material in the state and IDF archives have hampered research even in this restricted area beyond the necessary limits dictated by the continuation of the Israeli–Arab conflict. However, forerunners of the historical study of later issues such as the Lavon Affair and Ben-Gurion's retirement have already appeared.[61] Scholarly works dealing with the road to the Six Day War and the background of the Yom Kippur War are already under way.[62] In view of the excitement that critical examination of the first — and relatively consensual — decade (1948–1958) of Israeli history has exacerbated, it is easy to imagine the repercussions of a similar scrutiny of the second and third decades (1958–1978) — a period in which every measure, policy or expression has been controversial and a matter for public debate from the beginning, and whose events are masked by an ever-growing mass of irresponsible media coverage.[63] However, precisely for this reason, the continuous debating from the events themselves to the time of their historical study may reduce the shock when historians publish the findings of their research.

The main quandary in tackling the anticipated disputes is not agreement or disagreement among historians or between them and colleagues of other disciplines. Harmony is no less dangerous than rivalry, and arguments may well increase scholarship. Israeli historiography, however, has already lost its joint disciplinary basis, in other words — its common language. It is impossible to conduct a reasonable and constructive debate without shared terminology, principles and ethics. These prerequisites have apparently disappeared in the heat of the recent destructive polemics on the history of the first decade.

I end where I began: the Tantura affair. What would have happened if a scandal like this had taken place in chemistry or in sociology? If major discrepancies had been found between the experiment and the chemist's published conclusions, or the questionnaires and the sociologist's deductions — all the more so if the researcher had intentionally falsified the results — their academic colleagues would have unanimously condemned them as charlatans and expelled them from their ranks. In the Tantura case, Israeli historians have split: some — myself included — maintain that this has been an unprecedented disgrace, and others retort that this is a new zenith of scholarship. To restore the status of Israeli historiography, we should primarily determine what historical scholarship is and what it has in common with other types of knowledge. Furthermore, we should shape the specific criteria by which we decide whether a historical work qualifies as a bona fide piece of knowledge — or as a piece of propaganda and historical fiction.

NOTES

1 Amir Gilat, "Ha-tevah be-Tantura" (The Massacre in Tantura), *Maariv*, weekend magazine, 21 January 2000.
2 For all the polemics, legal documents, committees' reports, articles, letters to editors and other source material relevant to the Tantura affair, cf. the website www.ee.bgu.ac.il/~censor/katz-directory/.
3 For an example of ulterior motives behind the campaign to defend Katz and his thesis, see Ilan Pappé, "The Tantura Case in Israel: The Katz Research and Trial," *Journal of Palestine Studies*, Vol. 30, No. 3 (Spring 2001), pp. 19–39.
4 A good example is Judge Eliahu Vinograd's verdict in the libel case of Moshe Svorai against Anschel Spielman in 1992. See Yoav Gelber, "Ha-mesugelet maarekhet ha-mishpat ha-yisre'elit letapel be-mishpatim historiim?" (Can the Israeli Judicial System Handle Historical Trials?), *Ha-Umah*, Vol. 35, No. 129 (Autumn 1997), pp. 27–36.
5 Cf. Israel Kolatt, "Ha-akademizatsiyah shel toldot ha-tziyonut" (The Academization of Zionist History), in Yehiam Weitz (ed.), *Bein hazon le-reviziyah: Me'ah shnot historiografiyah tziyonit* (From Vision to Revision: A Hundred Years of Zionist Historiography) (Jerusalem, 1997), pp. 89–95; and Yoav Gelber, "Ktivat toldot ha-tziyonut: Me-apologetikah le-hitkahashut" (Writing the History of Zionism: From Apologetics to Denial), in ibid., pp. 67–76.
6 Yehuda Bauer, *Diplomatiyah u-mahteret ba-mediniyut ha-tziyonit, 1939–1945* (Diplomacy and Resistance in Zionist Policy, 1939–1945) (Merhavia, 1970), p. 232.
7 Arthur Eisenbach, "Nazi Foreign Policy on the Eve of Second World War and the Jewish Question," *Acta Poloniae Historica* (Warsaw, 1962), pp. 107–39; Tze'irei Agudat Yisrael (The Youth of Agudat Israel), *Srufei ha-kivshanim maashimim* (Those Who Were Burnt in the Crematoria Accuse) (Jerusalem, 1965); Avraham Fux, *Karati ve-ein oneh* (I Called and No One Answered) (Jerusalem, 1981); Lenni Brenner, *Zionism in the Age of the Dictators* (London, 1983).
8 Dan Michman, "Heker ha-tziyonut le-nokhah ha-shoah: Be'ayot, pulmusim u-munahei yesod" (The Study of Zionism in Face of the Holocaust: Problems, Controversies and Basic Concepts), in Weitz (ed.), *Bein hazon le-reviziyah*, pp. 145–69.
9 Aharon Cohen, *Yisrael ve-ha-olam ha-aravi* (Israel and the Arab World) (Merhavia, 1964).
10 Israel Kolatt, "Heker toldot ha-tziyonut veha-yishuv" (On the Research of the History of the *Yishuv* and the Zionist Movement), *Ha-Universitah*, December 1972, and "Al ha-mehkar ve-ha-hoker shel toldot ha-yishuv veha-tziyonut" (On the Research and Researcher of the History of the *Yishuv* and the Zionist Movement), *Cathedra*, No. 1 (September 1976), pp. 3–35.
11 Ibid., p. 23.
12 Ibid., pp. 24–5.
13 Ilan Gur-Zeev, "Sof ha-akademiyah?" (The End of the Academe?), *Ha'aretz*, 15 June 2001, and Asa Kasher's response, ibid., 22 June 2001.
14 I am grateful to my research assistant Ms. Maya Dar for collecting the data from the various universities and building the database.
15 Not in his capacity as a historian, Yehuda Nini made a highly significant contribution to the

awareness of the growing polarization in Israeli society by publishing his article "Hirhurim al ha-hurban ha-shlishi" (Reflections on the Third Destruction), *Shdemot*, Vol. 41, Nos. 3/4 (Spring 1971), pp. 54–61.
16. Ian Black, "Zionism and the Arabs, 1936–1939" (Ph.D. diss., University of London, 1978).
17. For a critical survey of historicism cf. Hans Meyerhof (ed.), *The Philosophy of History in Our Time* (New York, 1959), pp. 1–84; for a concise review of the development of the various historical schools until the middle of the twentieth century, cf. Fritz Stern, *The Varieties of History: From Voltaire to the Present* (Cleveland and New York, 1956).
18. Stern, *The Varieties of History*, pp. 120–37.
19. Karl Popper, "Has History Any Meaning?" in idem, *The Open Society and Its Enemies* (Princeton, 1950), pp. 449–53; Karl Popper, *The Poverty of Historicism* (London, 1957).
20. Kolatt, "Al ha-mehkar ve-ha-hoker" (note 10), pp. 5–6.
21. Carl L. Becker, "What Are Historical Facts?" *The Western Political Quarterly*, Vol. 8, No. 3 (September 1955), pp. 327–40.
22. Michel Foucault, "Truth and Power," in Paul Rabinow (ed.), *The Foucault Reader* (London, 1986), pp. 51–75.
23. For opposing views on this issue, cf. H. Butterfield, *History and Human Relations* (London, 1931), pp. 101–30, and Isaiah Berlin, *Historical Inevitability* (Oxford, 1954), pp. 30–53.
24. François Furet, "Quantitative Methods in History," in Jacques Le Goff and Pierre Nora (eds.), *Constructing the Past: Essays in Historical Methodology* (Cambridge, 1974), pp. 12–27.
25. Charles A. Beard, "Written History as an Act of Faith," *The American Historical Review*, Vol. 39, No. 2 (January 1934), pp. 219–31.
26. Hayden White, *The Content of the Form: Narrative Discourse and Historical Representation* (Baltimore, 1987).
27. Anita Shapira, "Politics and Collective Memory: The Debate over the 'New Historians' in Israel," *History & Memory*, Vol. 7, No. 1 (Spring/Summer 1995), pp. 10–11.
28. Simha Flapan, *The Birth of Israel: Myth and Realities* (London, 1987); Avi Shlaim, *Collusion across the Jordan: King Abdullah, the Zionist Movement, and the Partition of Palestine* (Oxford, 1988), and *The Politics of Partition* (Oxford, 1990); Ilan Pappé, *Britain and the Arab–Israeli Conflict, 1948–1951* (New York, 1988); and Benny Morris, *The Birth of the Palestinian Refugee Problem, 1947–1949* (Cambridge, 1987).
29. Ilan Pappé, *The Making of the Arab–Israeli Conflict, 1947–1951* (London, 1994); and Avi Shlaim, *The Iron Wall: Israel and the Arab World* (London, 2000).
30. Shapira, "Politics and Collective Memory," p. 12.
31. Cf. Benny Morris, "The Eel and History: A Reply to Shabtai Teveth," *Tikkun*, Vol. 5, No. 1 (1990), pp. 19–22 and 79–86.
32. Shabtai Teveth, "The Palestinian Refugee Problem and Its Origin," *Middle Eastern Studies*, Vol. 26, No. 2 (1990), pp. 214–49; and Efraim Karsh, *Fabricating Israeli History: The "New Historians"* (London, 1997).
33. See Ilan Pappé, "Israeli Perceptions of the Refugee Question," in Naseer Hasan Aruri (ed.), *Palestinian Refugees: The Right of Return* (London, 2001), pp. 71–6.
34. Yehoshua Porath, *The Emergence of the Palestinian-Arab National Movement, 1918–1929* (London, 1974), and *The Palestinian Arab National Movement: From Riots to Rebellion, 1929–1939* (London, 1977); Avraham Sela, "She'elat Eretz Yisrael ba-maarekhet ha-bein-aravit, 1945–1948" (The Palestine Issue in the Inter-Arab State System, 1945–1948) (Ph.D diss., Hebrew University, Jerusalem, 1987); Haim Levenberg, *Military Preparations of the Arab Community in Palestine, 1945–1948* (London, 1993); and Joseph Nevo, "The Arabs of Palestine, 1947–1948: Military and Political Activity," *Middle Eastern Studies*, Vol. 23 (1987), pp. 3–38.
35. For an up-to-date survey of Arab narratives of the war, see Eugene L. Rogan and Avi Shlaim (eds.), *The War for Palestine: Reviewing the History of 1948* (Cambridge, 2001).
36. Nur Masalha, *Expulsion of the Palestinians* (Washington, 1993); Walid Khalidi, *All that Remains: The Palestinian Villages Occupied and Depopulated by Israel in 1948* (Washington, 1992); and Rashid Khalidi, *Palestinian Identity: The Construction of Modern National Consciousness* (Chicago, 1996).
37. Edward Said, *Orientalism* (New York, 1978); On Said's Palestinian identity cf. Justus Reid

ZIONIST AND ISRAELI HISTORY IN ISRAELI UNIVERSITIES   153

Weiner, "'My Beautiful Old House' and Other Fabrications of Edward Said," *Commentary*, 16 September 1999. The reactions of Said and his admirers to this article have been furious and aggressive but did not contradict convincingly any of the points made by the author.. Alon Confino's review, "Remembering Talbiyah: On Edward Said's *Out of Place*," *Israel Studies*, Vol. 5, No. 2 (2000), pp. 190–8, is indeed more polite and sophisticated but he, too, does not refute Weiner's facts and focuses mainly on the psychological insight and aesthetic or literary merits of Said's personal narrative. Confino accuses Weiner of ignoring Said's subjective feelings of exile and dispossession, and reiterates that if Said says such and such he must be right — an irrelevant and invalid historiographic argument.

38 Uri Ram, "The Colonization Perspective in Israeli Sociology," in Ilan Pappé (ed.), *The Israel/Palestine Question* (London and New York, 1999), pp. 55–80, and Gershon Shafir, "Zionism and Colonialism: A Comparative Approach," in ibid., pp. 83–96.

39 Porath, *The Emergence of the Palestinian-Arab National Movement*, pp. 39–63; Khalidi, *Palestinian Identity*, pp. 96–111.

40 Recently, Derek Penslar has tried an interesting comparison between Zionism and Indian and other movements of national awakening in Asia. See his article in this volume, "Zionism, Colonialism and Postcolonialism," pp. 84–98. In my opinion, however, the comparison is hardly valid. While in Asia a meeting between two separate societies took place, the Jews of Europe were part of European society and separated from it for different reasons.

41 An undated list (probably from 1944 or 1945) of more than 50 Palestinian notables who sold land to Jews, including the offices the sellers held and the location of the sold parcels, Central Zionist Archives (CZA), S 25/3472.

42 Nachman Tal, "Tmurot bi-mediniyut ha-bitahon klapei ha-mi'ut ha-aravi, 1948–1967" (Security Considerations in Shaping Israel's Policy towards Its Arab Minority, 1948–1967) (Ph.D. diss., University of Haifa, 2001), pp. 60–5.

43 Two random examples are Lev Grinberg's course in the framework of Ben-Gurion University's program of Israel Studies "Nationality, Ethnicity and Racism: The Case of Israel," and his colleague David Newman's course "Space and Politics in Israel and in the [Occupied] Territories."

44 Yosef Grodzinsky, *Homer enoshi tov: Yehudim mul tziyonim* (Good Human Material: Jews versus Zionists) (Or Yehuda, 1998).

45 Idith Zertal, *From Catastrophe to Power: Holocaust Survivors and the Emergence of Israel* (Berkeley, 1998).

46 Daniel J. Goldhagen, *Hitler's Willing Executioners: Ordinary Germans and the Holocaust* (New York, 1996).

47 Interview with Zimmerman in the *Yediot Aharonot* network of local papers, 28 April 1995.

48 Pappé, *The Making of the Arab–Israeli Conflict*, pp. 12–13, and his interview with Yona Hadari in *Yediot Aharonot*, 27 August 1993.

49 Ilan Gur-Zeev, "The Morality of Acknowledging/Not-Acknowledging the Other's Holocaust/Genocide", *Journal of Moral Education*, Vol. 27, No. 2 (1998), pp. 161–77, and *Filosofiyah, politikah ve-hinukh be-Yisrael* (Philosophy, Politics and Education in Israel) (Haifa, 1999), pp. 79–98.

50 Ibid. pp. 99–123.

51 Uri Ram (ed.), *Ha-hevrah ha-yisre'elit: Hebetim bikortiim* (Israeli Society: Critical Aspects) (Tel Aviv, 1993); Uri Ben-Eliezer, *Derekh ha-kavenet: Yetzirato shel militarizm yisre'eli, 1936–1956* (Through the Rear-Sight: The Creation of Israeli Militarism, 1936–1956) (Tel Aviv, 1995).

52 Cf. Dvora Hacohen, *Olim be-se'arah: Ha-aliyah ha-gdolah u-klitatah be-Yisre'el, 1948–1953* (Immigrants in a Storm: The Great Immigration and Its Absorption in Israel, 1948–1953) (Jerusalem, 1994); Zvi Zameret, *Idan kur ha-hitukh* (The Era of the Melting Pot) (Sde Boker, 1993), and *Al gesher tzar: Itzuv maarekhet ha-hinukh bi-yemei ha-aliyah ha-hamonit* (On a Narrow Bridge: Shaping the Education System during the Days of the Mass Immigration) (Sde Boker, 1997); Hannah Yablonka, *Ahim zarim: Nitzolei ha-shoah be-Yisrael, 1948–1952* (Estranged Brothers: The Holocaust Survivors in Israel, 1948–1952 (Jerusalem, 1994).

53 For a critical analysis of the issue cf. Yoram Hazony, "Al ha-mahapekhah ha-shketah be-ma'arekhet ha-hinukh" (On the Quiet Revolution in the Educational System), *Tkhelet*, No. 10 (2001), pp. 41–64.

54 Daniel Gutwein, "Historiografiyah hadashah o hafratat ha-zikaron" (New Historiography or the Privatization of Memory), in Weitz (ed.), *Bein hazon le-reviziyah*, pp. 311–43. See also his article in this volume, "Left and Right Post-Zionism and the Privatization of Israeli Collective Memory," pp. 9–42.

55 Cf. Yoav Gelber, "Eduyot be'al peh ke-makor histori" (Oral Testimonies as a Historical Source), *Dapim le-heker ha-shoah ve-ha-mered*, Vol. 7 (1987), pp. 165–71; Zvi Dror, "Ha-ed veha-edut" (The Witness and the Testimony), ibid., pp. 173–92; Stephen E. Everett, *Oral History: Techniques and Procedures*, Washington 1992 (also on the website: www.army.mil/cmh-pg/books/oral.htm).

56 Asher Koriat, Morris Goldsmith and Einat Pansky, "Toward a Psychology of Memory Accuracy," *Annual Review of Psychology*, Vol. 51 (2000), pp. 481–537; Elizabeth F. Loftus, *Eyewitness Testimony* (London, 1979); and Elizabeth Loftus and Kathline Ketcham, *The Myth of Repressed Memory* (New York, 1994).

57 For a very nice fictitious illustration of micro-history based on oral memories, see Alexandar Hemon's short story "Exchange of Pleasant Words," in idem, *The Question of Bruno* (London, 2000), pp. 95–116. For a comprehensive and illustrative discussion of the essence of oral history in the eyes of its devoted practitioners, cf. Alessandro Portelli, *The Battle of Valle Giulia: Oral History and the Art of Dialogue* (Madison, 1997). For the treatment of oral history in the framework of folklore studies, cf. in particular Barbara Allen and William L. Montell, *From Memory to History* (Nashville, 1981), pp. 67–87.

58 Cf. Yael Zerubavel, *Recovered Roots: Collective Memory and the Making of Israel* (Chicago, 1995); and Nurith Gertz, *Myths in Israeli Culture: Captives of a Dream* (London, 2000).

59 For example: Ilanah Zur's *Altalena* (1995) and Dan Wolman's documentaries on Reuven Shiloah (1996), Yoland Harmer (1998), and Israeli Intelligence in the War of Independence (1999).

60 The reader is invited to surf the historical sites listed in the Ynet website and judge for him/herself.

61 Shabtai Teveth, *Kalaban* (Tel Aviv, 1992); Eyal Kafkafi, *Lavon: Anti-mashiah* (Lavon: Anti-messiah) (Tel Aviv, 1998).

62 Emmanuel Gluska, "Ha-derekh le-milhemet sheshet ha-yamim: Ha-pikud ha-tzva'i veha-hanhagah ha-medinit shel Yisrael lenokhah ba'ayot ha-bitahon, 1963–1967" (The Road to the Six Day War: Israel's Army Command and Political Leadership in face of the Security Problems, 1963–1967) (Ph.D. diss., Hebrew University, Jerusalem, 2000); Uri Bar Yosef, *Ha-tzofeh she-nirdam* (The Watchman Who Fell Asleep) (Tel Aviv, 2001).

63 For a forerunner of the anticipated debate on Israel's later political and military history and its obvious bias and shortcomings, see Benny Morris, *Righteous Victims: A History of the Zionist–Arab Conflict, 1881–1999* (New York, 1999), and Shlaim, *The Iron Wall*, and Anita Shapira's review essay of these books, "The Past Is Not a Foreign Country," *New Republic*, 29 November 1999, pp. 26–36.

History Textbooks and the Limits of Israeli Consciousness

Amnon Raz-Krakotzkin

School Curricula and Cultural Criticism

History in general, and the study of history in schools in particular, has been pivotal to the formation of modern national identities and the shaping of national memory and traditions. The past has played a determining role in the construction of the self-perception of the present and the definition of its boundaries and goals. The school curriculum constitutes one of the primary frameworks wherein the conception of a national history is relayed and assimilated, and the values and images attributed to the nation are expressed. History curricula and textbooks can be seen as mediating between "collective memory" and academic historiography, demonstrating just how problematic the attempt to distinguish between them is.[1] On the one hand, the aim of school curricula is to impart students with agreed-upon and up-to-date academic knowledge. However, they also play an important role in the transmission of national ideals and the shaping of national self-perception. The matriculation examination serves as a kind of rite of passage, wherein the student is expected to demonstrate his/her ability to memorize and repeat, illustrating that they have internalized themes in accordance with the directives of the Ministry of Education. The history curriculum should be examined alongside additional frameworks that contour memory, be they other school subjects such as Bible, literature, civics or "homeland" studies, or school ceremonies and field trips (subjects of growing discussion).[2] In some respects, the school curriculum is the last bastion of a decisive, monotonous voice that relays the "correct" version of the past, the framework wherein the "official" or "agreed" version is formulated.

As such, history curricula and textbooks can serve as a relatively accurate framework for the examination of the basic tenets that inform a cultural consciousness. Moreover, they can illuminate the concrete repercussions that certain conceptions of the past have on the boundaries of political, social and cultural discourses in the present, particularly with regard to matriculation exams — the setting wherein normative cultural knowledge is defined and conveyed. The curriculum can be considered an expression of the cultural consensus, of the "official" historical conception, at least at a given point in time.

Recent changes in the history curriculum in Israeli schools, and the publication of new high school textbooks, have triggered extensive public debate. Proponents and opponents alike have presented these revisions as evidence of a radical shift in the Israeli historical consciousness. On the one hand, these texts have been lauded for expressing a would-be new Israeli consciousness reflective of a courageous contention with the past. On the other hand, they have been assailed for reflecting a retreat from fundamental Zionist values and myths, and embracing so-called "post-Zionist" values instead. This public debate led to the eventual banning of one of the texts, authored by Danny Yaakobi — the only one published by the Ministry of Education denounced for deflating the fundamental myths of Zionism. On similar grounds, a book authored by Eyal Naveh also came under public attack.[3]

Indeed, in some ways these books attest to interesting changes in the Israeli consciousness, and to a new sensitivity towards issues that can no longer be suppressed and ignored. Nonetheless, the excitement, as well as the apprehension and resistance, that accompanied the publication of these books were both exaggerated and misleading. As I will attempt to demonstrate in this article with regard to central aspects of Zionist historical consciousness and self-perception, the new curriculum maintains the same discursive boundaries. Moreover, the gratification that accompanied the reception of the new curriculum, and its presentation as "objective" and "balanced," impede examination of central issues concerning the history and principles of Zionism and Israeli culture.

It must be stressed that my criticism is not directed at those responsible for designing the curriculum, nor at the authors of the textbooks. They express a serious and sensitive attempt to address controversial issues and to present new historical approaches. In many respects, the books intended for upper-division high school students[4] as well as those designed for middle school students, are commendable. Generally speaking, they are clear, interesting, and include spectacular pictures. Not only do some chapters reflect fresh attitudes towards the Israeli–Palestinian conflict,[5] they also provide the basis for a comprehensive discussion of both the past and the present. It is precisely the historical sensitivity that they display that invites pointed, rather than sweeping, critical discussion. It is not the curriculum and textbooks themselves that I want to investigate here but the assumptions that define the entire Israeli discourse. Nor is my criticism founded on an alternative narrative, a supposedly objective version in the face of another. The historical conception presented by the educational system should be examined with the purpose of revealing and illuminating fundamental cultural questions. However, we should distinguish between the much-needed historical and cultural-political discussion and the textbook debate. It is neither justifiable nor appropriate to transfer this debate to the students, when public debate on these matters remains so barren, and the issues under discussion are of such acute importance.

These issues are especially important in light of the fact that the formulation of the new curriculum, like its critique, is taking place at a time when the Israeli consciousness is in real crisis, a crisis expressed by multiple, heterogeneous reactions to the dominant narrative and the proliferation of alternative historic conceptions on many levels and from different, sometimes opposing, directions. Indeed, in Israel today there is no agreed-upon historic conception with regard to central matters, and at least since the advent of the Palestinian uprising in October 2000, the main factor that binds Israeli Jews together is their opposition to the Palestinians. In the period preceding this stage, the fissures between different groups within Israeli-Jewish society, on religious, cultural and ethnic grounds, received sharp expressions, testifying to the crisis of Israeli consciousness. Academic and nonacademic criticism has served to expose various aspects of the denial upon which the Zionist historical conception is based, but to date this criticism has failed to lead to any satisfactory alternative position with regard to central issues, namely the history of the Israeli–Palestinian conflict and the diverse histories/experiences of the Jews. A number of repressed and silenced voices have worked their way into the dominant culture, from competing directions, though none has yet led to the formation of an alternative framework.

The current curricular controversy stems, among other things, from this confusion. It is the product of a sincere and serious attempt to contend with critical approaches and attests to sensitivity to social and political criticism. But in the present state of affairs, it does not and cannot provide a coherent alternative framework for the simple reason that such a framework does not exist. In such a reality, the very formulation of a history curriculum is problematic, and recognizing this should be our point of departure. The critical examination of history textbooks is an attempt to contribute to this discussion. On these grounds, the critical approach I will present here should be seen as a participation in the process, and not as written from an external position. Sharp critiques, like that of Yoram Hazony, expressed a desire to return uncritically to what seems to them as the essence of Zionism. This is obviously an ideological position that failed to offer an alternative historical narrative. Its implicit demand is to ignore any critical approach. It looks like a hysterical response (temporally successful) that substitutes for serious discussion. This dogmatism prevents the discussion of some serious and productive remarks this criticism includes.[6]

The first problem that warrants mention in the current context is the fact that history studies still rely on the memorization of a single version, even if it is a relatively "updated" one. More than teaching history as a discipline, and studying and debating questions, history studies as we know them encourage the assimilation of specific historical perspectives presented as objective. On these grounds, the question as to whether the current version seems more or less "correct" than the version that preceded it is irrelevant. As long as this remains the paradigm for teaching history, it will be impossible to question basic historical assumptions. In this sense, the outrage of rightist critics was justified when, much to their surprise, they discovered the decision to make curricular changes that, as far as they were concerned, were fundamental, without first conducting public discussion on the matter, particularly when some of the issues at stake are of obvious contemporary significance. The only way to resolve this predicament in the school curriculum is by exposing students to historiographic arguments that present them with various approaches and positions.

The aims of the new curriculum are broader than the facets I discuss here. At its core, the new curriculum is an attempt to fuse "general history" with "Jewish history." In itself an important approach, this endeavor warrants a discussion all its own. However, in this article, I will limit myself to an examination of those issues that relate directly to Zionist history and make up the crux of the debate. Needless to say, this is an incomplete discussion whose purpose, more than anything, is to raise questions rather than to offer solutions.

The History of Zionism and the History of the Land

One of the more striking aspects of the Israeli history curriculum on all grade levels is the conspicuous absence of the history of the land. The land — defined as a homeland — has no apparent history of its own in Israeli textbooks. Its annals, from the destruction of the Second Temple to the onset of Zionist settlement are ignored, especially in upper-division high school courses. The civilizations it nurtured, as well as its affinity to the region and its cultures, are by and large eliminated from the Israeli student's consciousness. In the lower grades, the Israeli student encounters the Crusaders briefly, but mostly in the chapters having to do with Europe rather than those about the land.[7]

This is a central aspect of Zionist consciousness that distinguishes it from other national consciousnesses (though to a certain extent it is reminiscent of other colonial-national phenomena in the Americas, southern Africa and Australia). If in other contexts molding a national consciousness was premised on the shared writing of the history of the homeland as a platform for defining the collective, here national consciousness was premised on the active erasure of the history of Palestine. True, in other national contexts, "writing the nation" and contouring a homogenous national history also entailed the negation or substitution of local traditions. However, in the Zionist context, writing Jewish history as a national-territorial history was based on the negation of the country itself — Palestine/*Eretz Yisrael* — as a geographical-historical entity that includes various histories at different stages of its history. Thus, the land was rendered a mythic depiction, and its history the history of messianic-theological images. The deletion of its history was imperative for the fabrication of "historical continuity" from biblical times through the period of the Second Temple (a tenth grade pre-matriculation requirement) to the present. In this history, the land is not a historical-territorial entity, rather it is an image based on the scriptures and what is defined as the yearning of generations for Zion. This is true both for the secular public educational system and the religious public educational system.[8]

It turns out that the principle behind the incorporation of Jewish history into "general history" was forgotten when it came to Palestine/*Eretz Yisrael*. The country defined as the Jewish homeland (in modern national terms) has no history of its own, and its definition as such depends on the negation of its past. This is not to say that the notion of "a history of Palestine" is a clear concept, and that beneath the mythical conception lies another "correct" or "real" history, that should be taught instead. The history of *Eretz Yisrael*/Palestine is complex, and requires separate historical and cultural examination. Moreover, it is impossible to detach the study of the history of the land from the very images attributed to it by various peoples and faiths. In this respect, the history of the land could serve as a basis for the study of different traditions and cultures. However, as stated before, the present framework is premised on the denial of this complexity.

Zionist Settlement and the History of the Conflict

The negation of the history of the land receives its most blatant expression in the representation of the history of the land throughout the twentieth century — the period of Zionist migration and colonization. The new curriculum does not ignore the Arab presence altogether, yet it nonetheless preserves the image of an "empty land" settled by the Zionist movement. This distorted image is the outcome of a superficial separation between the discussion of the history of Zionist settlement and the discussion of the Israeli–Palestinian conflict, as though these issues were indeed separable. Jewish settlement is described as though it transpired in the mythical image of the land rather than the land itself, ignoring crucial aspects of its concrete reality: its population, their culture and their aspirations. The history of the land begins outside the country — with the fate of the Jews in Europe — with no regard whatsoever for the inhabitants of the country, including its Jewish inhabitants.

In order to avoid any misunderstanding, it is not that the Arab inhabitants of the country receive no mention in the curriculum. As in earlier texts, the revised books devote a number of pages to the development of the Arab national movement. But the purpose of these accounts is to preface the difficulties faced by the Zionist enterprise. There is some truth to the position that rejects the claim that the Zionist settlers ignored the native population of the land. However, it appears that the present curriculum continues to preserve the image of "a land without a people for a people without a land." The conflict and Palestinian struggle against the British Mandate and Jewish immigration are described as external, as a manifestation of inexplicable evil, as if they bear no relation to the process of colonization itself.

Nothing illustrates this point better than the fact that the textbooks do not feature a single map of the country during the period of Zionist colonization that includes all of the settlements existent at that time: the maps present only Jewish settlements (and at best mixed Arab-Jewish cities), as if at the time of colonization there were no Palestinian towns and villages, no people with desires, fears, conflicts and problems. These elements are excluded from the Israeli student's consciousness, just as they are absent from the Israeli consciousness in general. Thus, those pages dedicated to the (usually "balanced") description of the Arab national movement perpetuate the non-discussion of the social and cultural reality (in stark contrast to the important new chapters dedicated to the social and cultural development of the *Yishuv* — which ought to be applauded). The actual emptying of the land in 1948 and immediately following the establishment of the State of Israel entailed the expulsion — from the imagination as well — of a preexisting entity.

In the accepted narrative of Zionist settlement, as it appears in the textbooks, the very existence of the Palestinians is first acknowledged in the context of the struggle for the "conquest of labor" waged by Second *Aliyah* immigrants. In other words, the Arabs are referenced in light of the opposition of young, idealistic immigrants to their employment in the colonies (*moshavot*). In fact, the Arabs are not the subject here, but the objects through which the First *Aliyah* and the Second *Aliyah* are contrasted. As for the fate of the banned Arab laborers, they receive no mention, just as their plight was of no concern to the Socialist Zionist settlers.[9] While many of the demonizing descriptions of Arabs found in previous textbooks have been removed, the new texts keep the Arabs trapped in an ahistorical framework that precludes the possibility of historical understanding.

It should be clarified that the purpose of this commentary is not to denigrate the image of the Zionist settler by deflating myths or belittling heroes. There are doubtless many other sides to these historical actors and their deeds, which warrant further treatment in the curriculum. Generally speaking, the use-value of myth deflation strikes me as limited. It is not the settlers who are under scrutiny so much as our own contemporary consciousness which, by attempting to uphold the myth, reinforces the suppression of the context in which they were active and the implications of their ideas. Awareness of the consequences of their actions need not nullify noteworthy aspects of their activity. Rather, as will be emphasized further on, awareness should mean taking responsibility for the entirety of their deeds.

The fundamental point that must form the basis for any historical understanding is that the history of the Jews and the history of the Arabs in the twentieth century are not two separate histories, but one integral — albeit not identical — history. Each of the two collectives has had its own autonomous trajectory, and the circumstances that informed the development of each national identity should be examined on its own. However, it is impossible to write the history of the Jews whilst ignoring the Palestinians, and vice versa.

Of course, any adequate historical narrative of Zionist settlement must address the specific context wherein Zionism evolved: the crisis of Jewish existence in Europe and the transformation of anti-Semitism into a major facet of European consciousness. It seems to me that the different political, social and cultural approaches that grew out of the Zionist context, including non-Zionist Jewish approaches, warrant greater attention. However, the denial that informs the current historical conception must be acknowledged. This is a basic methodological question, which has obvious implications for the definition of Israeli political discourse. Describing the settlement project without describing the settled land negates its context — the basic constituent of modern historiography.

The 1948 War, the Establishment of the State of Israel, and the Palestinian Tragedy

The focal point of the public and historiographic debate over Zionism centers on the events of the 1948 War, Israel's War of Independence, central to which was also the Palestinian Tragedy — the *Nakba*. The official texts in use until recently afforded the Deir Yassin massacre modest mention as an "aberrant" action carried out by a minority group and "exaggerated by Arab propaganda...." The "emptying" of the land of its inhabitants was explained as "flight" in response to the call to do so by Arab leaders. The destruction of the Palestinian entity was not discussed, and the question of the refugees was altogether ignored.

The new textbooks undoubtedly express a new attitude. They address the refugee question and acknowledge the partial transfer of Arabs during the war.[10] However, this change clarifies the limits of the historiographical revision. A case in point is the textbook authored by Eyal Naveh and Eli Barnavi. This book includes a brief presentation of the refugee problem following a detailed description of the different stages of the war (though, again, divorced from the description of the actual battles). The authors then discuss the two existent explanations for the refugee problem: the Israeli version, which posits that it was Arab propaganda that encouraged the Arabs to temporarily flee their homeland, and the Arab version, which posits that the dispossession of the Arab population from its land and its subsequent expulsion were inherent to the Zionist plan. The authors reject both explanations, and determine instead that the "flight" (*sic*) was the result of war. According to this version, the war was caused by the Arab refusal to accept partition, though they do concede that in some locations Arabs were faced with "a local policy of intentional expulsion." A similar approach to this question can be found in other texts.[11]

This new version deserves serious attention. Its description of events coincides with the approach adopted by many Israeli circles in response to the publication of critical historical research and the "new history" polemic it has triggered.[12] If in the past expulsion was vehemently denied, today there is some recognition of the facts. However, what is most interesting is that the revised descriptions are accompanied by a refusal to assume historical responsibility. Instead, responsibility is thrust on the Palestinians for not accepting the partition plan and choosing war instead. In light of this, it is not surprising that the public tempest was triggered not by the outing of the fact of expulsion *per se* but by the challenge this outing posed to the version wherein the war was presented as a struggle between the few and the many, and the tacit acknowledgment that the external assistance (for example, from the Communist bloc) obtained by the Jewish forces was pivotal to determining the war's outcome.

The problem with reading this shift as fundamental is that fundamental questions are then neglected and the discussion of sensitive issues is avoided. The attempt to frame the new version as "objective" is misleading and even dangerous as its claim to be an alternative to two rejected versions strengthens its authoritative status. The fate of the Palestinians, as well as their consciousness, remains external to the historical debate. The need to recognize the expulsion has begot a new version that affirms the enlightened self-perception of the authors and places responsibility squarely on the victims. In both versions the question of the refugees is severed from the discussion of the establishment of the State of Israel.

The contention that the Palestinian rejection of partition triggered the war is certainly not baseless, though it is simplistic and fails to provide satisfactory historical understanding. Especially in light of the fact that the background to the refusal, like the Palestinian debate that took place (and continues) around this question, receives no mention. The version implicitly assumes that had the Palestinians accepted partition, a Palestinian state would have been established along the lines of the 1947 plan, and beside it a Jewish state whose population would have been comprised of almost 50 percent non-Jews severed by a border from their brethren. Such a reality would have brought about the establishment of an entirely different Jewish state or, conversely, resulted in the eventual expulsion of the Arabs (what happened in any event), especially considering the fact that the state as we know it was established upon the lands and homes of the expelled and by way of the adamant refusal to enable their return — aspects conspicuously missing from the "balanced" version.

The contention that the sole cause for the emptying (to use the most neutral term available) of the country was the war is far from accurate and ignores central facets of both the war and the policies enacted in its wake. The massacres (the only massacre that receives mention is the Deir Yassin massacre so as to emphasize the differences between the Haganah and the Etzel) might be attributable to the state of war, but not the expulsion nor the inducement to flee. However, expulsion continued long after the war ended and the state was established (not to mention continued confiscation of Arab lands). The textbooks do not mention Israel's absolute unwillingness to enable the refugees to return, despite explicit United Nations resolutions to that effect. It is common knowledge that this is also the case with regard to refugees known to have cooperated with the Israeli forces, like the residents of Iqrith and Bir'im. In any event, historically speaking, the state that was established, and its history, are inseparable from the question of the refugees.

The question is not whether or not the "transfer" of the population was premeditated, as a number of historians have argued. The issue at hand is that one cannot speak of establishing the state in its current form without addressing expulsion, refugees and the vehement Israeli denial of their right to return. The fundamental historical question precedes the question: did the refugees flee or were they expelled? Even were we to accept the Israeli version, the Palestinian tragedy remains just that, regardless of whether they fled their homes in the heat of battle or whether they were forcibly expelled from their lands. Either way, their dispossession is integral to the establishment of the State of Israel. Such an understanding need not lead to one political conclusion or another but it should trigger much-needed discussion on our present reality.

In this context, it is important to note that the partition plan itself, which is presented as the source of legitimacy for the state and informs the historical approach to the topic, is not taught in the schools. There is no Hebrew translation of the UN partition plan. The plan upon which the establishment of the state is premised is presented as the plan to establish the State of Israel, not as a plan to establish two equal states.

Once again, it must be emphasized that one cannot expect the textbooks to initiate this discussion. Particularly when it is clear that we are not dealing with mere historical questions, but rather questions that have acute political ramifications in the present. This has been, in my view, the shortcoming of the ongoing historical debate in Israel over the last 15 years. The working assumption, particularly following the Oslo Accords (the period when this debate came to a head), has been that the refugee question is not a contemporary one but rather a historical one. Despite the fact that the Oslo Accords left this question for the final status negotiations, debate and discussion have revolved around the critique of Zionism, not the fate of the refugees. Thus, paradoxically, it was critical historiography that reinforced the preoccupation with Zionism and kept the refugees forgotten. Critical discussion of Zionism is important and necessary. But the Palestinian victims, yet again, remain outside its scope. Though the "new historians" were accused of being political, in fact the academization of the discussion is associated with its depoliticization, namely the distinction between the discussion of the past and the discussion of the present. Meanwhile, in the context of the failure of the Israeli–Palestinian peace talks, it has become increasingly clear that the question of the refugees is not a question of the past but of the future.

In these circumstances, it is, of course, impossible to transfer the discussion of these existential questions into school textbooks. These questions are complex and open, and their general discussion heretofore was meant to demonstrate how the attempt to present the new consciousness as a meaningful contention with the past is both limited and dangerous, and how the very distinction between "old" and "new" historiography is insufficient. Of course, it is possible to present different historical approaches: those of the Jews and those of the Arabs, those of "conservative" historians and those of "progressive" historians, and to illustrate the problems this subject entails. Textbooks are certainly not the first place where we should expect to find a solution, though their content illustrates the urgent need for a complex discussion of the issues.

At issue is historical understanding, not condemnation or delegitimization of Zionism. Condemnation and negation are historically meaningless, and stand in opposition to the principle of responsibility I try to address here. Nor is it my intention to tarnish the image of the 1948 fighters. On the contrary, I believe that the approach I am arguing for makes room for their recollections as well — for difficult memories that have been suppressed for years. Beyond the importance of their subjective take on the war, it should be taken into account that they also bear the memories of mass exodus, death and dispossession. For many, these memories are unbearable and their suppression problematic.

Understanding Israeli sensitivity in the face of this question, and the anxiety it raises, is essential. The commotion stirred by Yaakobi's book for including photographs of Palestinian refugees teaches us much about Israeli anxiety. Indeed, it is difficult to figure what exactly Israeli students should make of photographs of refugees in today's political and cultural climate. But we should remember that denial only reinforces Israeli society's existential dread, and impedes the development of a pragmatic solution that takes into consideration the national rights of the Jewish collectivity and the historical background of its creation. The refugee question is no doubt complicated and has no simple answer. Yet, the political discussion and the historical discussion are intertwined, though not identical. Even if the anxiety is understandable, it does not justify a refusal to take responsibility — an act with obvious political repercussions. Both on the political and on the historiographic levels, Israeli discourse is characterized by the unwillingness to assume responsibility for the refugee problem. Accountability is understood as signifying a political solution that entails the full implementation of the right of return in total disregard for the reality created on the ground over the past 50 years. As long as these issues are ignored, anxiety will continue to dominate Israeli culture.

The principle of responsibility was central to Zionist ideology and the desire to transform the Jews into a sovereign nation. In this respect, assuming responsibility means recognizing that the fate of the refugees — the inhabitants of the country — is inseparable from Zionist history. Whether they fled or were expelled, even if they do bear some responsibility, it still falls within the domain of responsibility that must be claimed by the historian of Zionism. The intention is neither to blame nor to condemn but to construct the historical foundation that will enable us to contend with these very sensitive and politically complex historical questions. Assuming responsibility does not mean negating Jewish existence: it is a precursor to agreement over the Jewish collective's rights and boundaries. Precisely the Zionist principle of "a return to history" mandates the acknowledgment of history and its consequences. Again, the idea is not judicial responsibility but historical responsibility to facilitate discussion on the resolution of this problem — a problem that concerns both peoples.

Meanwhile, it is the history textbooks that demonstrate the limits of Israeli consciousness, though it is obvious why in the present reality it is impossible to write an all-encompassing narrative. The textbooks reveal that it is no longer practicable to maintain a state of denial, but their convoluted formulations reflect an attempt to reckon with historical knowledge without dealing with the fundamental questions it raises. For such a discussion, a history of events is not satisfactory. The fundamental questions are directed not at the past but at the future. The question is: how can we redefine Jewish existence on the basis of the recognition of Palestinian rights and the aspiration for equality between Jews and Arabs? Collective anxiety stems from the fact that answering this question would require a redefinition of the Israeli consciousness.

Zionist History and Jewish History

Not only the history of the country was denied in Israeli consciousness and school curricula but also the varied histories of the Jews. This is the flip side of the Zionist consciousness as embodied by the concept "negation of exile." Zionist historiography negated the history of the country while also negating the histories of the Jews.[13]

The new curriculum has added a few chapters on Jews in the modern world, but the number of class hours dedicated to this subject remains paltry. The fundamental questions that informed Jewish discourses across time and place are not raised, making it impossible to locate Zionism in a wider historical context. While some Jewish alternatives to Zionism, such as the Bund, are mentioned in the new literature, they are not discussed in such a way as to clarify the questions and circumstances that brought about their development. In particular, there is no room made for Orthodox Judaism, and the currents within it. History is written, as one might expect, from a secular Zionist perspective predicated on the assumption that it is history's ultimate conclusion.

This approach was reinstituted in 1991, during the previous reform in the history curriculum. Until 1991, matriculation requirements included a unit on Jews in the pre-Zionist era. Thus, the students were obliged to study, even if in a shallow manner, central aspects of premodern and modern Jewish history. Indeed, one might express reservations about the way this subject was taught, but certainly the removal of this subject from the Israeli high school curriculum altogether raises greater reservations. This decision (made when, of all people, the late Zevulun Hammer of the National Religious Party served as the Minister of Education) meant that Jewish existence in the "diasporic period" was no longer discussed in the upper grades, thereby perpetuating the image of exilic Jewry as nothing but a passive response to evil, and the total identification of Judaism with Zionism. The Zionist educational system, which sees itself as imparting Jewish history, reinforces the negation of that very history. The secular graduate of an Israeli high school lacks basic knowledge of Jewish literature and key elements of the various Jewish histories. S/he also knows little about the crises of modern Jewish existence, both in Europe and beyond, to say nothing of the different approaches that developed in response to these crises.

This framework, which creates a continuum between the ancient past and the present whilst ignoring Jewish exilic history, also draws a line from the Holocaust to the establishment of the state, impeding any constructive criticism of present definitions. Thus, the Holocaust becomes the distillation of history, and Zionism its ultimate conclusion. Moreover, while the Holocaust is afforded in-depth treatment (as well it should be), no satisfactory room is made for the annihilated themselves — for the Jewish experiences that preceded annihilation. The focus continues to be on the relationship between the Holocaust and the need for Jewish sovereignty. Of course, this issue deserves greater discussion which cannot be elaborated here.

Jewish History and Mizrahi History

While all Jewish histories are somewhat diminished, this tendency is especially evident when it comes to Jews from Muslim countries, demonstrating the Orientalist dimension of Zionist Israeli national identity — a dimension expressed through the perception of "general history" as applicable particularly to the history of Europe and the West. Indeed, in the new curriculum a number of chapters have been added that address Arab nationalism and political events in Arab states, but the term "history" remains attributable by and large to the West. The desire to define Israel as part of the West and in opposition to the Arab world has resulted in the erasure of the histories and traditions of Jews from Muslim countries.

Growing criticism on the representation of *Mizrahi* Jews in the curriculum has led to curricular changes, but more than anything these curricular adjustments reflect the essence of the revision itself: more than a concerted effort to address the complex histories of *Mizrahi* Jews, these changes are the fulfillment of an obligation to respond to public criticism. A number of years ago the artist Meir Gal produced a piece titled "Nine out of Four Hundred" — a photograph in which he holds up the few pages devoted to the history of *Mizrahi* Jews in the textbook *Toldot am Yisrael* (The History of the Jewish People) by Shimshon Kirshenbaum.[14] In so doing, he illustrated the prevalent attitude towards *Mizrahi* Jews in Israeli culture as a group without a history of its own, as well as the dominant conception of Jewish history as Ashkenazi history. This is but one expression of the attitude whereby the integration into Israeli society of Jews from Muslim countries was made conditional upon the negation of their memory, culture and traditions.

Since the publication of Kirshenbaum's book (which is no longer an assigned text), a number of changes have taken place,[15] but the overall picture remains the same. The number of pages devoted to the issue is still negligible, and what has been written may as well have been left unwritten. Even in the new texts, the number of pages is limited (13–15). A book published by the Zalman Shazar Center stands apart in this case, as it includes a number of matter-of-fact chapters on Jews from Muslim countries, written by Haim Saadon. Overall, the marginalization of the subject has been maintained. The only issue afforded elaboration is the participation of *Mizrahi* Jews in the Zionist movement and their subsequent migration to Israel. Other trends among *Mizrahi* Jews, such as their participation in non-Zionist and Arab social and political movements[16] or their migration to other countries, are barely mentioned, unlike trends among American or Soviet Jewries.[17]

Today, the "integration" of the *Mizrahim* into the school curriculum still requires melding their histories in the Arab world into the historical narrative of the largely European Zionist movement, without even exploring what distinguishes Zionism in an Arab context from Zionism in a European context. *Mizrahi* Jews remain stripped of their Arabic culture, the culture wherein they defined their Jewishness.[18] In contrast to the elaboration of European Jewry, which includes "portraits" — short pieces on prominent figures — when it comes to *Mizrahi* Jews even the new textbooks do not include a single public figure known for his/her activity, be it in a Jewish or a "general" context, as writers, political activists, musicians, etc.

Interestingly, the most prominent question pertaining to *Mizrahi* Jews in the matriculation exams administered to this day can be found, of all places, in the section on the Holocaust. Students are asked to prove that the final solution was directed at world Jewry, not European Jewry alone. In other words, they must detail Hitler's plans to annihilate the Jews of the Muslim world as well. This is a particularly strange question that chooses to focus on those who were not annihilated as a means for constructing a common Jewish history. The road to integration in Israeli society runs through Auschwitz, an illustration of just how problematic Holocaust memorialization is in Israel. While the complex and varied histories and experiences of *Mizrahi* Jews are not discussed, they are subsumed into a history to which they did not belong, to a catastrophe that was not directly theirs, admitted through the symbolism of hypothetical annihilation.

The new texts also devote scant discussion to the question of the absorption of *Mizrahi* Jews in Israel, demonstrating yet again the limitations of the supposed "balanced" approach. Indeed, the new textbooks address the "hardships" of absorption, as part of the repentance ritual implemented by former Prime Minister Ehud Barak. The texts present the insensitivity of the absorbing authorities as a misunderstanding and the result of an attempt to absorb masses in a short period of time with few resources. However, the underlying causes for ethnic discrimination — the subject of extensive critical discussion over the past few years — receive no mention. In Naveh's book, discrimination is presented as a "feeling of deprivation" on the part of *Mizrahi* Jews, explaining that "some felt that the absorption process was unjust and left them in a subordinate position vis-à-vis the veteran population. These feelings of deprivation continue to be expressed to this day."[19] The historian who possesses rational knowledge attributes "feelings" to *Mizrahim*, without addressing the concrete reality that triggered them. The issue is couched in subjective terms, adding insult to the injury suffered by *Mizrahi* Jews who were characterized as having "secondary retardation" in Israeli pedagogical treatises. There is no history here, no mention of the growing critical scholarship on the subject, only a description of "feelings." Naveh and Barnavi do admit in their textbook that the economic gap between *Mizrahi* and Ashkenazi Jews remains as it was, failing, however, to attempt to explain this phenomenon.

A similar trend can be found in Dumke's text. The book quotes a passage from an article by Aryeh Goldblum in the Israeli daily *Ha'aretz* on 22 April 1948, which describes the primitivism of *Mizrahi* Jews. The article from which the passage is extracted is rightly described as a reflection of the "ignorance and lack of understanding of the reality in the countries of origin of the immigrants as well as the needs of the new state." The article is said to have engendered angry responses, and for contrast the author quotes a piece by Efraim Freidman, an immigration agent who described the North African Jews as "rooted" (*shorshiim*). Goldblum's sentiments are described as marginal, an attitude that is "stereotypical and that's all."[20] This, however, is not the case. Goldblum's attitude was anything but marginal, and as a number of studies have established, it is reflective of the institutional treatment afforded *Mizrahi* Jews. Critical research has demonstrated that even had Goldblum's formulation been extreme, it represents the basic Israeli-Zionist attitude towards the *Mizrahim* and continues to direct the educational system in its perpetuation of discrimination.[21] Nor does the book tell the students that since the establishment of the state, not only did the ethnic divide not decrease, it increased considerably. The "ethnic problem" is presented in the past tense, as though it has no bearing on contemporary Israeli culture. Worse yet, pedagogical approaches, such as those advanced by Karl Frankenstein and Reuven Feuerstein that attribute "secondary retardation" to *Mizrahi* Jews, are still taught uncritically in some Israeli educational institutions.[22] Moreover, the presentation of the *Mizrahi* Jews as "rooted" does not constitute a counter-attitude; rather it reflects a blatantly Orientalist perception — the exotification of a people as the preservers of an ancient culture, not as a society with a dynamic, complex, tension-laden, contradictory and fascinating history.

Ultimately, this approach reinforces the very problem it aims to address: Ashkenazi–*Mizrahi* relations in Israel. It does not speak to or for *Mizrahi* Jews, who remain silenced, without any serious representation. It discusses the treatment of *Mizrahim* in Israel with an elusive allusion to *Mizrahi* struggle, whilst ignoring the concrete expressions of *Mizrahi* culture that developed both in response to, and despite, this treatment. It maintains the distinction between "Israel" and "the mass immigration" (*aliyah hamonit*), thereby redefining their exclusion. Certainly, this is not a "brave" confrontation on the part of Israel with its "past," which is also the present wherein these texts are being written. In effect, the treatment of *Mizrahi* Jewish history in the textbooks is indicative of the overall response to the criticism. At the same time, however, there is an attempt to rebuff it and to suppress the conclusions it provokes. Thus, the new school curriculum becomes an exercise in rhetorical acrobatics whose purpose is to preserve the existent consciousness by neutralizing the critical discussion developed over the last few years.

The question of the *Mizrahi* Jews and their histories is, as I have tried to demonstrate elsewhere,[23] critical to an overall principled interrogation of the Zionist conception of history and demonstrative of the Orientalist dimension that informs discussion on other discursive fronts as well. Again, one cannot expect school curricula to become the platform for such a discussion. Here too, my critique does not intend to promote a particular version of things but to clarify the present perspective, with the hope of offering a direction for constructive discussion.

Conclusions

The school curriculum constitutes a framework through which it is possible to examine certain aspects of our historical consciousness. Its obvious advantage as a unit of analysis is that it strives to impart more or less agreed-upon knowledge. However, this article deviated from a strict discussion of the curriculum and posed questions that Israeli society at large must contend with critically. The presentation of recent curricular revisions as fundamental changes impedes such a contention. Acknowledging expulsion is not commensurate with a serious discussion of the conflict, and the addition of five more pages on *Mizrahi* Jews cannot come at the expense of a thorough interrogation of the roots of discrimination in Israel.

At the end of the day, the questions are the same questions that directed the Zionist endeavor from its beginning: the Jewish question and the Palestinian question. The issue is not Jewish existence, as some try to misrepresent it, but rather how to redefine Jewish collectivity and Jewish sovereignty in a way that will account for their suppressive aspects. A brave confrontation with the past is ultimately a confrontation with the crises of the present. The curriculum demonstrates a serious and interesting attempt to broach this challenge; however, it does not provide a satisfactory framework for dealing with cardinal questions. Historical analysis and political discussion are not the same, and history cannot provide by itself satisfactory "solutions." But political discussion cannot rely on distorted or suppressed images of the past. The examination of the curricular reform brings us back to the essential questions the educational system cannot solve.

The different dimensions of suppression raised in this article are commonly discussed separately, as if they were different issues. There are those who concentrate on the Jewish–Palestinian conflict, others who emphasize the question of *Mizrahim*, while another group is occupied with the commemoration of the Holocaust.[24] It seems to me that this organization of knowledge perpetuates present assumptions and impedes comprehensive cultural discussion. Though each of the issues raised in recent academic controversies (including questions not discussed here) deserves a separate discussion, it is only the integration of all these aspects that can lead to a fruitful reevaluation of the past, and new opportunities for the future.

NOTES

1 See Amos Funkenstein, "Collective Memory and Historical Consciousness," *History & Memory*, Vol. 1, No. 1 (1989), pp. 5–26. Republished in idem, *Perceptions of Jewish History* (Berkeley, 1993), pp. 3–20.
2 See, for example, Ruth Firer, *Sokhnim shel ha-lekah shel ha-shoah* (Agents of the Lesson of the Holocaust) (Tel Aviv, 1989); Avner Ben Amos and Hana Bet-El, "Yom ha-zikaron ve-yom ha-shoah be-vatei ha-sefer be-Yisrael" (Ceremonies, Education and History: Holocaust Day and Remembrance Day in Israeli Schools), in Rivka Feldhay and Immanuel Etkes (eds.), *Hinukh ve-historiyah: Hebetim tarbutiim u-politiim* (Education and History: Cultural and Political Contexts) (Jerusalem, 1999), pp. 457–79; Rachel Elboim Dror, "Israeli Education: Changing Perspectives," *Israel Studies*, Vol. 7, No. 1 (2000), pp. 65–95, and *Ha-hinukh ha-ivri be-Eretz Yisrael* (Hebrew Education in the Land of Israel) (Jerusalem, 1986).
3 Danny Yaakobi, *Olam shel tmurot* (A World of Change) (The Department for School Curricula, Ministry of Education, 1999); Eyal Naveh, *Ha-me'ah ha-esrim:* (The Twentieth Century: On the Verge of Tomorrow, History for the Ninth Grade) (Tel Aviv, 1999). For a critique of Yaakobi's book, see Yoram Hazony, "Al ha-mahapekhah ha-shketah be-maarekhet ha-hinukh" (On the Silent Revolution in the Educational System), *Tkhelet*, No. 10 (2001).
4 Eyal Naveh and Eli Barnavi, *Zmanim moderniim* (Modern Times), Part 1, *1870–1920*, Part 2, *1920–2000* (Tel Aviv, 1999); Eliezer Dumke (ed.), *Ha-olam veha-yehudim ba-dorot ha-aharonim* ((The World and the Jews in Recent Generations), Part 1, *1870–1920*, Part 2, *1920–1970* (Jerusalem, 1999); Ketzi'a Avieli-Tabibian, *1870–1970: Idan ha-eimah veha-tikvah* (1870–1970: The Era of Fear and Hope) (Ramat Aviv, 2001).
5 For example, that authored by Motti Golani on the 1948 war in Dumke (ed.), *Ha-olam veha-yehudim*, Part 2, pp. 221–44.
6 Hazony, "Al ha-mahapekhah ha-shketah be-maarekhet ha-hinukh."
7 On the erasure of the country in Zionist historiography and the creation of the myth of a "continuous Jewish presence in Israel" see Yaakov Barnai, *Historiografiyah ve-le'umiyut: Megamot be-heker Eretz Yisrael ve-yishuvah ha-yehudi, 634–1881* (Historiography and Nationalism: Trends in the Study of the Land of Israel and Its Jewish Community, 634–1881) (Jerusalem, 1995). The emphasis on the Crusades, as opposed to other historical periods, attests to a particular cultural bias that privileges European penetration of the country/land over, say, Islamic conquests.
8 This is beyond the existent differences in the curricula. The main difference with regard to the history of Zionism centers on the beginning of Zionist settlement. While the secular public educational system sticks to the year 1881 as marking the radical shift in patterns of immigration to the country, the religious public school textbooks go back earlier to the Hassidic immigration waves of the late 18th century. This difference happens to be a well-known argument among historians, the obvious representatives of which are Israel Bartal and Aryeh Morgenstern. There is no reason why this argument, like others, should not be presented to the students, instead of each sector receiving its own absolute singular version of things.
9 This was already emphasized by Hannah Arendt in her still illuminating "Zionism Reconsidered," first published in 1945, republished in Hannah Arendt, *The Jew as Pariah: Jewish Identity and Politics in the Modern Age*, ed. Ron Feldman (New York, 1978).
10 It is worth noting that in the new texts the description of the war is relatively free of the mythological and ahistorical imagery so prevalent in the older texts. Particularly noteworthy is the chapter devoted to the topic authored by Motti Golani (see above, note 5). However in the book's other chapters on earlier periods, one still finds descriptions of "Pra'ot"

(pogroms) — a term borrowed from the East European context of pogroms, which receives no historical clarification.
11 Naveh and Barnavi, *Zmanim moderniim*, Part 2, p. 239. In the book edited by Eliezer Dumke, *Ha-olam veha-yehudim*, it is determined that "there were those who fled and there were those who were expelled" (Part 2, p. 285). In Avieli-Tabibian's book, a single convoluted paragraph is dedicated to the topic, in which it is emphasized that the "departure" of the Arabs was the result not of a master plan but of "hesitation and fear" provoked by the Arab leadership. (*1870–1970*, pp. 313–4). It is interesting that unofficial matriculation preparation texts do not mention the refugees at all and continue to uphold the previous version, demonstrating how marginal the issue remains even in the "updated" curriculum.
12 It goes without saying that the criticism articulated by Palestinian historians such as Rashid Khalidi, Nur Masalha, Mousa Boudeiri or Edward Said (each offers his own perspective) is not presented to the students. The same is true of the major facets of Israeli criticism elaborated by historians and sociologists such as Gershon Shapir, Baruch Kimmerling, Avi Shlaim and Ilan Pappé. The practice of asking essential questions regarding central dimensions of Zionism remains, by and large, off limits.
13 I have elaborated this theme in my "Galut mitokh ribonut: Le-vikoret 'shlilat ha-galut' ba-tarbut ha-yisre'elit" (Exile within Sovereignty: A Critique of the Concept "Negation of Exile" in Israeli Culture), *Teoriyah u-Vikoret*, No. 4 (1993), pp. 23–53, and No. 5 (1994), pp. 114–32.
14 Published in *Ha'aretz*, 14 February 1997.
15 Avner Ben-Amos, "An Impossible Pluralism? European Jews and Oriental Jews in the Israeli History Curriculum," *History of European Ideas*, Vol. 18, No. 1 (1994), pp. 41–51.
16 See, for example, the textbook, Haim Saadon and Yoel Rappel (eds.), *Ba-mahteret me-artzot ha-islam* (In the Underground from the Muslim Countries) (Jerusalem, 1997). This volume contains excellent chapters dedicated to Zionist activity in various Arab countries, while ignoring other issues that occupied these communities, and other cultural, political and religious trends.
17 Sami Shalom Chetrit, "The Ashkenazi Zionist Eraser: Curricula in Israel on the History, Culture, and Identity of Mizrahi Jews," *News From Within*, Vol. 13 (December 1997), pp. 21–8; Yehouda Shenhav, "Analyzing Jewish History Textbooks," ibid., Vol. 14 (1998), pp. 32–35, and "Mizrahim in Israeli Textbooks," ibid., Vol. 15 (1999), p. 26.
18 Ella Shohat, "Sephardim in Israel: Zionism from the Standpoint of Its Jewish Victims," *Social Text*, No. 19/20 (1988), pp. 1–35, and *Israeli Cinema: East/West and the Politics of Representation* (Austin, TX, 1989); Amnon Raz-Krakotzkin, "Orientalizm, mada'ei ha-yahadut veha-hevrah ha-yisre'elit" (Orientalism, Jewish Studies and Israeli Society), *Jama'a*, No. 3 (1998), pp. 37–60.
19 Naveh, *Ha-me'ah ha-esrim*, p. 156.
20 Dumke, *Ha-olam veha-yehudim*, Part 2, p. 316.
21 See Shlomo Swirsky, "The Oriental Jews in Israel," *Dissent*, Vol. 31, No. 1 (1984), pp. 77–91, and *Israel: The Oriental Majority*, trans. Barbara Swirski (London, 1989).
22 See, for instance, Karl Frankenstein, *Shikum ha-nefesh ha-havulah* (Rehabilitating the Battered Soul) (Jerusalem, 1971); and for comments, Shlomo Swirski, *Hinukh be-Yisrael: Mehoz ha-maslulim ha-nifradim* (Education in Israel: The Bastion of Separate Tracks) (Tel Aviv, 1990), pp. 31–35; and Meir Buzaglo, "Mizrahiyut, masoret, kur hitukh: Iyun filosofi-politi" (*Mizrahi*-ness, Tradition, Melting Pot: A Philosophical-Political Study), in W. Z. Harvey, G. Hazan Rokem and Y. Shiloah (eds.), *Tziyon ve-tziyonut* (Zion and Zionism) (Jerusalem, 2002, forthcoming).
23 Raz-Krakotzkin, "Orientalizm."
24 Interestingly, critics like Hazony do not mention the question of the representation of *Mizrahi* Jewish history at all. This internal Jewish issue is out of the focus of interest for the new defenders of Zionism.

Contributors

MICHAEL WALZER. Professor of Social Science at the Institute for Advanced Study in Princeton, New Jersey. He is the author of *Just and Unjust Wars* (New York, 1992), *Spheres of Justice* (New York, 1983) and is a coeditor of *The Jewish Political Tradition* (New Haven, 2000).

DANIEL GUTWEIN. Senior Lecturer in the Department of Jewish History, University of Haifa. His recent publications deal with the interrelationship of social and economic policy, collective memory and historical research in Israel.

URI RAM. Senior Lecturer in Sociology in the Behavioral Sciences Department at Ben-Gurion University of the Negev. He is the author of *The Changing Agenda of Israeli Sociology: Theory, Ideology and Identity* (New York, 1995) and the editor of *Ha-hevrah ha-yisre'elit: Hebetim bikortiim* (Israeli Society: Critical Perspectives) (Tel Aviv, 1993).

ANITA SHAPIRA. Ruben Merenfeld Professor of Zionism at Tel Aviv University. Among her books are *Berl, the Biography of a Socialist Zionist: Berl Katznelson, 1887–1944* (Cambridge, 1984) and *Land and Power: The Zionist Resort to Force, 1881–1948* (New York, 1992).

MARK LILLA. Professor in the Committee on Social Thought at the University of Chicago and author, most recently, of *The Reckless Mind: Intellectuals and Politics* (New York, 2001).

DEREK J. PENSLAR. Zacks Professor of History at the University of Toronto. His most recent book is *Shylock's Children: Economics and Jewish Identity in Modern Europe* (Berkeley and Los Angeles, 2001).

AVI BARELI. Lecturer in the Department of Jewish History, Tel Aviv University, and editor of *Iyunim Bitkumat Israel* (Studies in Zionism, the Yishuv and the State of Israel), Ben-Gurion Research Center, Ben-Gurion University of the Negev. He is currently completing a book on Mapai in the early years of the State of Israel.

YOAV GELBER. Professor in the Department of Land of Israel Studies, Head of the Herzl Institute for the Research and Study of Zionism, and Chairman of the School of History, University of Haifa. He is the author of numerous books, most recently *Palestine 1948: War, Escape and the Emergence of the Palestinian Refugee Problem* (Brighton, 2001).

AMNON RAZ-KRAKOTZKIN. Lecturer in Early-Modern and Modern Jewish History at Ben-Gurion University of the Negev. He is currently completing a book entitled *The Censor, the Editor and the Text: Catholic Censorship and Hebrew Printing in the Sixteenth Century* (in Hebrew).

Index

Abdullah, King (Transjordan) 72, 140
Abramson, Larry 48
 "double map" 49, 52
"academic freedom", meaning of 122
academic historiography of Zionism 13, 21–2
"adulation of powerlessness" 68, 71
"adversary culture" 79–82
Agnon, S.Y. 29
al-Arif, Arif 140
Alexandroni Brigade 62, 121
Alterman, Nathan 24
American neoconservatism 77–9, 82–3
American revisionists 4–5
Anderson, Benedict 90, 92, 94–5
anti-anti-revisionism 7
anti-intellectuals 77
anti-revisionism 5–7
anti-Semitism 97, 106
anticolonialism 85, 96
Arab–Jewish conflict *see* Israeli–Arab conflict
Arabs 9, 14, 22–4, 38
 anti-Zionist propaganda 125
 Ben-Gurion and 66
 Brit Shalom association and 65
 Canaanite program and 114
 defeated by IDF 64
 exodus of 19–20, 47–8, 105
 harsh military rule in Galilee and 97
 injustices against 62
 killings of Jews by 72
 labor in Zionist colonies 86
 narratives of the war 139
 potential for exploitation of 108
 racist views of Palestinian 84
Arafat, Yassir 55
Arendt, Hannah 143
Argentina 93
Armenians, genocide by Turks of 143
Aron, Raymond 136
Arya Samaj 89–90
Ashkenazi Jews 9, 51, 106, 114, 167, 169
Auerbach, Efraim 68
Azure 27–9, 32–3, 63, 78

babu, the 90
Baer, Itzhak (Fritz) 131
balabat, the 90
Balkan wars 137
Bar Ilan University 54
Bar-Kokhba stories 1–3, 46

Bar-Yosef, Rivka 145
Barak, Ehud 168
Barnavi, Eli 161–2, 168
Bauer, Yehuda 124, 131
Beard, Charles 136
Bedouin 86
Begin, Menachem 3, 51, 55, 69
Ben-Gurion, David 14, 19–20, 22
 confrontation with professors at Hebrew University 65
 courses on 128
 dispute with Sharett 21
 "guided democracy" 68–9
 on history 2
 the Holocaust and 143
 Jewish creativity and 74
 Jewish immigrants and Arab citizens 7
 Labor movement under 30
 as a symbol 72–5
 vision of Israeli statehood 6
 Yizhar and Alterman 24
 Zionism without Arab confrontation 66–7
 Zionist state as "Third Temple" 45
Ben-Gurion Institute 150
Ben-Sasson, Hayim Hilel 131
Benvenisti, Meron 70
Berdyczewski, Micha 91
Bhabba, Homi 102–3
Bilu, The 100
Borchov, Dov Ber 44, 91
Bork, Rork 82
Bosnian War 144
Brenner, Y.H. 29
Brit Shalom Association 65, 72
Britain,
 anti-Zionist policy 72
 Palestinian onslaught 139
 development of Jewish autonomy 108
 role of colonizing state 85
 Zionism 105, 141
British Mandate in Palestine (1918–48) 20, 107, 160
Buber, Martin 65, 68–9, 79
Bund, alternative to Zionism 166
Burke, Edmund 33

Cahana, Reuben 145
Cambodia War 144
Canaanism 114–15
Canaanite program 114

"Canaanites" 46, 114–15
capitalism 33–4, 80, 92, 107
Caucasus wars 137
Chatterjee, Partha 85, 90–96
Chattopadhyay, Tarnicharan, *History of India* 90–91
Chechnya, war in 144
citizenship 87–8
"civic Israelis" 43
civic nationalism 55–7
civic post-nationalism 59
classic Zionist narrative, Jewish-Arab relations and 64, 97
"classical"Zionism 58
classification 104
Clinton, Bill 81
Cohen, Hermann 68
Cohn, Geula 74
Cold War 137
collective identity 50, 59
collective memory 9, 22–6, 50, 155
   alternative Israeli 18, 26
   forgetfulness and 48
   history and 148
   post-Zionism and 38
   privatization of Israeli 35–8, 147
collective mentalities 102
collectivity, boundaries of 44
colonialism,
   Jewish historical existence and 123
   multifaceted concept 105
   narrow definition 104
   Zertal and 113
   Zionism and 84–5, 101
Colonialist School,
   arguments against 106
   explaining Zionism 111
   historical fiction 115
   methodological limitations 100
   Palestine/*Eretz Yisrael* 110
   "Palestinocentric" shortcoming 113, 115–16
   study of Zionism and Israel 99
colonized intellectuals 88
Commentary 80–1
"conditional justification", hegemonic memory (1948) 25
conservatism 30
counter-intellectual books 83
counter-intellectuals 77
creation of an anti-narrative 63–5
"Critical Sociologists" (1970s) 9
critical sociology 71
Croce, Benedetto 95
Crusades, the 158

cultural alienation, Israelis and Holocaust survivors 47
cultural consciousness 155
"culture wars" 43

Dayan, Moshe 24, 128
de-Arabization 48–9
Deir Yassin, massacre of Palestinians 24–5, 132, 161, 163
dharma 90
Dinur, Ben-Zion 124, 131
   Yisrael ba-golah (Israel in exile) 95
Dohm, Friedrich Wilhelm von 94
Don-Yehiya, Eliezer 47
Droysen, Gustav Johann 95
Dubnow, Simon 2

economic profitability, Zionist settlement enterprise 106, 109
Egypt 3, 88
Eichmann trial (1961) 47
Eilon, Emunah 27–8
Eisenstadt, S.N. 108, 145
Elizabethan England, English language and 96
Elkana, Yehuda 35, 56–7
   "In Praise of Forgetting" 55
emancipation 10, 87, 97
Enlightenment (*Ne'orut*) 125
Enlightenment, the 33–4
Eretz Kedem (the "Land of Old") 114
Eretz Yisrael (biblical Land of Israel) 44–5
   Canaanites and 114–15
   Jewish immigrants 141–2
   religious and historical yearning for 47
   Zionism and 100
ethical politics, *realpolitik* and 66
ethnic cleansing 9, 26
ethnic nationalism 50–55
ethnic neo-nationalism 59
ethnic problem 169
Ettinger, Shmuel 131
European colonialism, expropriation of native lands 85
European Jewry during the Holocaust, Zionist leadership and 10–11, 23, 38

Far East, "Asian values" 6
Fast, Howard, *My Glorious Brothers* 1
Feurstein, Reuven 169
Fieldhouse, D.K. 109
fin-de-siècle Europe, Zionist thinking and 84, 86
First Things (neoconservative religious magazine) 82

INDEX

Fisch, Harold,
  "double calendar" 52
  Palestinian nationality and 54
  Six Day War and 52–3
  The Zionst Revolution: A New Perspective 51
"forgetting Europe" 112–14
Foucault, Michel 133, 136
"Founding Villains, The" 4
France,
  Algeria and 97
  Jews to undergo "regeneration" 94–5
  school of *Annales* 131
  Siamese jurisdiction in Mekong river valley 97
  women's suffrage 91
Frankenstein, Karl 169
Fredrickson, George M. 109
Freidman, Efraim, North African Jews "rooted" (*shorshiim*) 169
Funkenstein, Amos 91

Gal, Meir, "Nine out of Four Hundred" (photograph) 167
galut Jews , "all the world against us" 2–3
Gaza Strip 50, 97
gdud (battalion) or *plugah* (company), related to labor 141
Geiger, Abraham 89
Gelber, Yoav 22
Gentiles, Jewish state and 7, 33, 52, 94
ger toshav (resident alien) 7
German states,
  "civil improvement" for Jews 94
  preconditions for citizenship 88
Gide, André, *The Immoralist* 87
global integration, supportive of post-Zionism 58
Golan Heights 97
Goldblum, Aryeh, primitivism of Mizrahi Jews 169
Goldhagen, Daniel, *Hitler's Willing Executioners* 144
Gorny, Yosef 108
goyim, Jews and 5, 7
Grabski, Wladyslaw, "Grabski's persecution" 72
Graetz, Heinrich, *Geschichte der Juden* 90
Gramsci, Antonio 78
Gramscian "passive revolution" 92
Great Britain, "War of Liberation" and 71
"green-line" borders (1948) 57
Greenberg, Clement 81
Grodzinsky, Yosef 143
Gross, Nachum 108
Grossman, David, "present absentees" 48

Guizot, François 95
Gur-Zeev, Ilan 145
Gush Emunim (block of the Faithful) 50–51
Gutman, Israel 144
Gutwein, Daniel 147

Ha-Kibbut Ha-Meuhad Publishing House 35
Ha-Po'el Ha-Tza'ir , East European intelligentsia 100
Ha-Shomer ha-Tza'ir, historiography inspired by 125
Ha'aretz (Hebrew daily) 35–6, 169
Habad movement 71
Haifa and Tiberias 24
Halakhah (Jewish codex) 50, 90
Hale, Nathan 3
Halperin, Israel 131
Hammer, Zevulun (Minister of Education) 166
Harkabi, Yehoshafat, critique of Bar-Kokhba "syndrome" 2–3
hasidim, zealotry of 1
Haskalah (Jewish variant of European Enlightenment) 2, 88–9, 96–7
Hayek, Friedrich 33
Hazaz, Haim, "The Sermon" 45
Hazony, Yoram 36
  Ben-Gurion, view of 72–4
  bringing counter-intellectualism to Israel 78
  classic Labor Zionist movement 68
  consensus and 67
  critical analysis of Zionist project 31–2
  emancipationist German Judaism 68, 71
  essence of Zionism 157
  Hebrew University 68–9
  "In Praise of Post-Zionism" 31
  history of Zionism and 65
  Israeli occupation and 70
  "Jewish State at 100 , The" (article) 7, 30
  Jewish State, The:Struggle for Israel's Soul 54, 63, 71, 77–80
  morality and 66
  "political anti-Zionism" 64, 67
  praise for Zionist-Canaanite sculpture 79
  roots of anti-nationalist tendencies and 69
  selectivity of 70
Hebrew cultural revolution 11
"Hebrew ideology" ("Canaanism") *see also* Canaanism 114
Hebrew language revival 100, 106, 115
"Hebrew literature" 29
Hebrew project, Jewish immigrants from Muslim countries 47
"Hebrew settlement, the" (*ha-yishuv ha-ivri*) 44
"Hebrew Youth, the" (Canaanites) 46

Hebrewism, Judaism and 47
Hebrews (*ivrim*) 44–6
Herzl, Theodor 19, 30–32, 68
  Altneuland 33
  controversy between Buber and 65, 69
  courses on 128
  Hazony's view of 73
Hinduism 89–91
historian,
  correct narrative and 17
  interdisciplinary research and 135–6
  numbers and statistics and 135
  role of 133–5
"historical continuity" 159
historical events, moral judgment and 103
historical libel cases, difficulties of 122
historical nationalism 44–7
historical research,
  collective memory and 22
  cultural-political event 15–16
historical revisionism, meeting point for left and right 11
historical Zionism 32, 37, 54
historicism 131–2
historiography,
  agents of collective memory 148
  Arab scholars and 140
  common language and 150
  criticism from scholars outside 136
  as a discipline 129–36
  emergence of 63
  Hindu (1870s) and Western norms 90
  niche between humanities and social sciences 129
  postmodern relativism and 136–7
  postmodernist attack on its qualification 122–3
  problem of individual memory and 147
  purpose of methodology in 132
  Western and Israeli 125–6
  Zionist–British relations and 125
history 1–2, 7, 62
  acknowledgment of and consequences 165
  backward looking 5
  as conspiracy 69–70
  contribution to shaping of identity 149
  curriculum 155–7
  economic 131
  eradication of Palestinians 48
  of the land 159–61
  memory and 147–9
  Mizrahi 167–70
  "official Mapai version" 27
  oral, difficulties of handling 147–8
  period ending with Sinai Campaign (1956) 150
  polarized society and 126–9
  in schools 146–7
  as selectivity 70–71
  sites of *Yishuv* and Israeli 136
  as terminology 71–2
  tools, broad education and language skills 130
  Zionist and Jewish 166–7
history teaching 146
history textbooks, 155–71 *see also* new textbooks
Hitler, Adolf 55, 111
Holocaust of European Jewry 43, 52
  Ben-Gurion and 72
  genocides in twentieth century 143–4
  Jewish identity and 142–5
  lessons from 56
  more than mass killing 144
  new curricula and 166–7
  "Sabra" offspring of Hebrews and 46
  separate discussion of 170
  Zionism's attitude during and after 124
Holocaust Memorial Museum (Washington) 144
Holocaust survivors 38
  Ben-Gurion and 73
  clandestine immigration to Palestine 113
  "Judaization" of Israeli culture (1950s) 47
  settlement in Palestine 99
Horon, Adaya Gur 115
Horowitz, Dan 108
Huntington, Samuel P., "clash of civilizations" 34
Hyman, Paula 90

ideological disagreements, Pappé and Morris 17
Idumeans, forced conversion 1
Ihud organization 65
immigration 63–4, 145, 160, 169
  America and mass 5
  Eastern Europe and 112–13
  Europe, Middle East and North Africa 47, 49–50
imperialism of the fin de siècle 84
Inbari, Assaf 30
"Towards a Hebrew Literature" 29
India 88–92
Indian wars, new American historians and 5
individualistic Zionism 32
Institute for the History and Philosophy of Science and Ideas 55
international Zionist movement, interwar period 94

INDEX

Internet, the 148–9
intifada 50, 55, 122
Ireland, Act of Union and 95
Israel,
  big kahal (medieval Jewish community) 6
  negotiations with King Abdullah of Jordan 72
  "new faith" 29
  redefined as "Jewish" 47
  refugee problem and failure to achieve peace 11
Israel Archives Law, amendment (1981) 15
Israel be-Aliyah Party 57
Israel Defense Forces (IDF) 19, 62, 64, 121, 150
Israeli Academe 35, 62, 123–5
Israeli anti-revisionism 5
Israeli anxiety 164–5
Israeli–Arab conflict 112, 150, 156, 159, 170
  Ben-Gurion and 73
  changing historiography of 137–9
  escalation of 49
  history of 64, 157
  MA thesis and 122
  partition failed to solve 28
  redefined Israel as "Jewish" 47
  Shlaim blamed Israel 66
  solution to 25
Israeli–Arab peace, Israeli hegemonic collective memory 25
Israeli civic-liberal paradigm 43
Israeli consciousness 157, 165–6
Israeli historical consciousness, radical shift in 59, 156
Israeli identity,
  "biblical lands of Israel" fundamental to 57
  collective 33–4, 43, 59
  Edot ha-mizrah (Oriental communities) 49
  Holocaust and Israeli–Arab wars and 48
  issues of 43
  lack of group 113–14
  neo-Zionism and collective 54
  "new Jew, the" and 3, 23, 30, 34
  Orientalist dimension 167, 169–70
  politics of 59
  privatization of 37–8
Israeli leadership 19, 21
Israeli memory of the war 24
Israeli Ministry of Education 146
Israeli myths 148
Israeli–Palestinian conflict *see* Israeli–Arab conflict
Israeli–Palestinian peace 5, 164
Israeli right, "new Mapai" 30
Israeli right-wing anti-revisionist campaign 5
Israeli scholars, study of Arab side of conflict 139
Israeli schools, changes in history curriculum 156
Israeli Society 28–9, 38
Israeli universities,
  fin de siècle high imperialism 84
  old-historiography and 15
  postmodern theories and 137
  revisionist historians and 139
  study courses 127–9
Israeli withdrawal from West Bank and Gaza Strip 26
Israel's Declaration of Independence, double chronosophy 52

Jabotinsky, Vladimir 74
  The Iron Wall: Israel and the Arab World since (1948) 66
Jefferson, Thomas 56
"Jerusalem School" of history 131
Jewish, meaning "non-Arab" 47
Jewish Agency for Palestine 93
Jewish Colonization Association 93
Jewish continuity 31
Jewish ethno-nationalist paradigm 43
Jewish Holocaust, Palestinian disaster (1948 expulsion) 55
Jewish immigrants, identity and 49
Jewish immigrants from Muslim countries 47
Jewish intelligentsia 91
Jewish philanthropic organizations 93
Jewish philanthropists 93
Jewish settlement in Palestine 107
Jewish social engineering 93
Jewish sovereignty 52, 67–8
Jewish state 1
Jewish–American neoconservatism 30, 32
Jewish-conservative approach 28
Jews 65, 92
  brutality towards 55
  cultural renewal 90
  diaspora 9, 10, 31, 38, 44–6, 92
  of Eastern Europe 99–100, 112
  emancipation on a quid pro quo basis 87–8
  ethnic 43
  European character of 106, 109
  expulsion from Spain 90
  from Central and Western Europe 68
  insidious pact with British imperialism 64
  Middle Eastern and North African countries 99
  "old" historians and 70
  Oriental 73
  Oriental and Semitic element 106

Orthodox 59
secular 71
unbounded nation 93
Judah Magnes organization 65
Judaism, universal values and 67
Judea and Samaria, war over territories 30
Judeo-conservatives, US 27, 32 see also New Conservatism

kabbalah 91
Kaniuk, Yoram, *Last Jew, The* 46
Kaplan, Marion 90
Katz, Jacob 68
Kaufmann, Yehezkel 1
Khalidi, Rashid 140–41
Khalidi, Walid 140
kibbush (occupation, conquest) 141
Kimmerling, Baruch 70, 99
Kirshenbum, Shimshon, *Toldot am Yisrael* (History of the Jewish People) 167
Klausner, Joseph 1
Knesset 121
Kolatt, Israel 126, 129
  "On the Research and Researcher of the History of the *Yishuv* and the Zionist Movement" 125
Kook, Rabbi Abraham Isaaac Ha-Kohen 31, 51, 71
Korean war 137
Koster, Sharl De, *Till Eulenspiegel* 149
Kristol, Irving, "On the political stupidity of the Jews" 32–3

Labor Ashkenazi elite 10
labor movement, influence of Russian Marxism 30
Labor Zionism 20–1, 25, 28, 30–32, 34–7
Labor Zionist leadership 20
Lauder, Ron 27
Lavon Affair 150
Lebanon, attack on Palestinians (1980s) 55, 69
left post-Zionism,
  "new historiography" 12
  privatization as emancipatory step 34
  privatized project and postmodern criticism 37
left post-Zionists, dissolution of Zionism 34
left and right post-Zionism,
  privatization of its collective memory 37
  radical-collectivist ethos of Zionism 34
  reject Zionism for Israeli identity 33
left-wing radicals 102
legitimization, delegitimization and 67–9
Leibowicz, Yeshayahu, "Judeo-Nazis" 144

liberal post-Zionism (1980s) 58
liberation 3
liberationists 3, 7
Liebman, Charles 47
Likud Party 57
Lissak, Moshe 108–9, 145
Lod (Lydda) conquest 20, 24
Lorch, Netanel 70
Losin, Yigal, *Amud ha-esh* (Pillar of Fire) 149

Maariv (daily) 74
Maccabees 1–2, 139
Magnes, Judah Leib 72
mainstream Zionists 73–4
Mandatory British administration 85
Mapai Party 21, 24–5
Mapam Party 20
Mapam-oriented Palmah 22
"market Zionism" 32, 37
Marxian criticism 103
Marxism 69, 131
Marxist-Leninist, theories of nationalism 123
Masalha, Nur 140
maskilim founded schools 90
matriculation requirements 155, 166
Mizrahi Jews 168
Matzpen (Israeli anti-Zionist ultra-left-wing organization) 12
Meiji Japan 88
"melting pot" policy,
  Ben-Gurion and 73
  left and right post-Zionism 11
  Mizrahim and 10
  multicultural society 145–6
  Zionist collective ethos 37
"Memorial Day for the Holocaust and Heroism" 46
methodological question 104
Metzer, Jacob 108
Michelet, Jules 124
Middle East 111, 123
Ministry of Defense publishing house 15
Mizrahi history 167–70
Mizrahi Jews, stripped of Arabic culture 168
Mizrahim (Jews from Muslim countries) 9–11, 22, 38, 59, 167
  integration into school curriculum 168
  oppression of 38, 145
  Orientalist dimension of Zionist national identity 167, 169–70
  "secondary retardation" and 168–9
modern national identities, study of history in schools 155
Moledet Party 57
morality, politics and 65–7

"morality of partition" 28
Morris, Benny 4, 14–16, 64, 138
  Birth of the Palestinian Refugee Problem (1947–1949) 19–20
  "charter essay" 66
  differences within Labor Zionism 21
  portrayal of "old historians" 67
  positivist 17
  refugee problem 23, 54
  term "new historiography" 22
  transfer idea and Zionist agenda 19
  Zionism and 17–18, 66
  Zionist ideology of expelling Arabs from Palestine 69
Movement for Greater Israel 51
myths 13, 18, 91, 148–9

nakbah (the Palestine Tragedy) 121, 161
narrative, ideological-educational superstructure 63
nation,
  space, time, community 57–9
national liberation 3–4, 6–7
National Religious Party (Mafdal) 57
National transformations 47–50
national-religious right, opposition to Oslo Accords 10
nationalism,
  algebra of modernity 96
  component of early Indian and Jewish 90
  German 96
  and Jewish sovereignty 67–8
  messianic 51
  modern European 95
nation-state and 3
  Palestinian 97
  sacrifice of Zionist 13
  territorial 111
  umbrella concept 105
  Yeshiva 30
nationalism of national liberation 6
nationalistic neo-Zionism (1970s) 57
Naveh, Eyal 156, 161–2, 168
Nazi persecutions and genocide 111
"negation of the diaspora" 11
"negation of the exile" 1, 7, 31, 166
Nekudah (settlers' journal) 31
neo-Zionism 43–4
  exclusionary nationalistic 58–9
  Israeli collective identity and 54
  Zionist and Jewish ingredients 57
neo-Zionist calendar 53
neoconservative books 77
neoconservatives, attacks on revisionism 5, 81–2

neoliberal policy, privatization of public sector 36–7
Netanyahu, Binyamin 27, 36
New Conservatism, US 27, 32
  see also Judeo-conservatives
new curriculum,
  the Arab presence and 159–60
  "balanced" approach 163, 168
  chapters on Arab nationalism 167
  "diasporic period" no longer discussed 166
  "general history" and "Jewish history" 158–9
  Jews in the modern world 166
"new faith" 29–30, 34
new historians 54, 63, 66, 71, 131, 138–9
  exodus of Palestinians (1948) 18
  intentions "academic and not necessarily political" 12
  issue of Jewish–Palestinian confrontation 64
  Palestinian as ultimate "other" 23
  trained academic historians 14
  uniform Zionist narrative 70
new historiography,
  academic historiography 12–13, 35
  alternative Israeli collective memory 22
  "discoveries", recycling of arguments 13, 26
  from historical research to collective memory 22–6
  Israeli adaptation of *nouvelle histoire* 16
  method and ideology 14–18
  praxis of 18–22
  rejection of "official Mapai version" 27
  relativization and 38
  support by post-Zionists 28
  term and Benny Morris 18
  "victims" of Zionism 38
"new Jew", Israeli identity and 23, 30, 34, 38
"New left" 4
"new society" 34, 37
new textbooks, 160–63
  Israeli consciousness 165
  Mizrahi Jews 168–9
  Olam shel tmurot (A World of Transformations) 54
  refugee question and 161
New York intellectuals, fundamentalist groups and 80
New York Times 4
New York-based Joint Distribution Committee 93
new-old historians,
  definition of 67, 71
  establishment propaganda 14
  studies for collective memory 22
  supporters of certain ideologies 22

universities and 15
Nietzsche, Friedrich 3, 102
"non-Arab" 47–8
North Africa 111
Nouvelle Histoire, postmodernism and 16

objectivity, historical truth and 132–3
October war (1973) 9, 51, 53, 126, 150
old historians 14, 19, 70, 139
old historiography 15
"Old" Zionism 34
Ophir, Adi 70
opportunism, new-old historians 14
Orthodox Judaism,
  Jewish codex (the *Halakhah*) 50
  new textbooks and 166
Orthodox Rav Shach movement 71
Oslo Accords 10, 26, 30, 164
"others" 25
  diaspora Jews as ultimate 31
  inclusion of forgotten 52, 58
  left post-Zionism support for 34
  and the "losers" 17
  Mizrahim and Arabs 9
  Palestinians as ultimate 23, 140
  positive discrimination and 139
Ottoman Palestine, "Christian colonizers" 112

Palestine,
  arrival of Zionist immigrants (from 1881) 44
  European immigrants 107
  Hebrew culture 45–6
  history of 158
  nationalism combated by Israel 97
  rebellion (1987) and *Intifada* 50
  Zionists bought lands in 141–2
Palestine Economic Corporation 93
Palestine/*Eretz Yisrael*,
  Colonialist School 110
  complex history 159
  exploitation or dispossession 99, 108
  negation of 159
  two national sectors 106–8
Palestinian Arabs 109,
  "Arabs of the Land of Israel" 86–7
  repression by Israeli Jews 55
  war of destruction (1948) 47–8
  Zionist scholars and 125
Palestinian Historiography 139–40
Palestinian refugee problem 9 *see also* refugee problem
Palestinian rejectionism 28
Palestinian uprising (October 2000) 157
Palestinians 38, 59, 138

"1948 War" (*al-nakba*) 72, 161
Begin government and 3
British Mandate and Jewish immigration 160
defeat of 110
expulsion of (1948) 19, 38
"forgotten" group 50
"non-nation" 54
partition 162
Pappé, Ilan 11, 12, 16–17, 99–100, 110–12
  collective memory 22
  difference between left and right Zionism 21
  link between Palestinians and Holocaust 144
  new narrative of Israeli and Palestinian histories 54
  Palestinian propagandists and 139
  relativism and 16–18, 138
  Zionism as colonialist movement 18
Partisan Review 81
Peel Commission 63
Polisar, Daniel,
  "Making History" 27
  new historians and 27–8
"political anti-nationalism" 68, 71
"political anti-Zionism" 64
"political correctness" 103
political Zionism 52, 71
Popper, Karl 131, 136
"populism" 81
positivism 17, 131
post-*Yishuv* Israeli society 145
post-Zionism 43–4
  Azure's attitude 28
  civic dimension of Israeli statehood 59
  delineating political discourse 12
  Elkana's position 57
  Israeli collective memory 18
  left and right versions 11
  libertarianism and openness 58
  mainstream scholars 71
  negation of Ben-Gurionist Zionism 31
  privatization of Israeli collective memory 35–8
  Zionism and 55, 143
post-Zionists 63
  alternative collective memory 38
  alternative research program 100
  Ben-Gurion 73
  "end of Zionism" 34
  Labor Zionism 36
  postmodernist school and 10
  Zionist consensus 67
  Zionist ideology and 9
postcolonialism, anticolonialism and 85

INDEX

postmodernism,
  concepts 10, 16, 35, 102–3
  criticism of Zionism 37
  historians and 133, 148
  relativism and 38, 136–7
pragmatic Zionism 51
Prawer, Joshua 68, 70
productivization and proletarization 45, 47
Prussian Colonization Commission 86
Public Interest, The 78, 80

Rabin, Yitzhak 31, 43
Rabinovich, Itamar 14–16
radical left 26
Rama IV (King of Siam) 88
Ramakrishna, Vivekananda 88, 91
Ramle, expulsion of Arabs 20
Ranke, Leopold von 124, 132
Ratosh, Yonathan, Judaism and 46–7
Rav Ovadiyah Yosef movement 71
Reagan, Ronald 81
Reform Judaism 89
refugee problem 9, 18–21, 23, 161–5
  Arab leaders 24
  Jewish responsibility 24–5
  United Nations and 163
relativism 16–18, 38, 136–7
religion, umbrella concept 105
revisionism 3–5, 7, 13, 84
Revisionist Party 66
Richelieu, *raisons d'état* 65
right post-Zionism 26–38
right-wing anti-revisionist history 7
right-wing governments 15
Rotenstreich, Nathan 68, 74
Rousseau, Jean Jacques, "social contract" 67, 79
Roy, Rammohan 89
Russian pogroms, "massacres" 72

Saadon, Haim 167
"Sabra" 46
Sagiv, Assaf (deputy editor of *Azure*) 29–30
Said, Edward 102–3, 123, 140, 144–5
Salem village, Palestinians and 55
Saravati, Dayananda 89
scandal, Israeli Academe (2000) 62
Scholem, Gershom 73, 79, 91
Schwartz, Delmore 81
Sde Boker archives 150
Second World War 65
secular Zionism 50
Segev, Tom 70, 72, 143
  One Palestine: Complete 85
Senesh, Hannah 3

Sephardi Jews 114
Seton-Watson, Hugh 111
settlement colonialism 85
Shafir, Gershon 99–100, 108–12, 115
Shalaim, Avi, Israeli–Jordanian collusion (1948) 54
Shalem Center 27, 30, 33, 36, 63
  ethno-nationalist thought 54
  Hazony and 78, 82
Shamir, Ronen 84, 99
Shapira, Anita 14–16, 22, 108, 138
Shapira, Yair, "In Praise of Post-Zionism" 31
Sharett, Moshe 21
Shelah, Uriel (poet Yonatan Ratosh) 115
Shlaim, Avi 66, 72–3, 138–9
  Collusion across the Jordan 72
Sienkiewicz, Henryk, *Pan Zagloba* 149
Sinai Campaign (1956) 150
Sinai Peninsula 97
Six Day War (1967) 50–52, 63, 69, 124, 126, 150
Smilansky, Yizhar (alias S.Yizhar) 24
Smith, Adam 33
Spanish Conquistadores 141
Spartan–Maccabee alliance 2
State of Israel (1948) 4, 10, 43
state legitimization, women's suffrage and 92
stateless Jewry 7
Sternhell, Zeev 70, 72
  Founding Myths 4
Stoler, Ann 87
"Students of Zionism", Zionist movement and 111
Switzerland, women's suffrage 91
Syrkin, Marie 3

Talmon, Jacob 68, 79
Tamir, Tali 48–9
Tantura (Arab village) 62, 121–2, 132, 139, 150–51
Tehiyah Party 57
Tel Aviv, "new" middle classes 58
Tel Aviv University 55
Tel Hai stand (1920) 63
Thai nationalism 97
Thailand (Siam) 88
Theory and Criticism journal 35
Thierry, Augustin 95
Tikkun (1988) 66
Tkhelet see Azure
Tkumah (Revival), T.V. series (1998) 54, 149
Tonybee, Arnold 123
"torah of God", "torah of man" 89
trahison des clercs 80
Treitschke, Heinrich von 95

Trilling, Lionel 79–81
Trumpeldor, Joseph 3
Tsuba (village near Jerusalem) 48
Tzomet Party 57

Ukraine 93
Ultra-Orthodox anti-Zionists (*haredim*) 10–11, 71
UN, partition of Palestine (November 1947) 63–4, 109, 163
Unification Church (Reverend Sun Myung Moon 80–81
United Nations *see* UN
United States,
  Jewish Agency for Palestine 93
  Jewish community 43
  liberationist history 4
  neoconservative counter-intellectuals 83
  Reform Judaism movement 68
  Zionist protégé 140
universal welfare state, dissolution of 36
University of Haifa 121–2
Upanishads 89

Van Leer Institute (Jerusalem) 35, 55
Vedata 89
Vietnam war 81, 137
Villari, Pasquale, *Volkgeist* 95
virtual history 149
Volpe, Gioacchino 95

Walby, Sylvia 91
War of the Day of Atonement *see* October War (1973)
War of Independence 47, 67, 71–2
  "conditional justification" of refugee problem 25
  dispossession of Arabs after 108
  fate of two Arab villages 121
  formative moment of Israeli identity 23
  founding event of statehood 64, 97
  Israeli historiography 14, 139
  Israeli leadership split 21
  Morris and 20, 69
  Palestinian Tragedy (the Nakba) 161
  Palestinians after 48–50
  Pappé on 17
  partition of Palestine after 63–4
  Tantura village and 62
  Zionist narrative 71–2
war in Lebanon (1982) 58, 144
Weber, Eugen, "peasants into Frenchmen" 95
Weizmann, Chaim Azrail 128
Wessely, Naphtali Hirsch, *Words of Peace and Truth* 88–9

West Bank 50, 97
"Western political conservatism" 33
White, Hayden 136
Wissenschaft des Hinduismus 89
Wissenschaft des Judentums 89–91, 96–7
women 59, 90
women's suffrage 91–2
World history, Israeli national history 147
World Zionist organization 86, 92

Yaakobi, Danny 156, 164
Yad Vashem (Holocaust memorial museum, Jerusalem) 56, 124, 144
Yediot Aharanot, "Who's Afraid of the Truth?" 27
Yehoshua, A.B. 48
Yesh Gvul ("there is a border/limit") movement 58
yeshiva nationalism 30–31, 37
Yeshivat Merkaz ha-Rav, Rabbi Kook and 71
Yishuv 20, 63, 65, 72, 84–6, 93
  Arabs accuse Britain of betrayal 139–40
  Bauer on 124
  interwar period and 94
  new chapters in textbooks on 160
  sites of history and 136
  study of in 1960s 123
  ultra-Orthodox members
  women's suffrage 92
Yizhar, S. 24, 48

Zalman Shazar Center 167
Zaritsky, Yosef (watercolourist) 48–9
Zertal, Idith 143
  From Catastrophe to Power 113
Zimmermann, Moshe 70, 144
Zionism,
  causes of 110, 113
  challenges to emancipation in the West 97
  collective nature 32
  colonial nature and ties with imperialism 11, 18, 96, 140
  colonialism and 71, 84–5, 99, 103–4, 109
  colonialist paradigm of 140–42
  compared with colonialist settlement 105–6
  condemnation by revisionist historians 125
  duality of 52
  enterprise of colonization 64
  Eretz Yisrael and 100
  historical understanding 164
  history of 123
  imperialist Britain 141
  integral "people" and 54
  legitimate national-liberation movement 18

INDEX

messianic 51
military force and 28
mission civilsatrice 94, 96
Morris and Pappé 17
movement of people of European birth 105
national facet 110
Orientalist elements 87
prewar ideological adversaries 143
stimulus behind 73
"the Jewish state" and 29
three "moments of truth" 52–3
ultra-Orthodox approach 51
vital historical and political element 101
"Zionism of Zion" 52
Zionist aim, "Jews into Israelis" 95
Zionist collectivist ethos 37
Zionist colonization 71
Zionist development 108
Zionist historians 1, 31, 111, 166
Zionist historiography,
   empirical-positivist approach 111

Israeli Academe and 123–5
negated histories of Jews and country 166
Six Day War (1967) 124
Zionist/*Yishuv*'s actions during Holocaust 142–3
Zionist ideology 91, 95, 111, 165
Zionist immigrants 112
Zionist left 23
Zionist movement 111, 113, 123
"Zionist nationalism" 13
Zionist "old guard" 13
"Zionist prism – not only prism" 16–17
Zionist settlement,
   compared with European in America or Africa 104
   history of the conflict 159–61
Zionist socialists 108
"Zionist, the" 34
Zionist *Yishuv*, transfer idea 20
Zukermann, Moshe 57
Zunz, Leopold 89

Printed in the United States
108240LV00002B/89/A